Dining In Corporate America

HANDBOOK OF
NONCOMMERCIAL
FOODSERVICE
MANAGEMENT

Edited by
Joan B. Bakos
Foodservice Editorial Consultant
East Hampton, New York

Guy E. Karrick
Society for Foodservice Management
Louisville, Kentucky

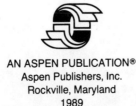

AN ASPEN PUBLICATION®
Aspen Publishers, Inc.
Rockville, Maryland
1989

Library of Congress Cataloging-in-Publication Data

Handbook of noncommercial foodservice management: dining
in corporate America/edited by Joan B. Bakos, Guy E. Karrick.
p. cm.
"An Aspen publication."
Includes index.
ISBN: 0-8342-0065-1
1. Food service management--United States. I. Bakos, Joan B. II. Karrick, Guy E.
TX911.3.M27D55 1989 647.95′068--dc20 89-6608
CIP

Editorial Services: Ruth Bloom

Library of Congress Catalog Card Number: 89-6608
ISBN: 0-8342-0065-1

Printed in the United States of America

1 2 3 4 5

Table of Contents

Contributors List

Editors

Joan B. Bakos
Foodservice Editorial Consultant
East Hampton, New York

Guy E. Karrick
Communications Director
Society for Foodservice Management
Louisville, Kentucky

Contributors

Bill Babcock
Principal
Babcock & Schmid Associates
Bath, Ohio

Steve Brennan
National Sales Director
Canteen Company
Chapin, South Carolina

Frank Burrows
District Manager
Lackmann Food Service, Inc.
Plantation, Florida

Clifton B. Charles
Food Services Manager
Steelcase, Inc.
Grand Rapids, Michigan

Martin Cherneff
President
M. H. Cherneff & Associates
Monterey, Massachusetts

John W. Chitvanni
President
National Restaurant Search, Inc.
Schaumburg, Illinois

Phillip S. Cooke
Executive Director
Society for Foodservice Management
Louisville, Kentucky

Elizabeth G. Flynn
Manager, Tower Dining Services
Procter & Gamble Company
Cincinnati, Ohio

Jack Galione
President
Corporate Food Services
New York, New York

Susan E. Guenther
Food Service Manager
Wisconsin Electric Power Company
Milwaukee, Wisconsin

Philip E. Hawkins
Manager, Dining Services
Procter & Gamble Company
Cincinnati, Ohio

Deanna Hormel
President
American Foodservices Enterprises, Inc.
Kansas City, Missouri

Paul Hysen
President
The Hysen Group
Livonia, Michigan

Dolores Juergens
Manager of Food Services
Northwestern Mutual Life
   Insurance Company
Milwaukee, Wisconsin

Guy E. Karrick
Communications Director
Society for Foodservice Management
Louisville, Kentucky

Bob Kilgore
Director of Marketing
CBORD Group
Ithaca, New York

Ronald Kooser
Senior Principal
Cini-Little International
Chagrin Falls, Ohio

William C. Lembach
Director, Food Service
Eastman Kodak Company
Rochester, New York

James Marvin
Vice President, Corporate Dining
Seiler Corporation
Waltham, Massachusetts

Neil S. Reyer
Vice President, Restaurant/
   Travel Management
Chemical Bank
New York, New York

Jacqueline M. Schoff
Manager, Cafeteria Services
Procter & Gamble, Inc.
Cincinnati, Ohio

Don Smith
Westin Distinguished Professor
Washington State University
Seattle, Washington

Charles Speller
General Manager, Business Food Service
Northern Trust Bank/Marriott Corporation
Chicago, Illinois

Carol Weisman
Manager, Dining Services
Procter & Gamble, Inc.
Cincinnati, Ohio

Candace Ann York
Food Service Manager
Texas Instruments, Inc.
Dallas, Texas

Beryl J. Yuhas
President
Beryl Yuhas Associates
San Raphael, California

Foreword

DON SMITH

Don Smith, BS, ME, is the Westin Distinguished Professor at Washington State University and received the Shell Award for Teaching Excellence. Previously, he served on the faculty of Michigan State University as director of the school of Hotel, Restaurant, and Institutional Management. In 1983, he was named MSU's Outstanding Faculty Member of the Year.

There is general agreement that employees are capable of contributing more than they do in the workplace. However, there is general confusion about how to tap this potential. I am satisfied that there is no simple recipe or set of actions that will influence employees to give their personal best and sacrifice their goals for those of the organization. For as you know, the organization is the cold, faceless entity most often represented by some acronym in the business section of the *Wall Street Journal*.

But of this I am certain: a person in line at the teller's window or a sales counter knows if somebody really cares about his or her welfare. I can assure you that the effort each employee is willing to put forth is directly related to his or her perception of how much the boss really cares.

The importance, theories, and practices of serving food and hospitality a few minutes every day to American workers are what this text is about. In its simplest vernacular, it is called Business & Industry foodservice, or B&I. B&I foodservice encompasses over 25,000 corporate outlets and represents 7.1 percent of today's $230 billion dollar foodservice market. In 1988, $15 billion dollars was pumped into the American economy through the business of dining in industrial plants, banks, and corporate suites. The future of B&I appears bright as it keeps pace with the growth in the gross national product.

Yet, even with lucrative careers and a more appealing life-style than the commercial sector, the vital B&I sector has long been the Cinderella of hospitality education. Why are more graduates and managers not breaking down the doors of the foodservice contractors and self-operated enterprises in search of careers?

This text, *The Handbook of Noncommercial Foodservice Management: Dining in Corporate America,* explores the nature of this unique business and shares the guarded secrets of successful operators. It has been too long in coming. *Dining in Corporate America* dispels the dull image and obsolete concepts of serving the "captive market." The only captive audiences left today are either in penal institutions or intensive care units of hospitals. The forerunners in B&I know that there are unlimited growth and extraordinary new opportunities on the horizon for those who see themselves as contributing to the quality of life of the American worker. To do this they must compete with the leaders in the commercial sector. Gone are the images of tired unfeeling people, bleak dining rooms, and the cold stainless steel cafeteria line filled with monotonous gray and brown food. In fact, today's B&I foodservice establishment is a *restaurant*—driven by the objective of the customer's satisfaction.

THE AGE OF THE BIG BUSINESS PROFESSIONAL

Among today's leading foodservice contractors are such billion-dollar companies as Marriott, ARA, Canteen, Service America, and Morrison's. These giants have brought with them economies of scale, sophisticated research techniques, systems, computer analysis, and commissary production. Of course, there are many excellent smaller regional contractors. Nor should one overlook the major "self-operators" that include such companies as Motorola, Eastman Kodak, Hallmark Cards, Martin Marietta, and Morgan Guaranty Trust.

Today's mega-foodservice companies have also ushered onto the B&I scene a new type of professional: the HRIM (hotel, restaurant & institutional management) graduate.

In over 12 years of university teaching and counseling, I have only recently observed a greater number of high achievers and class leaders entering the noncommercial foodservice sector. In the past, most graduates gravitated to the more "glamorous" sectors of hotels and upscale dining. They have not been attracted by the "9 to 5" life-style nor the challenge of satisfying the changing consumer's needs in the workplace and battle for market share in the B&I sector.

THE REVOLUTION IN CORPORATE FOODSERVICE

There is no question that many of America's "smoke-stack" industries have moved abroad. Today's corporations are not only experiencing a reduction in their workforce but also a change in its nature. Today's employee is more educated and enlightened and has heightened expectations, different problems, and different tastes. Organizations experiencing a reduction in their workforce are moving out of old bleak factories and into smaller buildings in industrial parks that often accommodate 500 employees or less. Such branch locations are simply too small to support a full-sized restaurant for employees; however, the need still exists for quality foodservice.

Meeting this challenge of employee satisfaction and motivation often comes into conflict with corporate cost-effective financial decisions; e.g., many large corporations are unwilling to put big dollars behind foodservice at facilities with 500 or fewer employees. Today's industrial leaders are moving from subsidized employee meals and are striving for break-even meal service. In the future, companies will see their foodservice managers as employee morale and service managers, creatively engaged in operating potential profit centers. Such profit centers may include not only foodservice but also such auxiliary services as take-home foods, photographic services, health and beauty aids, video rentals, libraries, and courses in self-help study.

Future B&I managers will need to understand how to market to a limited universe. Unlike their commercial counterparts, they must appeal to the same guest, day in and day out. The true measure of success will be the ability to influence the frequency of the current user and size of the average check.

I am very pleased to have been asked to write the foreword to this long-needed text, *The Handbook of Noncommercial Foodservice Management: Dining in Corporate America,* I hope that, after reading and studying this text, the best of you will be attracted to careers in dining and services to employees at their places of work. It will take great innovation and courage to cope with the exciting changes in the American workplace. I can assure you that B&I foodservice is no place for the timid.

A Special Acknowledgment

The Society would like to recognize Lease Plimpton's contributions to the book. Without her involvement this project would never have been completed. As a vice president of the Society for Foodservice Management, Lease served as chairperson of the Society's Book Committee responsible for producing *Dining in Corporate America*.

Lease Plimpton is special services manager at MIT Lincoln Laboratory in Lexington, Massachusetts. Lease joined Lincoln in 1976 with the responsibility of overseeing the company's foodservice operations. She has supervised the renovation of two cafeterias, contracted a professional management company to operate the foodservice, and watched both participation and revenue increase by more than 400 percent.

The Editors

This book is the result of efforts by many Society for Foodservice Management members. As you read each chapter, the strong personalities of the authors are evident in the varied and highly individual use of words. All of these writers project professionalism about a segment of the foodservice industry that is still a "sleeper." This knowledge and the generous sharing of it are hallmarks of both Business & Industry and the Society for Foodservice Management. We are deeply grateful to each chapter author for sharing his or her vast knowledge and experience. As a person with a nonprofessional background thrust into the foodservice liaison job, I know how much I needed this book in 1976.

Over the years, this industry has simultaneously challenged me and taught me. The help I have received made it imperative that I contribute to the industry. So, even though chairing a committee ranks with going to the dentist or washing windows, this has been an invaluable experience. To all of you who contributed in so many ways, my unending gratitude.

We have had the incredible good fortune to have Joan Black Bakos, former editor of *Restaurant Business* magazine, edit this book for us. Last, but far from least, we are all indebted to the efforts of Guy E. Karrick and Phillip S. Cooke at SFM headquarters for guiding the project to a successful completion.

Let us know how you like the book, and what you will need in future revisions as our industry evolves. All of us welcome your comments, your questions and your input. Good luck!

Lease Plimpton

Introduction

PHILLIP S. COOKE

Phillip Cooke is president of Foodservice Associates, a corporate communications and association management firm specializing in the foodservice industry, and executive vice president of the Society for Foodservice Management. Before forming Foodservice Associates in 1969, he served as editor-in-chief of Restaurants & Institutions *Magazine, editor of* Chain Store Age, *managing editor of* Restaurant Management, *and editor of* Restaurant Equipment Dealer. *Following graduation from Grove City College in Pennsylvania with a degree in journalism, he began his career at the New York* Times.

Business & Industry foodservice is one of the most dynamic segments of the foodservice industry. It is a segment with apparently unlimited growth potential, some interesting new opportunities on the horizon, and a willingness to experiment and try new ideas to remain competitive with the commercial marketplace.

We have seen B&I foodservice change its image from that of a stodgy, boring, battleship-gray environment to one in which both decor and menu almost exactly mirror the commercial segment. The most accurate descriptive term today, in fact, for a B&I foodservice establishment is *restaurant*.

The players in B&I foodservice are divided into three categories. First, of course, are the contractors. These are the companies that operate foodservice for the client on a contractual basis. Second are the self-operators, those companies that still elect to operate their own foodservice. Third are the liaison personnel. This group has recently begun to come into its own. The liaison is charged with the responsibility of translating corporate philosophy to the contractor and of overseeing the contractor to make certain that it abides by the terms of the contract. Traditionally, liaison personnel were pulled out of almost any department within the corporation and hurled into foodservice with little background or preparation. Today, that is changing. We now see professional foodservice management executives, often with HRI degrees, entering the liaison ranks. This is a healthy development for all concerned.

Who are the decision makers in B&I? If the client is lazy or unschooled in the ways of foodservice, often the decisions concerning layout and design, menu, and other basic areas are left to the contractor. However, it is much more desirable to assign an experienced and knowledgeable liaison person representing the corporation to the development of a new foodservice facility. The contractor should be involved as a partner in the decision-making process, but not as the sole arbiter in matters relating to design and menu. Increasingly, corporations are beginning to see the value of a knowledgeable liaison person representing their corporate interests. In the future, the liaison will become increasingly involved in the decision-making process.

Today, we are experiencing a revolution in B&I foodservice, with liaison personnel no longer accepting, and often rejecting, products and services offered by the contractor that do not measure up to the specifications of the contract or do not reflect the corporate philosophy accurately and favorably. As corporations move from subsidizing employee meals and closer to a break-even meal service, the liaison will assume an increasingly important role in the decision-making process. The day is not too far off when many corporations will begin to see their foodservice operations as potential profit centers.

Today, contractors hold 80 percent of the B&I market, with self-operators responsible for the remaining 20 percent. The trend to contract out foodservice will certainly continue and by the end of the century over 90 percent of operations will be run by contractors.

One interesting trend is that the so-called regional contractors are no longer necessarily willing to stay within their geographical boundaries or settle only for the smaller pieces of business that traditionally have been offered to them. There now seems to be a willingness, even an eagerness, to go up against the national contractors in the fight for market share. Regional contractors position themselves as being flexible, wiry, adaptable, and quickly responsive. Their strategy seems to be paying off.

B&I foodservice reached $13.8 billion in sales in 1987 and exceeded $14.6 billion in sales in 1988. This market had a 1.8 percent real growth rate for 1988, reflecting a 2.9 percent increase in the number of employees served nationwide, who are predominantly white collar. B&I foodservice, encompassing over 25,000 units currently, has a 7.1 percent share of the total foodservice market. It is predicted that B&I foodservice will continue to grow at a steady, although not overly dramatic rate of 1 to 2 percent each year between now and the year 2000. Although no one seems to have an accurate count of the total number of daily meal occasions in B&I foodservice, we are currently estimating that 37 million meals are served daily, exclusive of vending.

One of the most significant trends in B&I facilities design is the downsizing of employee cafeterias. During the past decade, America's economy has moved from traditional manufacturing to a more service-oriented business environment. Companies experiencing a decline in the size of their work-force are moving out of old facilities and into industrial parks or smaller office buildings. Products and services are also being produced so rapidly that they often become obsolete within 5 years. As a result, companies are opening more and more smaller buildings designed to accommodate 500 or fewer employees. In some instances, employees moving out of a main office building and into a small office complex feel isolated; they perceive that company benefits, such as foodservice, are being taken away from them. Usually these branch locations are simply too small in terms of space or workforce to support and justify a full-sized cafeteria. However, the need still exists to provide quality foodservice.

In addition, increased internal pressure has forced most foodservice operations to reduce expenditures and improve productivity. In such an environment, it is not always realistic to construct a full-sized cafeteria. Rather than make a multimillion dollar investment in capital equipment, the downsizing concept offers a viable solution. Smaller cafeterias and the downsizing of existing facilities will continue as a trend well into the future.

One of the treasured perks of the American corporate executive traditionally has been access to the wood-paneled, hallowed halls of the executive dining room. But now the future of the executive dining room is uncertain. Certainly, banks and brokerage houses will still use executive dining rooms as a marketing tool to woo and impress clients. Yet, as the democratization of the American corporation continues, the walls separating the executive dining room from the employee cafeteria will come tumbling down. Private meeting rooms will remain and be available to all employees for meetings and special occasions, but the majority of corporations will probably abandon the idea of executive dining well before the year 2000.

One of the most exciting developments in B&I foodservice is the advent of shops offering such auxiliary services as greeting cards, film development, health and beauty aids, videotape rentals, jewelry, and gift items. These shops, ranging in size from 300 to 1000 square feet and normally staffed by one employee, offer a dizzying array of products and services. In addition to those already mentioned, an employee may also buy candy, cigarettes, magazines, newspapers, soda, juice, and snacks. Even laundry and dry cleaning drop-off and shoe repair are increasing among the array of services offered. The design of these shops sets the tone for the product offerings. Tastefully upscale in appearance, they present an image that is not quite commercial, yet is user-friendly and colorful.

There is a tendency to overlook the importance of vending in B&I food-service, yet vending represents $1 billion in sales annually. It is still extremely important for feeding late-night shifts and small office staffs for whom cafeterias are not warranted and for sales of subsidiary items, such as soft drinks and snacks. Thirty years ago the vending industry made a concerted effort to replace manual foodservice with all-vended facilities. This dream on the part of the vending companies never materialized, but vending has found an honorable and acceptable place in the scheme of B&I foodservice. It should not be discounted as a contributor to bottom-line profitability.

Another trend is the emergence of multi-tenant buildings with one centralized foodservice facility available to all. It certainly makes a great deal of sense for several smaller corporations to take advantage of a single foodservice operation for their employees, rather than each tackling the problem of providing foodservice on an individual basis. Contractors initially saw this new expanding market as a bonanza, but have come to find that there are some problems inherent in the concept. Namely, the return on investment has not been as great as originally anticipated. Although a multi-tenant building may be 100 percent leased, in many instances the offices are more "mail drops" than fully functional offices. Office personnel are predominantly in sales positions and are on the road a majority of the time, resulting in a "ghost" population that is not present to avail itself of the dining facility. Increased profitability may be achieved by some form of foodservice that uses little space and offers take-out and take-home foods in addition to on-premise dining to help recoup costs. The auxiliary services shops will also have a strong role to play in connection with the multi-tenant facilities. The combination of food and retail will, in all probability, make these facilities economically viable.

Another trend is the return of the commissary. With the introduction of new cooking techniques, such as *sous vide* and quick-chill, we are almost certainly going to see the establishment of central commissaries providing products to individual contracted units. In cases where self-operators are large enough, such as at Eastman Kodak, we will see the establishment of these commissaries to feed the corporate population.

B&I foodservice operators have also become extremely adept at studying and then mimicking their commercial counterparts. Fast food, including the ubiquitous hamburger, French fries, and pizza, has found its way onto the B&I menu. Recognizing that these are not the healthiest of all possible foods, B&I has also generously borrowed the salad bar concept and a heavier reliance on seafood and fresh vegetables for those who are both diet and nutrition conscious. The increased emphasis on wellness and fitness programs in the corporate environment in recent years is complemented by the foodservice menu offerings.

There is a trend toward fragmentation of the service area going far beyond the traditional cafeteria scatter system. We now see make-your-own sandwich bars, salad bars, make-your-own dessert and sundae bars, fresh fruit stations, pizza stations, ethnic food stations with Mexican and Italian being the most popular, and almost any other kind of make-your-own participation food station imaginable. The traditional steam table has shrunk almost out of existence as fun foods and fad foods have dominated the available space for merchandising and presenting food.

What all of this means, in terms of equipment and facilities design, is that today's B&I foodservice operator requires flexible, mobile equipment that can easily be moved, rearranged, and utilized in a number of situations. A most recent trend is the use of carts similar to those used by street vendors in New York City. These can be rolled out at various points of service and then can just as quickly be rolled away. Overdesigned and overequipped kitchens and foodservice facilities are things of the past.

In the past few years, the B&I segment has emerged from the position of red-headed stepchild, unloved and unnoticed, to one of the most sought-after segments in the industry. The volatility and flat sales of the commercial market, a decrease in new restaurant openings, and an apparent unwillingness or inability of potential customers to pay for goods and services have turned many manufacturers and suppliers away from the commercial market and toward the noncommercial segments. Even though its growth rate slowed somewhat in 1988, B&I remains ahead of all other noncommercial segments, which in the aggregate report 1.1 percent real compound growth. However, it is still behind the commercial market, which reported 3.2 percent growth for 1987. Yet, the stability of the B&I segment makes it the more attractive of the two when viewed on a long-term basis. The renaissance of the American corporation, the resuscitation of the Rust Belt, and the development of new service industries all forecast continued growth for B&I foodservice for many years to come.

PART I

Types of B&I Foodservice

1

Self-Operating Foodservice versus Contract Management

GUY E. KARRICK

Guy E. Karrick is communications director for the Society for Foodservice Management. In this capacity, he is responsible for all the Society's publications including the SFM Report, SFM Annual, *and special reports published on a timely basis. Guy joined the association in 1984 upon graduating from the University of Kentucky with a B.A. degree in Communications. He served as the project director for* Dining in Corporate America.

External governmental pressure and internal fiscal constraints have forced more and more corporations to reduce the operating subsidy of their food-service operations and to take a closer look at the bottom line. Corporate cafeterias are not only becoming break-even operations, but many are even expected to show a yearly profit.

As a result, the movement within the industry has been toward hiring foodservice management companies to operate corporate foodservice operations. Most companies are not in the foodservice business, but are in the business of producing something else. Ford Motor Company, for example, is in the automobile industry, not in the foodservice business. That is why corporations ask themselves, "Why do we have to make a commitment to foodservice? Why don't we put the burden on someone else by hiring a foodservice contractor?"

Where does this type of reasoning leave the self-operators? Are companies that contract out not as committed to foodservice? Are self-operators truly becoming a dying breed? This chapter examines the answers to these questions by providing insights of many prominent B&I foodservice managers.

This chapter was adapted from the article "Are Self-Ops Becoming Extinct?" *Society for Foodservice Management Annual,* 1987.

ADVANTAGES AND BENEFITS OF
SELF-OPERATING FOODSERVICE

Although self-ops are becoming few and far between, there will always be a niche for them in the industry. Even though foodservice contractors offer a high level of professional expertise, many corporations who have made a strong commitment to operating their own foodservice in the past will continue to do so. Depending on the corporation, self-ops have the resources and capabilities to do as good a job—and in some cases even better—than a contractor. For instance, "I am basically providing a level of service and quality of food that would be hard to match by a contractor," says Richard McQueen, manager of foodservices for Bausch & Lomb in Rochester, New York. "We are also meeting all the financial goals with our foodservice." According to Tom Ney, director of the food center at Rodale Press, "We have a very strong corporate philosophy at Rodale where we practice what we publish and translate it into practical sense. Quite frankly, it would be difficult for a contractor to meet the stringent nutritional requirements and aesthetics of our foodservice operation."

Greater control is among the main benefits experienced by corporations that decide to operate their own foodservice. Policy changes and other alterations can be implemented quickly, whereas a contractor may typically need to cut through a myriad of bureaucratic levels to institute changes.

"There is generally more red tape to cut through when instigating policy and procedure decisions with a contractor, that I could otherwise make instantly," states Dolores Juergens, manager of foodservices at Northwestern Mutual Life Insurance Company. "In most situations, a liaison must negotiate for certain provisions to which my company has already made a strong commitment."

Craig Smith, manager of food services at Steelcase, Inc. concurs, saying, "Having total control and direct access to the people who are doing the job are the biggest advantages of operating your own foodservice. It's very easy to lose control of your operations when someone else runs your foodservice. You tend to be much more involved when you operate your own foodservice—you have to be," adds Craig.

Foodservice employees working with a self-op environment tend to exhibit more dedication and loyalty toward corporate goals. They are providing foodservice to their fellow employees. They experience none of the conflict engendered by working for one company while being paid by another. Bill Lembach, foodservice director at Eastman Kodak, explains,

> By operating our own foodservice, we have a better understanding of the company we work for and show allegiance toward that

company. People who actually work for us have allegiance to the company as well. They are company employees.

Gary Gunderson, regional manager in Austin, Texas, for Motorola, Inc., adds, "Our foodservice employees provide personalized service and have a more vested interest in serving their fellow employees."

Another advantage of self-op foodservice is having only one central authority. The contractor must always take direction from its own company procedures, as well as from the client. And, on some occasions, these directions can conflict.

WHY CONTRACT MANAGEMENT COMPANIES SUCCEED

The chief asset of most professional contract caterers is their ability to manage the foodservice at a lower operating cost than a self-operator. Corporations operating their own foodservice must generally pay higher wages and offer benefits comparable with other corporate employees. Contractors are not required to pay these corporate benefits; therefore, they are in a position to present a better financial package to prospective clients.

To complement their own professional foodservice expertise, contractors are able to call on a strong back-up management staff at their company headquarters. According to Martin Cherneff, president of M.H. Cherneff & Associates, "Contractors provide good management depth and solid back-up support for each unit manager. Generally, self-ops have little support or anyone to turn to. Through the sharing of knowledge, however, professional associations such as SFM can provide self-ops with a viable resource base."

Does the buying power of some of the national contractors give them an advantage over self-ops? Not according to Marty Cherneff. "It doesn't affect the bottom line that much to have the purchasing power of a major corporation versus the astute purchasing ability of a strong foodservice operator."

Michael Barclay, vice president of Southern Foodservice Management, describes the advantages of contractors in this way.

In general, contractors offer the professional expertise of a food-service management company and in some cases, the ability to purchase on a national scale. However, the single greatest advantage in hiring a professional management company to operate the foodservice is lower labor costs.

GOVERNMENTAL PRESSURE—UNCLE SAM INTERVENES

In December 1985, the IRS issued new temporary regulations of the 1984 Tax Reform Act regarding meals provided in subsidized company cafeterias. In 1987, the IRS issued regulations allowing only 80% of all business meals as deductible. Although commercial restaurants have been affected by this legislation, many non-commercial foodservice operators have reported an increase in their in-house corporate dining rooms.

What effect have these two bills and other governmental regulations had on the industry? Although no one can accurately predict the full impact of the new tax bill, companies are encountering increased pressure from the government to operate their foodservice in a profit/loss arrangement, reducing and sometimes even eliminating their subsidy. This competitive environment favors contractors because lower labor costs put them in a better position to reduce the operating subsidy.

If a self-op foodservice can continue to satisfy corporate objectives and meet all financial goals, it will remain self-op. However, if a professional contractor can operate the foodservice more economically, then the trend will continue toward hiring management companies.

Richard McQueen elaborates,

> Unless contractors inherit a problem with the IRS, they will continue to grow and consolidate at even greater rates. The efficiency in their sheer numbers in areas, such as test kitchens, centralized menus, and major purchasing programs, will allow them to hold their end up because they can keep the cost down. However, this becomes a labor issue and not a food issue. Foodservice is based on providing quality food and good service, but is not a financial issue. In short, the new tax law means we're all in the same boat to break even.

The new 80/20 bill has provided keen foodservice managers with a tremendous opportunity to promote their own in-house guest or executive dining rooms. By saving an additional 20 percent deductibility, business executives have a financial incentive to entertain in-house, not to mention the time-saving advantages.

MERGERS AND ACQUISITIONS BY NATIONAL CONTRACTORS

What effects have the recent mergers and acquisitions by some of the national contractors had on the industry? Do these rounds of consolidations and mergers signify the end of self-op foodservice?

Although mergers and acquisitions have certainly made contractors more visible, they should not have a dramatic impact on corporations who desire to continue with self-operation. "Mergers and acquisitions have mainly resulted in the development of strong regional management companies," says Marty Cherneff. "But the mergers in no way represent the last vestiges of self-operated foodservice."

Large companies are frequently viewed as being impersonal and unresponsive. The foodservice industry is a very personal business; therefore, responding to the client's individual needs is one of the keys to success. The industry will continue to see the emergence of smaller regional contractors and clients looking for personalized foodservice.

Most large contractors also tend to move their employees around often, resulting in a high turnover of top management. Because management personnel differ in operating philosophy and ability, these moves can potentially affect the client adversely.

Other potential problems can surface in the relationship between the foodservice contractor and the company liaison manager (see Chapter 2 on the role of the liaison manager). In many situations, the liaison has come out of personnel, human resources, or even the comptroller's office and has no foodservice experience. "In the end, the smaller regional contractors will prosper and eventually come into their own. Regional contractors have the ability to provide their clients with outstanding, personalized service," says Beryl Yuhas, president of Beryl Yuhas Associates.

HOW WILL SELF-OPS REMAIN COMPETITIVE?

In order to survive in an increasingly competitive marketplace, self-ops must continue to offer creative foodservice. Foodservice managers in most self-op situations have a free hand to be creative and make on-the-spot decisions. By taking full advantage of their resources and facilities, self-ops will continue to succeed. Larry Appleton, manager of food and vending operations at Martin Marietta, notes,

> Although there have been some challenges set by foodservice contractors, we have become more creative and very competitive in nature. We shouldn't just throw up our arms and say, "Leave it to the foodservice contractor." The self-ops that will be successful will be the ones who are creative, daring and audacious.

Self-ops must turn to other markets, such as carry-out and breakfast programs, to generate additional revenue from their foodservice operations. Such programs as one-stop, take-out dinners for the entire family are a great source of untapped income.

Marketing and merchandising techniques can be used by foodservice managers to increase sales. The bottom line in foodservice is still variety, service, and quality. Those companies that can excel in these areas—going the extra mile and treating their customers like royalty—will succeed. Dolores Juergens of Northwestern Mutual says,

> Everyone in the industry is not solely dependent upon the bottom line. Sometimes service and quality as well as other intangibles overshadow the bottom line; companies develop a strong pride of ownership philosophy. Northwestern Mutual has been self-op since 1915 and we see no reason to change now.

Another area of concern is the number of qualified foodservice managers in the B&I segment of the foodservice industry. Is there a shortage of quality management personnel? According to Craig Smith, there is no shortage.

> I am not finding a shortage of good management personnel in the Midwest. A lot of people are looking for jobs in B&I foodservice. For some managers, it's more desirable to work in a self-op environment where you have a greater amount of control. There also tends to be less corporate rules and guidelines to follow, resulting in a greater opportunity to be more creative.

However, Deanna Hormel, director of foodservice at Hallmark Cards, disagrees. "Most foodservice managers are trained for hospitals, hotels, and restaurants. It is vital to contact students and make them aware of opportunities in B&I food service."

OUTLOOK—WHERE DOES THIS LEAVE SELF-OP FOODSERVICE?

In these turbulent times of increasing governmental regulation and decreasing company subsidies, the trend toward hiring professional contractors will continue. "We will continue to see a trend to hiring contractors, but eventually it will end with those corporations who have made a strong commitment to foodservice and feel it is a vital part of the company remaining self-op," says Craig Smith.

Michael Barclay concurs, saying, "The industry as a whole will continue to favor contractors. However, those companies who have professionally trained individuals to manage the foodservice and have made a strong commitment to quality will remain self-op."

Bill Lembach agrees.

> More companies will take the easy way out to reduce payroll and labor costs by hiring a contractor to operate the foodservice. Self-ops who want to survive, however, know we must meet our competition head on and Kodak is willing to do that. We're willing to show that we can compete effectively and do a better job than a contractor.

Overall, the B&I segment continues to grow at the real growth rate of 1.3 percent. Although mergers among some of the industry's biggest companies have eliminated some of the players, sales and customer counts are expected to increase.

When deciding whether to operate their own food service or hire a professional contractor, corporations must determine the type of commitment they are willing to make to foodservice. Contractors and self-ops both have the skills and resources to provide quality foodservice, but each one has distinct advantages. Contractors offer lower labor costs; self-op arrangements allow total control of the foodservice operations.

"I am still scratching and clawing at my little corner of the world," says Richard McQueen. "I'm independent and have a free hand to do just about anything that I want. And I'm having fun doing it."

2

Corporate Liaison Management

PART A: THE INTERMEDIARY ROLE BETWEEN THE CLIENT AND FOODSERVICE CONTRACTOR

GUY E. KARRICK

In an effort to explore the role of the corporate liaison and enhance the professionalism and stature of the position within the corporate environment, the Society for Foodservice Management conducted a series of liaison roundtable seminars throughout the country in 1987. This chapter is based upon the information gleaned from these meetings.

Corporate foodservice liaisons have been in existence since corporations began contracting their employee foodservices out to professional management companies. In the fifties and sixties, when a corporation needed to communicate with its foodservice contractor, someone within the corporation who had some extra time would fill the role. The thought of hiring a full-time professional to assume this role was inconceivable.

However, the corporate world has experienced dramatic and complex changes. More and more jobs within the corporate setting are becoming increasingly specialized, requiring professionals to fill them properly. Managing a typical B&I employee foodservice operation has become such a position. It has become far too important a function to be left to someone underqualified or faint of heart.

In its simplest terms, the corporate liaison is the individual employed by the client/corporation who has the responsibility of coordinating the activities of the contractor with the needs of the corporation. The liaison's job is extremely diverse and complex, although largely behind the scenes. The biggest challenge facing all corporate liaisons is balancing financial controls while maintaining the customer base by providing perceived foodservice quality and dollar value.

The liaison's position is so diverse and ever changing that there is no standard job description for the industry as a whole. A corporate liaison's responsibilities and job description ultimately depend on the priority and commitment to foodservice of the corporate management. In the past 10 years, the role of the liaison has evolved into a prominent part of the overall corporate structure.

Today's corporations are placing more emphasis on human resources and employee benefits than in the past. They are also striving to create a more positive working atmosphere and improving the overall quality of life for their employees. Well-managed corporations have realized there is a solid return on the investment of providing the benefit of a well-run foodservice operation for their employees. Not only do the employees have an opportunity to receive a quality meal (often subsidized by their company) but corporations also enjoy increased productivity by keeping their employees on-site during lunch and other meal occasions.

The Liaison's Job Description and Responsibilities

Although there is no formal job description for the liaison, some basic functions are performed by most liaisons and are written into most foodservice contracts. Exhibit 2-1 is a brief list of a liaison's duties.

The liaison's most important function is to make certain that the foodservice contractor performs consistently to the standards of the agreement with the client/corporation. It is the liaison's responsibility to be sensitive to the corporate philosophy. On occasions when the contractor's and the corporation's philosophies are incompatible, the liaison must ascertain whether to make a change and, if so, to evaluate proposals and select a new management company to operate the foodservice.

Foodservice is a major investment by any corporation. A large amount of dollars are necessary to support such an employee benefit as a quality foodservice operation. That is why corporations should select a liaison of the highest professional caliber: one who possesses a strong foodservice background either through education or practical experience to manage the employee foodservice operations. In many cases the knowledge is hard won through experience in an unfamiliar position. Good managers from other disciplines have learned as much as possible and as quickly as possible in order to perform this new or added job assignment for the company. Many non-foodservice professionals have found surprising satisfaction in their interactions with the contractor and the foodservice community.

The liaison's role will continue to prosper and flourish as many companies move toward contract food management and from self-op. A foodservice contractor should never be left to operate a foodservice facility without receiving some type of formal direction or feedback from the corporation. In addition, foodservice contractors should not have to report to many masters or top executives at the client/corporation. Someone (the liaison) has to establish objectives and specifications for the foodservice and provide direction for the contractor. That individual must also develop a realistic working budget, review the budget, and then implement the budget.

Exhibit 2-1 Duties of a Corporate Liaison

Financial—Working with the contractor, the liaison is responsible for developing a workable foodservice budget.

Purchasing—Although food management companies use their own suppliers, most contracts are written to allow the client (liaison) the latitude to add or remove suppliers from the list on an as needed basis. Because most corporations provide space and facilities for the foodservice operation, it is usually the liaison who makes decisions about equipment, smallwares, and furniture purchases. Liaisons also choose consultants for small or large operational and design tasks.

Hiring and Salary Decisions—Foodservice management personnel are selected according to both an interview process involving both the contractor and liaison. The liaison participates in all hiring, transferring, promoting, terminating, and salary determination activities. Before employees of the foodservice contractor may assume a management position at the unit level, they must fullfill all corporate qualifications. The liaison influences that determination.

Incentive Fee and Bonus Payments—The liaison always determines these payments on behalf of the corporation.

Promotional Calendar and Ideas—In addition to embellishing any promotion or theme day implemented by the contractor, the liaison may create an in-house promotional calendar.

Menu Planning and Design—By communicating corporate customs and preferences to the contractor, the liaison has direct input into developing all menus to ensure that they meet all corporate guidelines regarding nutrition.

Management and Policy Decisions—Any major policy decisions requiring the expenditure of funds or dramatic changes in the corporate quality of life vis-a-vis foodservice are approved through the liaison's office.

Food Committees—In most B&I settings, a committee of employees is formed to monitor the foodservice operations and make suggestions or recommendations to improve service levels. The committees vary in size, but always report directly to the liaison.

Human Resources—The liaison handles specific customer situations to prevent them from becoming a problem. For example, customers with complaints should always report them to the liaison.

Sanitation—This may be handled by the client/company, the contractor, both, or an outside source. Usually this responsibility is carefully spelled out in the foodservice contract.

Negotiation of Contracts—The crux of the liaison's role is reviewing the contract and ensuring that the contractor is faithfully adhering to the agreement. Major revisions are made only after the liaison meets with the food management company to develop a written proposal.

This role of liaison is very proactive and should be performed by an individual with a strong foodservice or management background. The liaison must first and foremost understand the needs of the client/corporation and the real world of contract management in order to join both sides together to fulfill the corporate philosophy and foodservice objectives of the client. The liaison must interpret that philosophy and be able to translate it into a workable foodservice program understood not only by the contractor but also by the client/corporation and its employees—the B&I foodservice customers.

In corporations where there is no liaison role, the foodservice contractor is in a position to do as it pleases, which may or may not be in line with corporate goals or philosophy. In such a situation, every customer becomes a boss; all senior management personnel within the corporation become bosses. Contractors do not know what are the foodservice objectives or goals. Sooner or later, chaos ensues.

As its agent, the food management company is spending the client/corporation's money. It is dangerous to assume that all contractors will always spend the company's money wisely. What prevents the contractor from going over budget or hiring an inordinate amount of labor? Because the typical B&I foodservice requires a large amount of capital and dollars to operate effectively, a foodservice professional employed by the client/corporation should always monitor those expenditures and ensure the most efficient use of those funds. What the client thinks it is paying for in terms of quality, it should in fact be receiving.

When hiring a food management company to operate the foodservice, the liaison must ensure that the contract is in compliance with all existing local codes of health and sanitation, fire safety, and employee safety. It is also the liaison's responsibility to ensure that the foodservice contract is always being followed. Because the liaison serves as the primary point of contact with the contractor, in essence, the liaison becomes the client.

It is the liaison's role to articulate the corporate foodservice objectives to the contractor in language it can understand. Conversely, the liaison must translate the contractor's needs into language the client/corporation can understand. A liaison's continual challenge is balancing the needs of the contractor and the needs of the corporation to avoid an adverse relationship. A good liaison will engender an "us" relationship by building trust and credibility.

The liaison must ensure that the relationship between the corporation and contractor is a solid, long-term relationship that works for everyone involved to meet the foodservice objectives on a day-to-day basis. To accomplish this goal these elements should be clearly specified from the beginning of the relationship—food quality, price structure, what level of service needs to be provided, and what times of day that service will be provided.

Keeping communication open and establishing a relationship of trust are the keys to successful liaison management. The client/corporation and contractor must work together. The contractor's employees have to feel a part of the client/corporation's team even though they are on the contractor's payroll. Yet, although it is tempting for the liaison to become actively involved and to assume a physical role in the day-to-day operation of running a restaurant, the liaison must be careful not to interfere with the responsibility of the contractor's on-site unit manager. The contractor's employees should never receive two or three different directions. They should only receive guidance from the unit manager. If the liaison wishes to voice a concern, it should go directly to the unit manager.

Establishing credibility is crucial. A strong liaison must be willing to come to the contractor's defense when the client/corporation is in the wrong. Conversely, the liaison must side with the corporation when the contractor is in the wrong. Because the liaison is on the client's payroll, balancing this relationship becomes very difficult.

A successful liaison is always honest with the contractor. When policy changes are instituted, a contractor should immediately be told what the new procedure is and why the decision was made. However, the contractor should not always feel obligated to say yes to the change. A contractor should have the right to say no and present an alternative solution to any problem.

When a corporation decides to change its foodservice contract, the decision is usually attributed to a lack of communication between the contractor and client/company. At times, contractors may take it for granted that they are irreplaceable. They are not! The contractor should always make available top management people with decision-making authority to stay in touch with the liaison. A routine phone call every two weeks or an on-site inspection every 2 months is desirable. A client will go out to bid when it feels the contractor is not listening or making any attempt to respond to the liaison's suggestions. It is the liaison who will ultimately decide whether to change food management companies.

As previously mentioned, the liaison's role should be assumed by an individual with a strong foodservice management background or a formal management background in accounting, finance, controls, and human resource development. In spite of the current emphasis on participative management, the amount of money invested by some corporations into foodservice should not be left to someone with no previous experience; on-the-job training is not always the best course to pursue. Liaisons must also be prepared to assume collateral responsibilities within their companies. During the 1980s, more and more liaisons have assumed additional auxiliary responsibilities, such as travel, company protocol, conference and meeting planning, and other human resource activities.

Outlook

The liaison in a B&I foodservice situation faces the challenge of finding people willing to deal with unique customer relations situations. Unlike the commercial sector, B&I foodservice managers must deal with the same customer base daily. These customers also feel the foodservice should be provided for them as a benefit. Therefore, they expect to pay lower prices even for superior products.

As corporations in all industries continue to merge, consolidate, and diversify, the role of the corporate foodservice liaison will become more important. A successful liaison will be an individual who can grow within today's complicated corporate structure. A liaison cannot rest on his or her laurels as a foodservice manager only. A successful liaison must be able to blend a variety of experiences and be willing to assume ancillary responsibilities, such as design projects and financial planning.

The liaison of the 1990s is likely to combine an HRI degree and strong business background with customer relations aptitude. An astute awareness of the industry is also necessary to tie these skills and experience together. Liaisons must also dedicate more time to the industry and community by joining professional organizations, attending industry seminars, and giving guest lectures at colleges and universities. To attract new people to the industry, liaisons must be willing to give to the educational process what it gave them.

To compete in today's fast-paced and ever-changing corporate environment, the liaison should visit other foodservice operations (both commercial and noncommercial) to gain ideas for continually developing new, fresh, and exciting foodservice programs. Liaisons should also think in terms of working for a club whose membership is restricted. Once liaisons adopt this philosophy, it becomes second nature to treat each customer as special—which is what the foodservice business is all about.

Wearing many hats and assuming additional responsibilities present an opportunity for liaisons to gain entry into senior management positions within their corporation. Assuming the management responsibility for auxiliary projects will not only benefit the corporation but will also enable liaisons to develop more skills, which enhances their position within the corporate structure. By being involved with a corporation's foodservice operations, liaisons also have a unique opportunity for high visibility because, as with almost every other aspect of foodservice operation, liaison management is often management by crisis. Fast responses combined with confident experience create a situation where the liaison as leader can shine.

PART B: WHAT IT MEANS TO BE A CORPORATE LIAISON: WINNING WITH AN RFP

RONALD KOOSER

Ronald Kooser is senior principal at Cini-Little International, the foodservice industry's largest and most diversified consulting firm. Headquartered in Wash-

ington, DC, the firm has offices in Boston, Chicago, Cleveland, Miami, Los Angeles, San Francisco, New York, and Toronto. Ron has worked extensively with health care, foodservice, laundry and solid waste facilities, developing programs, systems and designs. Cini-Little provides foodservice consulting and support service consulting in laundry, solid waste management, health care and other areas of hospitality and related industry.

Some see the Request for Proposal (RFP) process as a burden instead of what it truly is: a very important ingredient in the success formula for selecting the best possible contractor in any type of industry.

An RFP is as advantageous to the contractor as it is to the service provider. It provides the only way by which all bidders—whether they are convention centers, stadiums, factories, office buildings, restaurants, or correction facilities—can make a proposal on the same basis and be fairly evaluated by providers. The competitive bidding process provides an opportunity to select the most favorable financial arrangement.

Typically, the RFP process is conducted before starting up a new operation. Usually it is not conducted again unless there is a rebidding process, which normally occurs 5 or 6 years after a contract is let.

Objective Assessment

An RFP permits a corporation to conduct an objective assessment of all management companies in a given area of expertise, whether in foodservice, health care, construction, or other services.

An RFP also can serve as a catalyst for the corporation to become better organized in its approach to the desired service, as well as in laying groundwork for an effective reporting relationship between the corporation and contractor. A side benefit is that the contract administrator can learn a great deal about the service being offered by going through the RFP process. Use of an RFP can eliminate time-consuming sales presentations that usually are not objective.

The first stage is screening, during which a corporation learns about a management company's background and experience, as well as makes telephone reference checks with its current accounts. At this point, bidders can be screened out who do not meet the objectives of expertise, similar types of accounts, and strength in the corporation's geographical area. Too often, an RFP is initiated without the prequalification step. It is begun either with a small list of potential bidders that may exclude capable and qualified firms (too narrow) or a large group of companies that do not match the basic requirements of experience (too broad).

Three key parts to an RFP document are

1. specific instructions, conditions, and bid submittal requirements
2. detailed operating specifications
3. specific requirements of each party, i.e., obligations, limitations, restrictions, etc.

These elements help eliminate distortions in the bid response. An RFP that is not specific but simply requests ideas and proposals for how bidders would run the operation produces bid responses that are very diverse and difficult to evaluate objectively. In contrast, a specific RFP covering expected financial arrangements, will enable the evaluating team to compare bids and permit enhancements and creative thinking by the bidders.

Rebidding Cuts Complacency

With rebidding, both parties win. Rebidding eliminates any sense of complacency on the part of the contractor. It also corrects any dissatisfaction felt by the corporation and enables an examination of the market to compare what other concepts rival contractors have developed during the course of the contract. This re-examination also allows the incumbent operator to demonstrate a revitalization of his or her program and approach to the business.

Rebidding should be done every 5 or 6 years. If a contract runs longer than 5 to 6 years, the rebid should be done at the end of the contract. In the rebidding process, the incumbent operator has the advantage of knowing the corporation better than other contractors.

It is vitally important for the client's evaluating team to be wary of promises that appear too good to be true and of financial projections that are very far above the incumbent's performance. The team needs to examine projections for staffing and financial results carefully, as well as talk with the bidders' existing accounts before making a decision.

Assuming a detailed RFP is issued, listing the specific requirements (hours of operation, estimated guest counts, level of service) of the program, the bid response should be evaluated on the following points.

- *Experience level* (if not already determined in the screening stage)—Does the bidder have experience in the same *types* of operation, *levels* of service, and *size* of operations? Does it have capabilities in the immediate area—is it established or *new* to the area?

- *Concepts, menus, services descriptions*—What will the contractor provide? This is the most creative section of the RFP; bidders really must know their client's objectives to complete it properly and then have the talent to produce and implement it
- *Staffing*—Does the bidder show an organizational chart for the unit, the resumes of key management staff, and a carefully worked out staffing plan?
- *Financial information*—How well does the bidder justify its estimates and does it avoid "making it look good;" i.e., is it a realistic picture? Is it competitive in fees or commission structure?
- *Sanitation and safety practices*—Will the bidder provide a program for the standards, inspections, and action plans to correct deficiencies?
- *Labor and training practices*—Does it have established criteria and a thorough, effective training program for both wage and salaried employees?

PART II

Styles of Service

3

Styles of Service (Manual Operations)

JAMES MARVIN

James Marvin is vice president of corporate dining for Seiler Corporation, a foodservice contractor. He is responsible for the corporation's $40 million in sales, predominantly from clients along the Eastern seaboard from South Carolina to Maine. With a Bachelor of Science Degree in Hotel and Restaurant Management from Cornell University, he previously worked for the Wood Company and Servomation.

B&I foodservice has adopted many operational styles in order to serve food and related products to its customers. Service styles are dictated by how much time, space, and money are directed toward the foodservice operation. The amount of company resources used for foodservice is a reflection of management's attitude toward the importance that employee dining has within the corporation. Building designs and management attitudes are changeable, and as a result, foodservice operations have to be flexible.

There are, however, certain basic styles of service under which most food operations can be classified. They are as follows:

- full-service cafeterias
  1. straight line system
  2. scatter system
  3. mobile system

- limited-service cafeterias (made up of components of a full-service cafeteria)

- fast food service

- cart and mobile service

- waitress or waiter service dining rooms

- executive dining operations

FULL-SERVICE CAFETERIA

Cafeteria-style service grew out of a need to provide dining accommodations to large numbers of people with a minimum amount of labor requirements. A full cafeteria comprises several service areas designed to meet the many tastes of a large audience. These areas can be either manned with personnel or constructed for self-service by the customer.

These stations are found in a full-service cafeteria.

- **Entrees or hot food**—This area provides the customer with prepared hot main course selections, vegetables, starches, and soups.
- **Grill**—The grill provides the customer with popular food items, such as hamburgers, hot dogs, steak sandwiches, grilled cheese, Reubens, breakfast items, etc. The grill area is also equipped with a deep-fat fryer to allow for service of French fries, onion rings, chicken nuggets, fried fish sandwiches, and similar items.
- **Deli counter**—At the deli station is found a selection of cold sandwiches that may be either prepared or made to order. The made-to-order deli has a full selection of fresh and processed meats, as well as various sandwich spreads, such as tuna, chicken, ham, and seafood salad. Sandwiches made to order are served with garnish and perhaps chips or a cold salad accompaniment.
- **Salads and salad bar**—This station is almost always designed for self-service. Preplated garnished salads and salad platters of all portion sizes are merchandised for sale. All items should be attractively plated and colorful and ready for customers to select as they pass by.

  The popular salad bar in public eating establishments was quickly adopted in B&I cafeterias. Many salad bars in industrial and corporate settings are as extensive and attractive as in the finest restaurants.
- **Desserts**—The dessert station is also a self-service area. Most always, a full selection of pies, cakes, puddings, cookies, gelatine, and more fancy desserts is offered.
- **Beverages**—In the beverage station in a full-service cafeteria there are a large variety of beverages. Coffee and tea, a selection of varietal teas, cold soda drinks, milk, various drink mixes, and real fruit beverages are some of the selections. Many of the cafeterias offer only cup beverages with lids for carry-out, whereas others offer a variety of self-contained drinks either to be consumed in the cafeteria or taken back to the employee's work area.
- **Specialty sections**—Many full-service cafeterias are now providing a station that can be used as an exclusive service style area; for instance,

a health food station, ethnic foods location, self-service soup location, sundae bar, or cookie bakeshop location. The use of this special section can be as wide and varied as the creativity of the manager allows.

These stations are laid out in one of three ways: the straight line method of service, the scatter or scramble system, and the flexible mobile concept.

Straight Line Method

In a straight line cafeteria presentation all service stations are lined up immediately following the other. This system enables the full-service concept to be designed into smaller locations and can also reduce equipment needs. Often, one piece of equipment can double as preservice preparation equipment and for the service of prepared products in front of the customer.

Generally, in a straight line cafeteria patrons enter the line at one end, obtain their tray, and pass through the entire service line selecting the menu items they desire. For the customer's convenience a tray rail usually runs the full length of the cafeteria line; the patron may rest the tray on the rail while moving through the line.

The major drawback to the straight line service is the inefficient way in which large numbers of people move through a single area in short periods of time. The straight line service method grew out of the military where selections were limited and the time of usage was strictly controlled.

Scatter or Scramble System

The need to satisfy the customer's desire for variety and management's desire to control the time of employee meals gave rise to the scatter or scramble system (see Figure 3-1). In this design, customers can go directly to the service station that meets their need for that meal. For example, in order to get to the deli bar, they do not have to wait in line behind the individual who wants an entree. Each service station is separated from the other and designed to offer a particular item.

Flexible Mobile Concept

The third method of cafeteria service is a totally flexible one. All the service equipment is mobile and designed to be moved as the situation dictates. This style of service is most useful to accommodate small but growing service areas and also in plants and areas where employee popu-

Figure 3-1 Many corporations are adopting a scatter or scramble system in the cafeteria to ease customer flow and make the foodservice operations more efficient. (Photo provided by Corporate Public Affairs Department, ARA Services, Inc.)

lation relocations occur frequently. The service can be expanded and/or reduced as needed.

Each method of service in a full-service cafeteria is supported by a kitchen that contains equipment sufficient to produce the majority of products on location. Most often, corporations that are willing to allocate large amounts of space to the service and seating areas also have kitchens with ample equipment to receive, store, prepare, and service all the stations in the cafeterias.

LIMITED CAFETERIA SERVICE

Not all locations have a need or desire for a full-service cafeteria and kitchen. Many corporations are in constantly changing environments and do not want to commit large amounts of capital to employee food service. A limited cafeteria-style service was developed to meet this need.

A limited cafeteria service can feature many of the food delivery stations of the full-service cafeteria, but the number of pieces of equipment is reduced.

The selections offered are limited to those items that can be prepared in a small on-site kitchen or by commissary support from an off-premise food production facility.

The scope of service offered in a limited cafeteria is as follows:

- **Entrees**—Service is limited to one entree, one vegetable, and a starch. Many locations also feature a hot sandwich, which adds variety to the menu. If there is a small prep kitchen on location the kinds of entrees offered can be extensive. When the food is prepared at an off-site location, the entrees are limited to those products that maintain their quality when held at proper transporting and service temperatures for long periods of time.

  If the cafeteria is extremely small the entrees might be provided through convenience products that are prepared, canned, and frozen elsewhere and reconstituted at the location. Under these limited conditions the entree may be a stew or extended item that includes meat, vegetable, and starch in one selection. Menu cycles with this limited style of service are very short, and variety is extremely limited.

- **Grill**—Those limited cafeteria services that provide a grill build the majority of their hot food service around this feature. Hamburgers, hot dogs, steak sandwiches, and popular fast food items are promoted heavily. Breakfast items may also be marketed.

  Some of the smaller limited services do not provide a grill, but can accommodate a hot dog roller or steamer and a small hot plate for preparing and heating some selections.

  With the advent of the microwave, limited service cafeterias that are commissary supported can offer prepared hamburgers, grill products, and breakfast items in refrigerated stations. The customer can heat and finish these products in the microwave.

- **Deli**—A limited-style service very rarely has both a deli operation and a grill. Service is built around one station or the other.

  A service with a full deli location provides all selections of sliced meats and cheeses and salad mixtures to prepare sandwich items in front of the customer. In contrast, a service without a full deli prepares sandwiches of all kinds, whether on location or in a commissary, and presents these items attractively for the customer's choice.

- **Salads and Salad Bars**—Salads are popular and colorful and are most often part of the selections offered in a limited service. The number of types of salads is limited in order to control prep time and service space.

  Salad bars are very effective in increasing the customer appeal of a limited-service cafeteria; where space is adequate, they are pleasantly received. Products for the salad areas can either be prepared on-site if space allows or by a central commissary kitchen. Freshness and product quality are essential.

- **Desserts**—Desserts are limited to those that are prepared and cut for service on location. Selections are minimal due to space allocations. Occasionally, a special dessert of the day or week is offered to stimulate interest and create variety.
- **Beverages**—Many limited cafeteria services are supported by vended beverages. This provides a full variety of selections while limiting labor costs and space requirements on the serving line.

    If space allows, many customers prefer fresh-brewed urn coffee, which enhances a limited service by its aroma alone.

A limited service can be arranged in a straight line configuration or a scatter-style system. Either works effectively.

The limited cafeteria service minimizes equipment needs and labor. In some organizations sufficient planning allows limited cafeteria set-ups to be expanded to full-service cafeterias as the corporation grows.

FAST FOOD SERVICE

The popularity of the fast food chains cannot be disputed. Any food item that can be packaged for easy transportation and quality preservation is a likely candidate for fast service. Some B&I locations are perfect for fast food, and some of the major fast food chains have established locations in large industrial settings.

Fast food is food designed to be prepared and served quickly and efficiently from the operator's point of view. This efficiency is achieved by building a very systematized operation. The menu is selective, and the service area and kitchen equipment are designed around the menu.

Most fast food menu items are packaged for easy handling. Many are in their own portable containers, thus eliminating the need for plates or trays. Much of the food is designed to be hand eaten, which eliminates the need for service utensils.

Although a fast food operation works best when it is built around one type of food production, many business dining accounts have incorporated many fast food concepts into one location. A typical location may feature a walk-up service counter with items fresh from the grill or fryer, attractively packaged and convenient for customer self-service. This same location may feature a pizza shop or Mexican-style foods.

Fast food areas save space and labor, and because of the limited menu they may be tightly controlled. Some corporate locations with multiple dining operations use the fast food concept as an additional service to enhance overall employee satisfaction.

Just as the commercial arena has spawned all kinds of business around the fast food concept, business dining can create a fast food image in any of the service stations in a cafeteria. Hot food entrees to salad shops to ice cream parlors and pizza houses—if the need is there the concept can be developed.

CARTS AND MOBILE SERVICE

In some locations the employees do not have enough time to leave their work area for breaks and lunch. The need therefore arose to develop mobile service (see Figure 3-2).

Mobile service can be as simple as a coffee cart that is wheeled or driven to the employee location. Or, it can be as complex as a catering-style van that is virtually a kitchen and service area on wheels.

Coffee carts provide workers with the convenience of a coffee, beverage, and snack without their taking the time to travel to a location away from their immediate work station. The carts dispense both hot and cold beverages, carry snacks and pastries, and contain a change drawer for cash. Each cart is inventoried as it is prepared for its service rounds and re-inventoried when it returns. Cash control is critical because very few carts are large enough to accommodate a cash register.

Mobile meal service can range from a refrigerated sandwich cart moving to different areas within a plant to a full-sized catering van equipped with a selection of premade sandwiches, grill items, salads, desserts, and hot and cold beverages. The mobile trucks are supplied from a central location. All products should be prepared fresh daily. Control over inventory, product, and cash is essential.

WAITER- OR WAITRESS-SERVICED DINING AREAS

Serviced dining areas in the business community are actually restaurants created for a limited audience. Most locations that have dining areas with waiter or waitress service allow the employees of the corporation to use the dining areas for their business and personal needs. Whether entertaining a prospective client or having lunch with a spouse or a good friend, the

Figure 3-2 Modular, flexible equipment, easily moved (such as the food cart pictured here), allows creation of "instant" foodservice areas and can bring foodservice to the customer's immediate work environment. (Photo provided by Hallmark Cards, Inc.)

convenience of having the service at work is great. It is also, of course, an excellent time saver for the employer because it keeps employees close to their work.

Dining rooms that employ service personnel are set up according to a large variety of styles. Some are full menu operations with hot selections, cold selections, appetizers, and desserts; others only provide the service of setting the table, cleaning the table, and serving beverage or dessert.

The dining areas themselves also may vary a great deal. Some corporations create rooms that can rival fine restaurants, and others simply partition a portion of their regular cafeteria.

EXECUTIVE DINING

Some business locations provide special dining services for their corporate officers. These operations can be among the finest in America. Many are the settings for multimillion dollar decisions, and the quality of their design, service, and product reflects this importance (see Figures 3-3 and 3-4).

Service standards are extremely critical in these locations. Personnel must be trained in the fine arts of all styles of service and decorum. Confidentiality is a must.

The quality of the china and tableware is first rate, and special handling is needed to maintain its fine appearance.

Often a chef is assigned solely to the executive dining operation. The chef trains and guides the kitchen crew to provide absolute freshness of product with superb presentation. Menus are styled after restaurant presentations, with specials offered daily and items served upon request.

Providing this style of executive dining is costly, and this style of service on a daily basis is slowly disappearing. More often, these important serviced

Figure 3-3 Gannett corporate headquarters has three executive dining rooms which are available to employees on a reservation basis only. Gannett is known for its exquisite dining facilities and first-rate foodservice. (Photo provided by Scott Maclay, Gannett Co., Inc.)

Figure 3-4 The White Room at the USA Today building seats 20 people at an oval table made of heavy lacquered goat skin. The room also affords an excellent view of Washington, DC and the Potomac River. (Photo provided by Scott Maclay, Gannett Co., Inc.)

functions are provided on a special request basis. This eliminates the necessity of carrying the cost of the operation on a day-to-day basis.

DIVERSITY

Business dining at one time or another uses all service styles. The needs of a business organization parallel the needs of many communities. After all, the employees who work in the marketplace live in the marketplace. It stands to reason that the wide range and styles of foodservice that appeal to people while they are away from work may also be used to satisfy them while they are at work.

4
Vending

STEVE BRENNAN

Steve Brennan is national sales director for Canteen Company, responsible for sales and marketing activities in the eastern half of the United States. His primary responsibilities at Canteen include managing a sales force of 25 representatives and maintaining client relations with a number of key accounts. Before assuming his present position, Steve was president of Cape Fear Valley Canteen (a franchise of Canteen), national accounts manager for Canteen, and a sales representative in Texas and North Carolina.

PROLOGUE

I didn't see her first. I wish I had; then maybe I could have positioned myself for more appeal, smiled winsomely, maybe even puffed up and preened a bit.

But it didn't happen that way; in fact, it was more like a high school dance. Everyone was there and our group—eight or nine of us that went everywhere together—were huddled on the dark side of the room, shoulders squared, backs to the wall, not concerned with anything in particular. Music was playing, but the real noise in the room came from the mix of voices—conversations drifting from the pairs and knots of people gathered at different points in the cafeteria.

Then . . . silence! Not even a random murmur assailed the ear. I glanced up, then gasped. I'd never seen a vision like this—she was gorgeous—the kind of woman that made you want to send a thank you note or an architectural award to her parents. She commanded every eye in the room and she knew it.

Conversation started again, excitedly, as she moved fluidly across the room toward us. We didn't quite know how to act. Be cool, ha! Panic was more likely as she was coming right at us. "Come on guys," I finally stammered, "grow up, just pretend it's. . . ." My voice was hoarse and drifted off. She was right in front of us now, looking us over, shopping us to see who or what appealed. She was next to me, ignoring me. Instead she gazed at him—my best friend—looked right into his soul and then lightly ran her fingers over his chest.

For a moment nothing moved but her eyes, darting here, there, left, right, and then, a smile lit her lips. Deftly she plucked something silver from her purse—a few shiny coins. I was dying to know what he'd offered her— what his appeal was over mine. She took a step back and turned to go and then I saw it—the long, thin, green wrapper of granola. Wouldn't you know it, a health nut. If only she smoked, then I'd have had a chance. Maybe I could have felt her light, warm touch on my chest. But it won't happen. I'm stuck, immobile, watching, longing, aching as she melts away.

A NEW PERSPECTIVE

The prologue to this chapter encourages you to think of vending in a new light. Forget the old cliches, stereotypes, and shop-worn concepts. Bury the negative phrases—"that won't work," "but we tried that once," "this is just vending." Open your mind to the possibilities of vending as an exciting entity within the restaurant community. What if, as suggested in the pro- logue, vending machines were imbued with physical and emotional attri- butes? What if they could cleanse and groom themselves, accentuating their personal characteristics to make their contents more appealing? We know they cannot do that on their own, but they can be made more appealing through the commitment of their owner, operator, or service person.

That is what I am addressing in this chapter—commitment to an under- lying operational philosophy that mandates that vending enhance and con- tribute to the totality of the employee dining, corporate dining, and company restaurant experience.

Those with any more than minimal exposure to the vending industry will immediately recognize the oversimplified maxim: "clean, full, and work- ing." That was the charge of vending managers to their employees for years.

- Keep them clean!
- Keep them full!
- Keep them working!

And the customer had an almost equally naive perception of vending: "sim- ple as one, two, three."

1. One—put in your money.
2. Two—push a button.
3. Three—enjoy your purchase (or curse, kick the machine, rattle the knob, punch the button, and go back to Step One).

Yet, this perceived extremely simple business is, in truth, quite complex and, contrary to what many believe, has been around for several centuries. However, the practical impact of vending on our society and our economy was not recognized until after World War II. With the arrival of the microprocessor, digital displays, aseptic packaging, enhanced shelf-stable products, debit card access, and other more recent developments, we have still not fully appreciated the potential impact of vending.

HISTORY OF VENDING

The trivia buffs among our readers can note that, in 215 B.C., the mathematician Hero produced a book entitled *Pneumatika,* in which he described many of his own inventions and those of his teacher, Tesibius. Hero lived in Alexandria during the golden age of Greece, and though his original manuscript is lost, it was copied. In 1587 a copy of *Pneumatika* with accompanying illustrations was translated into Italian. In it Hero illustrated a coin-activated device to be used for vending sacrificial water in Egyptian temples. Completely automatic, the device was activated by the insertion of "a coin of five drachmas," equivalent to approximately $2. Whether the holy water vendor was the invention of Hero or Tesibius is not clear from the manuscript nor is there any substantive evidence that the device was widely used.

From the time Hero wrote his book until the Italian translation there is no indication of other inventors developing vending machines. However, the translation of Hero's work may have revived interest in the idea of vending because snuff and tobacco boxes, activated by the insertion of coins, appeared in English taverns and inns in 1615. These seventeenth-century tobacco and snuff vendors were not particularly sophisticated and, like the modern "honor systems," relied to a considerable degree on the honesty of the user. A number of these early vending machines were brought to the American Colonies, and a few survived in museums and in private collections.

Among the interesting items that were vended in the nineteenth century were "outlawed" and "banned" books (England, 1822); handkerchiefs, cigarettes, and confections (Germany, 1867); envelopes and paper; postcards and stamps; boiling hot water used by the drivers of horse-drawn cabs in Paris to warm the feet of passengers; French wine, bon bons, gum, and perfume; and an early "strength tester" (1897). The first U.S. patent for a vending machine went to W. H. Fruen in 1884 for an "Automatic Drawing Device," which bears a very close resemblance to Hero's holy water dispenser.

Perhaps the most unusual idea for vending emerged in 1895 in the wild American West. The automatic divorce machine vended, for a while at least, entirely legal divorce papers in Corinne, Utah. Any citizen interested in obtaining a divorce could insert $2.50 in half or silver dollars and pull the machine's lever; a cash-register-style drawer then popped open and delivered the divorce papers. Then the papers could be taken to a local law firm, the name of which was imprinted on the form, where the names of the divorcing parties were written in and witnessed. "No fault divorce" is not a recent phenomenon.

For those interested in an in-depth history of vending, G. R. Schreiber's *A Concise History of Vending in the U.S.A.* published in 1961 offers a detailed description of vending's evolution.

The *vending experiment* of centuries past has evolved to become the *vending industry* of today. From a few drachmas in ancient Egypt the sales volume of the U.S. vending industry has grown to $18.9 billion in 1987. Numbers in the billions are often difficult to grasp, but think in these terms. In the next 15 minutes over 3 million coins will be deposited in vending machines across the United States—over 12 million coins per hour or 200,000 coins every minute of the day. On a per capita basis Americans spend about $75 annually in vending machines, and within the corporate environs the averages are substantially higher. What began with gum machines on the elevated train platforms of New York City in the 1890s has evolved to a full-blown love affair with sophisticated technology, product development, and complex merchandising considerations (see Figure 4-1).

MODES OF VENDING

Although there are literally dozens of combinations for vending as a source of food and drink, there are basically three primary vending modes.

1. Refreshment vending, also known as the "4 Cs" (candy, coffee, cold drinks, cigarettes), is designed to fulfill a limited role in the workplace. It provides convenient refreshment to employees at break times, before or after work hours, etc.
2. Full-line vending provides the products discussed above, but also includes an expanded product line. Soups, sandwiches, fruit, juice, salads, milk, ice cream, and other ancillary products are vended for employees. This service is typically accompanied by condiment counters, microwave ovens, bill and coin changers, and some type of comfortable seating.
3. Either of the above modes of services can be combined with a full-service cafeteria or dining program. Vending is thus used to provide

Figure 4-1 A well-managed vending operation is an excellent source of incremental revenue and can contribute significantly to any foodservice operation's bottom line. (Photo provided by Canteen Company.)

products and convenience to those isolated from the cafeteria, to speed service by providing an alternate source of refreshment to employees who do not want a full cafeteria meal, or to provide a high-quality alternative to cafeteria service on less-populated work shifts.

The above description is an extremely simple version of what exists in the marketplace. Another element related to vending lends itself to extreme simplification; that element is service or, put another way, who fills the machine and takes the money. If the corporation does it itself, which is fairly rare today, vending is *self-operated*. If another company handles the vending needs, then it is a *contract operation*.

PLANNING A VENDING SERVICE

Whether the vending service is self-operated or contracted out, its quality is a reflection of the host corporation's employee relations attitude and philosophy. Those who care, those who recognize the substantive benefits to be derived from a positive quality of worklife environment take the steps necessary to provide (or have provided by their contractor) a responsive, contemporary, affordable vending service. Naturally, the converse of the above position also holds true.

Assess Your Goals

At the outset in planning for vending services, you should focus on the goals of vending in your corporation. Ask yourself or your superiors or your management committee, What do we want to accomplish through vending? Pay attention to the answers. Some companies want convenience. Some want revenue. Others want to eliminate the expense of a cafeteria. Still others do not want vending at all, but recognize that it is necessary. Whatever the circumstances, define your goals and plan your selection of a vendor based upon them and the likelihood of realizing them. For those readers who did not do this planning initially and who already have a vending service in place, it is not too late to focus on goals. Assess your goals now, evaluate your present service in light of those goals, and take the necessary actions to correct any deficiencies. However, remember, do not be too hasty to condemn your present vendor. If you have never defined your goals or communicated your expectations, then it is not always the vendor's fault if your program falls short. A good vending operation requires cooperation and communication. Initiate an open dialogue with your service supplier and approach the task together. Your mutual accomplishments will be greater and you will improve your success potential.

Decide between Contracting or Self-Operation

The next logical step is to make an "either/or" decision. *Either* you are going to provide the vending yourself, *or* you are going to obtain a vending service company to manage the function for you.

Most of the quality vending operations in corporate America are handled by firms that specialize in vending and contract foodservice management. The reasons are fairly obvious why corporations contract their services. Professional vending operators know which equipment to buy; they know about reliability, capacity, the right machine for a particular location, transaction time, and service scheduling. They not only know what to buy but they also make the investment with their capital. Some of the sandwich and food machines, high-capacity cold beverage machines, and the newer specialty machines cost more than a low-priced automobile, and industry-wide the average cost of all machines is hovering near $3000. When you list the machines that comprise a typical full-service location (hot drink, cold drink, candy/snack, milk, sandwich, ice cream, cigarette, bill and coin changer, condiment stand, microwave ovens) it becomes readily apparent that substantial money is at risk.

Professional vending companies are also committed to the business as their primary function; it is not an ancillary activity with them. Therefore, they have an established, trained service organization and, most important, a maintenance staff. They have a supplier network for products, and they are familiar with the local market's brand preferences.

In recent years, slick promotional approaches have been used to make operating one's own machines sound very tempting and very profitable. In most instances, however, the advantages are exaggerated and the drawbacks do not become apparent until later. Keeping up with innovations in equipment, knowing which machines work well and which do not, and keeping track of desirable products and how to merchandise them are very difficult for the unwary do-it-yourself vending operation. Rarely are the promised higher profits realized, or even when they are perceived to be realized, a more in-depth analysis will often reveal increased costs or diminished productivity in other areas. If you hire an employee (or two or ten) to service and maintain your vending, then you must factor in additional wages, fringe benefits, insurance, supervisory time, etc. You must warehouse products (storage), provide someone to receive and issue products and control inventory, and have the machines cleaned, fixed, and replaced. The list goes on. And those who say they will not need to hire, but will assign vending duties to existing employees, should ask themselves what those present employees do now.

This is not meant to condemn self-operation totally. It has worked, it does work, and in certain circumstances it can make sense. But usually it does not. So before you undertake it, examine self-operation closely.

RESPONSIBILITIES OF THE PROFESSIONAL VENDING OPERATOR

Before beginning operation, a professional vending operator has to procure licenses, understand the local and state regulations that govern the business, and know what tax obligations exist for vended revenues. Each of the 50 states has a different sales tax structure, and thousands of counties and municipalities have their own tax codes. In many areas of this country identical products in identical machines across the street from each other are subject to different tax structures. In fact, in some places the tax can differ in the same building because vended food is taxed as in a restaurant if there is seating provided in the area, but if the machines are located in a refreshment center with no dedicated seating, then there is no tax. Cigarette tax stamps vary in every state; dairy-producing states do not tend to tax milk products, which are subject to tax in states without a dairy industry.

The vending operator must know how to select and buy machines that are reliable, that have the capacity to serve their intended audience, and that are compatible with other equipment used by the operator. In addition to purchasing machines, the operator must purchase parts—many of them for all types of machines—and expensive parts, such as coffee brewers, ice makers, compressors, coin mechanisms, and magnetron tubes for microwaves because some inconsiderate user (who was not even a customer) brought food from home in aluminum foil or a metal container and burned up a $600 oven.

The vending operator must meet the fleet requirements: big trucks for machine delivery and removal, refrigerated trucks for perishable products, step vans or similar vehicles for route service and delivery personnel, and, of course, vehicles for the maintenance staff to obtain those expensive parts when they are needed. All those trucks require care too, so arrangements must be made for gas, oil, maintenance, tire rotation and replacement, truck washing and cleaning, and more.

The vending operator needs an operations center, shop, office space, warehouse, and adequate parking for the fleet at night and the employees' vehicles during the day. That entails real estate considerations. Once established, the operator must select and warehouse hundreds of products that will sell quickly and be of the right size and in the right package to be compatible with vending merchandising.

Perishable and limited shelf-life products are particularly problematic because if they fail to sell within the allotted time they must be removed and thrown out, thereby negatively affecting operating expense and profit. Perishables such as baked goods, sandwiches, salads, and fruit, must either be made by the vending operator or purchased from someone who does. So the operator must build, establish, and operate a commissary (kitchen production facility) or locate someone who has the type and quality of product that is needed at an affordable price because it will be marked up further to the customer.

Another element tied closely to the success of any vending operation is productivity—maximizing the efficiency of the employees while catering to the needs, preferences, and schedules of the customers. A tremendous amount of time, planning, and scheduling is dedicated to organizing the route delivery schedule. Scheduling is influenced by the location of clients in relation to each other, the work schedules and break times of the client employees, the amount of equipment in each location, and the volume of usage or machine; that is, the volume of product through the machine. Some machines require service daily or even several times per day; others require it less frequently. In low- and medium-volume locations "jump route" service is common, with one person serving multiple clients in different physical locations. In high-volume facilities, hostess or attendant service is typical, with the vending service person dedicated to filling and maintaining a fixed number of machines in a single location.

Whatever the situation, scheduling a large vending service operation is as complex as setting up class schedules in school, or bus schedules, or even airline scheduling. In the latter case, in which on-time performance counts heavily, most vendors do it better.

Other requirements for a professional operation are a network of effective supervision and sound internal management, sophisticated coin counting and money handling capability, accurate accounting and auditing systems, an active preventive maintenance program, on-location machine repair capability, client and customer relations development, and close involvement with the industry's technology to keep pace with the latest developments.

HOW TO MAXIMIZE THE SUCCESS OF A VENDING OPERATION

Creating and maintaining a successful vending operation is like a *Mission Impossible*. Think about that for a moment and let your imagination wander.

> Your mission, should you decide to accept it, is to build and operate a highly successful restaurant operation. Your restaurant will be confined to a space of between 50 and 150 square feet. Within the confines of that space you will be expected to provide a full range of food and beverage products, including hot and cold drinks, snack foods, fresh soups, salads, health foods, deli items, entrees, and tempting desserts. You will also offer a selection of ice creams, fresh popcorn, appropriate condiments, and clean napkins. Many of your customers will be carrying the wrong type of currency to indulge their cravings, so you will need to provide a currency exchange within the restaurant.
> This will be a restricted access restaurant. Your customers will not come in and out as they choose, but rather will crowd in—

large masses of humanity unchained from the rigors of their daily routines for brief 10-, 15- or 30-minute periods. Your mission will be to serve them all quickly, quietly, and efficiently and to send them back to their routines refreshed and replenished for several more hours of work. If you fail, you will be beaten, kicked, defiled, and defaced. If you succeed, no one will even say thank you. And finally, your host (some call them clients) will expect you to pay a substantial portion of your sales revenue to them for the privilege of accepting this assignment.

That is an accurate description of the vending challenge. The average machine occupies between 8–12 square feet of floor space. Machines heat, refrigerate, and freeze and dispense everything from a quick cup of coffee to a full meal. Bill and coin changers are like a mini-bank, and microwave ovens bring a working kitchen to the workplace. A full array of machines, including condiment counters and bill changers, occupies less than 150 square feet and can provide necessary refreshment and lunch service to approximately 300 people.

However, successful vending operations *are* possible and occur with far more frequency than you might suppose. Whether they are in plants, office buildings, or institutional facilities they all share several elements in common. First, client management has determined carefully in advance what it expects of the operation for its employees. In addition, the client has (1) researched who are the available and suitable contractors, (2) established an objective contractor selection and bidding procedure and, most important, (3) provided for a logical interface of client management and contractor management once the contract is approved.

The objectives of the vending operation should spell out how vending fits into the employee benefit program, what services are desired, and on what level. Attention should also be focused on what role the vending operation will play in employee motivation and productivity and how it fits into the other activities carried on at that particular location.

Each vending operation will vary because each client has different objectives. If the host company has a beautiful cafeteria that is easily accessible to all employees, then perhaps the vending may be needed only for beverage refreshment and an occasional snack. However, if there is no cafeteria (and there are more businesses without cafeterias than with them), then vending takes on a new role. The vending room, in fact, becomes the dining room. The sandwich machine is the restaurant, the soda machine the fountain, and the pastry machine becomes the bakery. If vending is the only available foodservice, then it is essential that it be the best vending available or an important element in the employee relations portfolio will be missing.

Give careful thought to the location of the vending operation. It should be reasonably accessible to the majority of employees.

Client and contractor need to communicate and work cooperatively to highlight the quality of the vending product, the reasonable level of its price, its reliability, and its convenience. Good positive positioning will make your vending program a major component of a progressive, contemporary employee relations program.

Your survey of available and suitable vending service contractors should be thorough and comprehensive. Do not be afraid to ask for and check references and to check them carefully. If a contractor has a poor reference because of prolonged inferior service, that is a red flag. However, the contractor may have lost a contract because the client wanted more commission and the contractor was better off without that business. A vending contractor is a businessperson entitled to a fair return on his or her time and investment. Many clients are in the habit of holding a gun to their contractor's head: "Pay me more commission or I'll switch suppliers," "give me more machines or I'll change to another company," "you can't raise prices now; it has only been 12 years since we raised prices the last time." These responses are all too typical.

There is a vast misconception in the business community that vending companies garner huge profit margins. Nothing could be further from the truth. Most vending companies' profits are less than a nickel on each dollar of sales—before taxes.

On average about 45 percent of each dollar goes to product cost and another 25 percent to direct labor, support labor, and administration. Operating expenses (trucks, gas, oil), overhead (building, utilities, warehouse), equipment purchases, depreciation, and investment charges are also sizeable. Sales tax is another component of the price. At the restaurant or retail counter, sales tax is added to what is purchased. Because that is impossible in vending, the sales tax is included in the price. Thus the value of every dollar deposited in a machine is reduced by the prevailing tax at that location. According to the studies done annually by the National Automatic Merchandisers Association (NAMA), the average commission paid by contractors to clients across our nation is 8 percent.

It does not take long for that vending dollar to shrivel and shrink. Vending operators that achieve close to a nickel of profit on the dollar are fortunate and astute businesspeople. The vending business is similar to the retail grocery business in that it is low margin and dependent on high volume. Sufficient volume per machine and per location is the key to success and a company's prosperity. In days gone by the prevailing attitude was that, when two people stopped somewhere to talk, you put a candy machine next to them. No more! Today, success comes from wise machine placement, proper route scheduling, effective merchandising, rational pricing, purchasing and a plethora of other important activities.

So when you look for suitable contractors, look for successful companies with a track record of honesty and integrity. Most important, look for local representatives who communicate well with you. Remember that you, the client, are going to deal with local representatives. Although a big vending company may have support services, central accounting and research centers in another area, your machines will be serviced by members of your community under the management of your fellow members of the local business community.

After completing your search for suitable companies to provide your services, the next steps are the actual bid process and the selection of a contractor. The bid process need not be overly complicated or accompanied by a lengthy RFP or an army of consultants. The important factor is that your bid specifications be uniform and *realistic* and that adequate information is provided to all the companies invited to participate in the review. Sharing historical and statistical information on your facility enables the bidders to provide you with a more accurate financial projection of your account's potential.

When it is time to select your operator, weigh all the factors. No decision of this type will ever be totally objective. The chemistry of the relationship with the contractor's management, their commitment to service, a caring attitude, and other factors are truly subjective. Of course, there are objective components to the decision process as well: are the machines new, how many are offered, what type of product quality will you get, is it route service or attendant service, and what is the commission?

Commissions are based on sales. If contractors pay too much commission they have to recoup their expense somewhere—in product quality, service frequency, or equipment quality and replacement. Once service or quality is diminished, sales fall off; commissions as a percent of sales likewise spiral down and everyone suffers. The message is clear—a contractor who does a professional job, who provides excellent service and product, who builds customer satisfaction in your employees, and who pays you 5 percent may, in the long run, put more money in your pocket (and more good will) than the contractor who promises 15 percent and then compromises quality to make the bottom line.

Having selected a contractor, you have an obligation to establish a clear liaison with the contractor. Responsibility for supervision of the contract performance should be clearly spelled out and accurately communicated. There should be a clear understanding of how the contractor and client will interact to make the operation successful.

The client liaison should make it a point to solicit employee feedback. Do not wait for a problem to arise. If the contractor is doing a good job 29 days a month let him or her know and then work to solve the problems on the other one day. Stay in touch with employees and monitor their product preferences and ensure that they are offered consistently. When your contractor has a problem, help explain it to employees so that they will understand and be realistic in their expectations.

Vandalism and abuse do occur often, perhaps because personnel are not manning the machines. These are not new problems in vending. In 1886 an Englishman, Percival Everitt, applied for a group of patents at the U.S. Patent Office. Some were for original machines, some for improvements on earlier models. An indication of the trials and tribulations of the early vending machine designers (and for many of us in years to follow) is contained in Everitt's patent application. Everitt observed that his patent (No. 374, 297) was an invention improving an earlier patent dated July 28, 1885. He wrote,

> It has been found in practice, that although the apparatus is perfectly successful when not designedly misused, articles, such as paper, orange-peel, and other rubbish, have been maliciously placed in the slit provided for the admission of the coin, and that in consequence the channel provided for the passage of the coins from the slit became blocked.

It would seem that early in the development of the vending machine the American public came to regard these silent salesmen as fair game, either to "beat" the machine or, failing that, to stuff an orange peel down its innards to put it out of commission. Reckoning with this perversity is still a mighty challenge for designers and engineers in our modern era.

Of course, the typical customer retort is that the machine "took my money" or "I didn't get what I wanted." Machines do malfunction, but a good operator minimizes down time with a strong preventive maintenance program and a quick repair when needed. The response of a vending contractor to a problem is faster than any other service industry. Not long ago, I sat in a hospital emergency room with an injured child and watched a vending machine malfunction. The vending company fixed the machine before the child saw a doctor.

For readers who want a more definitive discussion of the technical complexities of the vending industry there are a number of industry periodicals, and a wealth of material is available from NAMA. Representatives of local vending contractors are a good source of information about their services and the industry as well.

FUTURE OF VENDING OPERATIONS

During the past 30 years the vending industry has grown tremendously as vending machines have become an accepted part of our modern life-style. Vending is no longer a new way to do business and serve customers but a commonplace part of the workplace and public facilities.

In the years ahead the industry will not have the spectacular expansion of the past two decades. Yet, the vending business will advance in part because of the new generation of equipment, those with computer microchip technology. Vending companies will receive computerized feedback on what was sold, how much money was taken in, how long it took to service the machines, and when the machine sold out. Fed into home-based computers, this information will enable improved scheduling, service frequency, accounting, warehousing, purchasing controls, and more.

From the customer's vantage point, these newer machines will expedite trouble-shooting to correct malfunctions, provide better and faster feedback on customer product preferences, facilitate greater selection, and offer enhanced money-handling capability.

With the possible reintroduction of an acceptable $1.00 coin in the United States (Canada has one) and the new dollar bill acceptors, vending will expand to provide higher-priced products. This coin will eliminate the need to carry and use an excessive number of coins, which produces a built-in resistance to higher-priced items. Batteries, film, paperback books, over-the-counter medications, and more up-scale food products will be sold. Chicken fingers with honey-mustard sauce, shrimp cocktail or crab claws, escargot swimming in garlic butter, tins of gourmet pâté, and other similar items will become standard vending fare in and out of the workplace.

One of the more popular "new" items for the future will be an old item— water. With waste dump contamination polluting ground water at an increasingly alarming rate and the earth's aquifers continuing to be threatened, people are becoming more concerned with what they drink. Purified water by the glass at work and by the gallon to carry-out or take-home will be an increasingly popular component of the vending contractor's product line.

One of the newest developments is the application of the credit and debit card principle to vending. Already frequently used in Europe, machines using this principle are receiving more than casual attention in the United States. The economics of their application to employee dining and employee vending programs has to be more satisfactorily addressed for them to receive wide acceptance, but it will happen. The all-debit-card-system is easily workable now; the debit card and cash system creates problems for most contractors, but they will ultimately be resolved. An industry that could provide an automatic divorce in the 1800s will not be stymied for long.

The vending industry and business is a people business. It serves people and it is serviced by people. That will continue. It is a daily challenge to keep the business running smoothly and profitably, but the dedicated people in America's business community will make it happen. And, as I implied in the prologue, vending machines are almost human; they do a great job, they provide a needed service, and they do it well so give your machine a hug.

Acknowledgments

I would like to thank the National Automatic Merchandisers Association, the publishers of *Vending Times,* and the publishers of *American Automatic Merchandisers* for the source material and timely articles they provided. Additionally, I would like to thank my colleagues at Canteen Company and my associates throughout the foodservice industry for the information and inspiration they have and continue to provide.

For those readers who would like a more detailed look at the technical elements of vending and an analysis of current or developing product preferences, I recommend a thorough review of *American Automatic Merchandisers'* annual industry census issue. That issue provides a wealth of demographic information on the industry, as well as very clear, easy-to-digest visual materials on market share, product distribution, labor costs, and other pertinent data.

5

Multi-Unit Foodservice Operations

FRANK BURROWS

Frank Burrows is a district manager for Lackmann Food Service, a regional foodservice management company headquartered in Woodbury, New York. Before joining Lackmann, Frank was a regional manager at Motorola, where he was responsible for the company's foodservice operations in Florida and Texas. At Motorola, he was instrumental in implementing automated systems in the corporate-wide foodservice organization, which allowed electronic transfer of data throughout the units.

Satisfying the customer, producing the best quality food, training and developing staff, and operating within budgeted guidelines are the objectives of unit and multi-unit operations.

IDENTIFYING MULTI-UNIT OPERATIONS

What is a B&I multi-unit foodservice operation? A foodservice operation that provides food and beverages to employees at their work location, usually for the convenience of the employer, is a B&I foodservice unit. An operation with more than one operating unit or profit center may be classified as a multi-unit operation. That classification is given when the operation can be divided into measurable profit centers. Dollar volume or geographical location plays no part in determining the classification.

These types of operations—vending, cafeteria, delivery carts, catering, office coffee, employee store, and executive dining rooms—may be combined to form a multi-unit. Multi-unit operations range in size from a very small single-address operation comprising a small cafeteria and vending or office coffee service that is possibly a satellite or part of a chain to a large operation with multiple cafeterias and other services at a single address. Units are located in both rural and large metropolitan areas.

Satellite

A satellite is usually a small operation with little or no food preparation area. The hours of operation are generally from 6:00 A.M. to 2:00 P.M. Monday through Friday, unless there is service for second and third shifts. This unit orders all of its supplies from the home unit or a supplier designated by the home unit. A supervisor is responsible for placing orders, tracking sales, directing employees (usually three to six), preparing daily reports, and relating on a day-to-day basis with the customers. This is the smallest part of a multi-unit operation.

These units usually provide beverages, cold sandwiches, salads, snack items, soup, chili, and hot dogs to between 150 and 750 customers per day. Limited hot entree service may or may not be available.

Cafeteria

Single-address cafeterias vary in size from serving 300 to 3,000 customers. They are self-sufficient and have adequate storage, preparation, service areas, and dining areas to serve their customers. Hours of operation are usually from 6:00 A.M. to 2:00 P.M. Monday through Friday, unless there is service for second and third shifts. The manager supervises a staff of from 6 to 30 employees. This unit achieves multi-unit status by being part of another operation, such as vending, employee store, etc.

Cafeteria, Vending, Office Coffee Service

Typically this operation serves a minimum of 1,000 employees. The cafeteria is self-sufficient, coffee supplies and equipment for office coffee services are provided, and the vending may be contracted or managed by a separate division. Hours of operation are usually from 6:00 A.M. to 2:00 P.M. Monday through Friday, unless there is service for second and third shifts. The manager supervises a staff of from 6 to 30 employees.

A cafeteria serves salads, beverages, desserts, hot entrees, soups, chili, grill, and snack items.

Cafeteria, Vending, Catering, Executive Dining, Employee Store, Etc.

The population at these facilities is usually a minimum of 1,000 employees. This type of unit may be very complicated, because of the unique demands of executive dining, employee store (sundries), and the other operations. Hours of operation are usually from 6:00 A.M. to 2:00 P.M. Monday through Friday, unless there is service for second and third shifts. The manager supervises a staff of from 6 to 30 employees.

Executive dining rooms vary in size, level of service, and menu, but they are critically important to a multi-unit food service manager. Attention to detail is crucial to the success of these operations. One of the unique problems of executive dining rooms is billing the customer. This operation is very similar to private club management.

Catering primarily provides beverage and snack service at meetings and some working lunches. These events present excellent opportunities to "show off" new foodservice items and the overall quality of the foodservice program. Of course, if you forget to make a coffee delivery or forget the knife to cut the cake, you may be out of a job! Catering is the chance to have fun with food, do something different for your customer, and make some extra profit.

COMPUTERIZING MULTI-UNIT OPERATIONS

The gathering of information on cash collection, item sales reports, sales by the hour, and sales by category has been facilitated by the computerized point-of-sale cash register. The central office gathers information on individual unit operations and produces statistical models to determine strengths and weaknesses. These models compare sales to labor ratios and meals served to labor ratios among units with similar populations and type of business to measure performance and success of marketing programs, menus, and personnel.

Purchasing has likewise been facilitated, as almost all suppliers, including the small Mom and Pop bakery, are computerized. Invoices and order forms are legible, and order input has been computerized in some instances. Fax machines are used by most major suppliers, and many multi-unit facilities have access to fax machines. Personal computers are used to track purchases and in some cases to send the order to the supplier's computer. Personal computers are also used to prepare budgets, extend inventories, prepare weekly operating reports, do word processing, track payroll, gather and consolidate information from satellite operations, send data to central offices, track vending and office coffee sales, and do accounts receivable and accounts payable.

Desk-top publishing software and laser printers and scanners are providing multi-unit operations the capability to design marketing programs and to print catering brochures, flyers, newsletters, employee handbooks, and other information that once had to be done by a graphic artist and print shop.

MANAGING A MULTI-UNIT OPERATION

In the 1960s and 1970s controlling food costs was the biggest problem for foodservice managers, but in the 1980s labor costs started to become a problem. In the 1990s foodservice managers' biggest problems will be customer quality and value perception and motivating employees to work in the service industry. Staffing will be difficult, and training programs will be necessary to educate employees in math, the operation of more and more sophisticated foodservice preparation equipment, special nutritional programs, and new or different methods of food preparation and presentation.

Food Costs

Menus based on regional food preferences, nutritional considerations, standardized recipes, and available foodservice preparation and service equipment are the basis for achieving predetermined and budgeted food operating costs. A kitchen preparing food for more than one operation must have a system to transfer the cost of food and labor to each profit center. A transfer system is necessary to match costs to sales and to detect problem food cost areas. Single-unit operations usually do not have transfer systems, but those single-unit managers who have developed good purchasing and inventory systems will appreciate the importance of a good transfer system to track costs and manage the food cost percentages when they become unit managers.

Labor Cost

Hiring the right person in the first place sounds so simple, but will continue to be very difficult. Hiring a trainable, enthusiastic person and building a team through an extensive training program will be the only ways to survive in the future. The high cost of medical benefits, workers' compensation, and other fringe benefits makes training the key to controlling labor costs. Learning about the latest foodservice equipment and challenging foodservice manufacturers to produce new equipment to reduce labor and to reduce employee accidents will be critical. Equipment to receive, prepare, serve, and clean will be changing in renovated and newly constructed facilities. You may have seen 30-year-old kitchens or dining rooms with brand new pieces of equipment. Ask yourself if the new equipment is state-of-the-art or a replacement of the same 30-year-old model. It will be essential for multi-unit managers to be aware of the latest equipment on the market and to specify the equipment most appropriate to serve the food on the menu.

Multi-unit managers are challenged to cross-train employees in many different aspects of service. Employees in a multi-unit operation with a cafeteria, vending, employee store, catering, executive dining, and airplane foodservice need to be trained to work in all of these very different areas.

Temporary help agencies are also being used in multi-unit operations to fill in during vacations and medical leaves. The use of these temps has been growing and will become a way of obtaining enough labor to serve at openings, special events, and other busy times during the year.

Training

Employees want to enjoy their jobs, to have fun, to learn, and to make more money. Restaurants and other service industry companies are offering the available labor pool many of these benefits, and we have to realize that we are in competition for the same group of employees. Our most important asset is our customer, and our employees are the key to satisfying the customer and enabling the customer to feel good about eating in our foodservice operations.

Vocational schools affiliated with public school systems can be a source of help in developing and instituting a training program in a multi-unit operation. Foodservice associations provide training films and books, and foodservice equipment manufacturers hold seminars and provide videotape instructions on repairing and operating foodservice equipment. Multi-unit managers must devote a great portion of their resources to training.

Retired people and other older people are going to be a key source of personnel in the future. Programs to attract and motivate this group have to be developed.

6

Options in Employee Dining

PART A: EXECUTIVE DINING

JACK GALIONE

Jack began his career in a family-owned restaurant and then worked 12 years with a national food management company. He founded Corporate Food Services in 1971, which today has over 1,000 employees and over 50 corporate accounts in New York, Connecticut, and Ohio. In 1983, he received the coveted IFMA Silver Plate acknowledging him as foodservice operator of the year in the B&I segment.

I started my company with one concept in mind: to bring restaurant quality to employee foodservice. Everything we have developed, innovated, and implemented has been done to reach that goal.

Food is a form of energy. A foodservice supplies the energy required by clients to conduct their businesses and professions. It supplies that energy in a healthful, appetizing, and appealing way.

Menu Development

Foodservice contractors must know and understand thoroughly the needs of every client, their employees, and the business environment in which they operate. Every menu, every service system, every dining room, every promotion has to be developed for each particular client. Clients have a wide variety of requirements, tastes, preferences, and demands. The emphasis on healthy eating and sound nutrition, coupled with a growing sophistication in food tastes, has challenged us to be innovative and creative in designing our menus.

From the beginning—when I started my company, Corporate Food Services, over 15 years ago—I insisted on hiring chefs for each unit. I insisted on chefs, not cooks, because I felt, and still do feel, that restaurant-quality food could only be provided by professionally trained chefs. I looked for general managers who would be committed to the level of quality and service that I insisted on delivering. I felt and still do feel that high-quality service and commitment will be found only in high-quality employees at all levels, but especially at the managerial level.

From the outset, I concentrated my sales efforts on professional companies in New York City, a segment of the market that I felt was not being served by the foodservice contractors. I also concentrated my efforts in New York City because it is home base for me and it is a city I know very well. Today, my company's clients include investment bankers, law firms, insurance companies, and other professional corporations. Although it has recently expanded beyond New York City, Manhattan remains the core of the company's business.

My clients are used to quality in their business lives and in their personal lives. They will accept no less from my company. They are also used to delivering a high-quality performance to their clients, and they expect that same level of commitment from us. That means we must go beyond the routine delivery of product and service and be prepared to meet their requirements, no matter how "extraordinary" they seem at the time.

Most of our clients, by the very nature of their businesses, work in a crisis atmosphere so we must be prepared to provide not only the regularly scheduled breakfast, lunch, and dinner menus but also foodservice throughout the night and on weekends. Every one of our clients can expect foodservice within the hour of an emergency call. "Black Monday," the stock market crash in October 1987, and the ensuing weeks sorely tested our ability to not only keep up with, but also anticipate our clients' needs.

In one law firm, for instance, we were told of an emergency situation on a Friday afternoon. The client planned to have its employees working through the night Friday and all through the weekend. We organized our staff to meet their foodservice needs that weekend, providing beverages, sandwiches, snacks, and dinner. We were able to respond to their emergency situation with the same quality and dedication that this law firm brought to its clients' demands.

Today 99 percent of our clients require breakfast service. In the modern life-style, many employees skip breakfast at home and eat something at work. Many of our clients request a basic continental breakfast of juice, rolls, coffee, and tea. Others, however, have more extensive requirements. For them we add hot and cold tables to the continental breakfast. On the cold breakfast bar we feature a variety of cereals, fresh fruit, granola, and yogurt. The hot section offers the traditional breakfast of cereals, eggs, bacon, and other breakfast meats.

Lunch

Lunch is, of course, our biggest meal. Health and weight concerns seem to drive the changing appetites of our customers. Our clients' interest in healthy eating is reflected not only in the food we serve but in our methods of preparation as well. We use all fresh vegetables, and we always serve sauces on the side. We now grill some vegetables, such as zucchini and squash, because we have found that grilling retains the color and texture of the vegetable. When we stir fry, we use low-cholesterol oil for frying. Because our customers have a hearty appetite for soup, we offer two soups a day; in the summer one of the daily soups is a cold soup.

Sixteen years ago I introduced a salad bar into a facility I was managing. It was such a phenomenal success that I have made salad bars an integral part of my business. Salads are popular throughout the year in all our locations. Last year, we started to serve salads by the ounce in some units, which has been very popular with our customers.

Over the years we have seen many changes in food tastes. Today, beef consumption has decreased while veal and chicken are significantly more popular. Pork consumption remains steady, but the demand for fish and seafood continues to climb.

We do not use additives and are very careful in the use of salt, although we make effective use of herbs and other seasonings. We are after all running a foodservice, not a health care facility, so we must prepare our food to be appetizing and attractive, as well as healthful. Yet, dessert sales have never been higher. However, it is our experience that customers are more likely to buy a spectacular dessert, rather than spending their calories on ordinary dessert. We make spectacular desserts.

A typical lunch in one of our employee cafeterias is

- Soup: Chicken broth with dumplings, Split pea and ham with croutons
- Deli: Baked Virginia ham
- Special sandwiches: Smoked turkey with chutney on Russian black bread
- Entrees: Calves liver sauté with sherry vinegar and onion, Navarin of lamb with baby vegetables, Canneloni Florentine

A typical a la carte lunch in a private dining room is

- Appetizers: Old Dominion Cheddar cheese soup, Terrine of garden vegetables, Quiche Lorraine
- Entrees: Linguini with bay scallops in fresh tomato sauce, Chouchroute garni with smoked pork chops, Avocado stuffed with crabmeat and shrimp ravigote, Grilled breast of chicken with pommery mustard, London broil with Dijon mustard
- Desserts: Poached pears in Riesling, French apple tart, Chocolate mousse

Dinner Service

In brokerage firms and law offices, it is not uncommon for some employees to work through the dinner hour and late into the night. Rather than allocate funds for employees to dine in local restaurants, our clients (about 20 percent of them) require us to provide on-premise dinner service, which keeps the employees in the workplace, eliminating the time they would lose if they went out to dinner, and thereby improving productivity.

For dinner, we provide a salad bar, a grill for entrees, a special roast carved to order, and of course desserts. We also offer a basic menu, such as the following:

- Soup: Beef with vegetables
- Entree: Rack of lamb provencale
- Vegetables: Acorn squash with maple syrup, Roasted red potatoes with rosemary sauce

Special Services

To be successful in this business, you must be constantly creative and innovative. Employees in the brokerage houses for which we provide food-service have some special requirements. The traders never leave their desks during the day; they are constantly in touch with the market and their clients. In response, we developed a packaged lunch for them, which we deliver to their desk. We provide them with a menu and they need only order before 11 A.M. to be served as they work.

For our suburban locations we created "Get A Way Gourmet," which provides high-quality foods, casseroles, pizzas, breads, and cakes for employees to pick up after work. Although this system may not work in Manhattan where employees must rely on public transportation, it is very effective in the suburbs where most employees drive to work.

Although basic menu items will always be the mainstay of our business, we keep trying new food items and new presentation and service ideas. We always offer grilled cheese sandwiches, hamburgers, ham and cheese sandwiches, tuna fish, and pizza on the menu, but we also present more adventurous food.

We have developed a fresh pizza program at all our facilities, which is very popular. We also offer a basket of steamed vegetable dim sum. In one unit we installed a Bake-Off station. In order to bring some personal service to the line, we hired a talented baker to work behind the counter, meeting and serving the customers. She has developed products unique to our facility, and she enjoys the daily exchange with the customers. Adding this kind of excitement to the service line is very important.

In some units a 6-foot space on the line is devoted every day to a different item prepared to order. One day someone might prepare omelettes to order, the next day it could be tacos with a variety of fillings, and another day we do a stir fry, with the customers choosing from the variety of meats and vegetables offered. The employees never know what the special selection will be, and it keeps an air of expectation and excitement in the facility.

Over the years our business has grown and has certainly changed. Today, with so many two-income families and single-person households, as well as the trend away from cooking at home, many employees prefer to have their major meal of the day at the workplace where it is subsidized and then have a lighter meal in the evening at home.

With the change in life-styles has also come changes in food preferences. Today because Italian food is very popular, pasta is now a menu mainstay in all types of facilities. Chinese food is next in popularity, with Mexican and German behind. American cuisine, using the foods and dishes of our own country, is quickly gaining in popularity.

The employees of many of our clients work irregular hours on a regular basis. Vending facilities allow us to supplement our regular foodservice and provide around-the-clock service in some locations. Vending provides sandwiches, beverages, and snacks for employees no matter when they are required.

We have made an interesting observation about vending sales. They are the highest in law firms and investment banking companies. These are high-pressure jobs, and our customers working under such constant pressure need the "instant energy" obtained from snacks and sodas. Many of our clients have asked us to remove the cigarette machines from their premises. We also do a large volume in hot popcorn sales.

Growth

When I started my company, the initial program was to contain our business in New York City. The types of clients we targeted were certainly prevalent in the city.

Yet, gradually, we moved to the suburbs as our clients began to expand their businesses outside the city. In 1986 we expanded to New Jersey, and in 1987 further expansion brought us to Connecticut and Cleveland. We now have more than 1,000 employees in over 35 locations and have reached our present limit of expansion beyond New York. We, of course, want to grow and continue our level of expansion, but we have always believed in programmed and controlled growth. We must be convinced that we have the management in place not only to maintain our standards but also to improve them. Our growth so far has been made possible because of the development of our computerized control system, which gives us immediate access to the data we need to manage our business and maintain the standards we have set for ourselves and the standards our clients have come to expect. From the day we wrote our first business plan to the day we opened our first facility and all the years and all the facilities since, we have maintained our original goal: to bring restaurant-quality food and service to the institutional field. Although there have been many changes in our business over the years, that goal has never changed, and we are constantly looking for new ideas, new systems, new products, and new approaches to provide restaurant-quality service to our foodservice clients.

PART B: WHITE COLLAR DINING

The five sections of this part of Chapter 6 are written by members of the Dining Services department at Procter & Gamble.

Philip E. Hawkins joined Procter & Gamble in 1973 as cafeteria manager of its Winton Hill Technical Center. He was later promoted to manager, Dining Services at P&G's world headquarters building in Cincinnati. Philip is currently zone manager at P&G's Sharon Woods Technical Center where he is responsible for two dining operations, vending, and two sundry shops selling company products.

After graduating from Miami University in Oxford, Ohio, with a Bachelor of Science Degree in dietetics, Elizabeth G. Flynn, RD, went to work in the foodservice department at Procter & Gamble. Since 1986, she has served as manager of Tower Dining Services at P&G's corporate headquarters in Cincinnati, where she is responsible for all cafeteria and guest services.

Carol C. Weisman is Dining Services Manager at Procter & Gamble's Ivorydale Technical Center in Cincinnati. Before that, she was manager of Tower Building Dining at P&G's corporate headquarters. After graduating from the HRI program at Michigan State University, Carol joined the ranks at Procter & Gamble in 1981 as cafeteria manager of the central building complex.

Jacqueline M. Schoff, RD, is a cafeteria services manager at Procter & Gamble in Cincinnati. In this capacity, she is responsible for operating one employee dining room, providing coffee cart service to meeting rooms, and catering special events and all conference room luncheons. Before that, she was a clinical dietitian and foodservice director for ARA Services at St. Paul's/Gray's Convalescent Home in Chicago. A registered dietitian, she holds a Bachelor of Science degree in dietetics and nutrition from the University of Kentucky.

Section I: Dining Services Goals

PHILIP E. HAWKINS

At Procter & Gamble's General Offices we currently serve 1,264 customers per day in two corporate cafeterias and with table service dining. Within the greater Cincinnati area, our foodservices provide meals for 5,215 customers per day.

Since 1985, when the change in tax law made it unfeasible for corporations to subsidize their foodservice operations, Procter & Gamble's Dining Services' financial goal has been to recover fully direct food and labor costs. In order to achieve this goal, several adjustments have been necessary, including a reduction of cafeteria labor hours and menu revisions. It is necessary to monitor our progress toward this goal frequently and adjust our course when indicated.

Another important goal is to train our staff effectively. Ideally, we strive to provide courteous and caring service for lunch, coffee cart services, and at special group meetings where Dining Services support is requested. The time and effort directed toward this goal result in better service and satisfied customers. We focus on doing the right things right in our operations.

Another goal of Dining Services is to provide a convenient site that attracts employees for meals. A variety of nutritious meal options are provided at a reasonable price and are served by an attentive service staff. The driving force here is to enhance employee productivity at the office. Our objective is to see the employee returning to work refreshed and energized after lunch in the cafeteria.

To enhance service and customers' perception of our service, we select key employees for customer contact areas. These employees should enjoy serving so that their caring attitude will be obvious to our customers. The bottom line is that good service results in more satisfied customers who are better able to be productive while at work.

At P&G, we also provide coffee cart, vending, and beverage services for group business meetings and for other events, such as retirement receptions. These services should be available at convenient locations and are justified where the population is large enough to support the service.

Our Dining Services functions in downtown Cincinnati, a very competitive environment. Just a few blocks away there are many local restaurants where employees may opt to eat lunch, instead of eating in-house. Our mission is to create a cafeteria where the food, service, and ambiance are attractive and interesting enough to motivate employees to eat lunch in the building instead of going out.

To stay on target, our prices must be competitive with nearby restaurants. Achieving this goal is an ongoing challenge, which includes frequently revising our menu. However, competitive pricing is imperative if we expect to enhance office productivity for our employees and compete effectively in the downtown environment.

How do we monitor our success in achieving the goals as defined above? We have been most successful in understanding customer perceptions through focus groups and surveys. These marketing tools help convey employee perceptions and opinions that are otherwise unknown to Dining Services. When customer perceptions are known to the Dining Service team, we can immediately take steps to meet those needs. This is the first positive step.

Next, we meet with our foodservice staff. Together we discuss and plan the best strategy to meet customers' needs by providing quality food at a reasonable price. As we succeed, we have a positive and direct effect on corporate productivity because the time of employees is saved when they eat lunch in-house. We believe that this time savings directly improves bottom line results in other departments throughout the company.

Section 2: Cafeteria Services

ELIZABETH G. FLYNN

The stereotype of an employee cafeteria is that of a dingy lunchroom serving cold and greasy food in the basement of a building. Procter & Gamble's cafeteria is very different from the stereotype. We recognize that our competition is fierce. Our challenge is to dispel that stereotype and operate a profitable in-house cafeteria facility. Meeting this challenge requires studying our customers and their needs, the physical design of the cafeteria, the menu, and employee training on an ongoing basis.

Our mission is to provide employees with a high-quality, reasonably priced meal. Our corporation believes that eating in-house can enhance productivity more than can dining at a restaurant. Our cafeteria allows employees to eat in a relatively short amount of time and maintain a high level of productivity in the work area.

Who are our customers? They are men and women, some just beginning employment at Procter & Gamble and some with many years of service. Some want a hearty meal, whereas others opt for low-calorie selections. Although they enjoy the cafeteria, they may also want to try one of the 80 restaurants in the downtown area, do some shopping, or just take a walk and enjoy the Cincinnati skyline. The customer group is certainly diverse. They present many challenges, but also many opportunities for us to serve them and motivate them to eat in our cafeteria.

A key to customer satisfaction is providing high-quality food. We are continuously evaluating our menus to keep up with market trends and competition. Our 6-week cycle menu ensures variety, but customers also know that their favorites will return. Computerized records track the success of an item, and cycle menus are revised accordingly. In keeping with market trends, we have incorporated several ethnic menu items, such as Oriental and Mexican dishes. Some specialty items include the "Super Spud" stuffed baked potato and our homemade pizza. For customers desiring a more traditional meal, we still offer such old favorites as meat loaf and fried chicken. For the more nutrition-conscious customers, we offer extensive salad bars with items varying daily.

In order to compete with the many restaurants in the area, we strive to create an attractive atmosphere where employees can escape their office pressures. The physical design of our cafeteria captures this atmosphere well. It is decorated with warm colors and attractive planters. Large windows let in natural sunlight to create a pleasant dining experience.

A cafeteria's physical design should enhance customer flow and reduce the amount of time spent waiting in lines. Procter & Gamble's cafeteria has a scramble system design. The servery is made up of several food stations, such as Hot Food, Grill, Cold Food, and Soup and Deli. Customers need only stop at the food stations serving their meal-item choices, which considerably speeds service.

A unique feature of our cafeteria is the point-of-sale cash register system that allows customers to charge their lunch through automatic payroll deduction by using their employee identification card. The average check total is higher when customers charge their meal, rather than pay in cash. This has had a positive impact on our profitability.

Ongoing employee training is essential in the successful operation of our cafeteria. We strive to make our employees feel that they are an integral part of our operation and to have pride and ownership in their work. We encourage them to make suggestions and pass along comments from customers. Training is provided in suggestive selling, portion control, proper safety, and sanitation procedures. Employees have identified what they believe constitutes good service and have been challenged to provide that daily. Above all, good and friendly service is the key to customer satisfaction.

Cafeteria service in a business setting is an area of continuous change and challenge. Competition is always present, and we must find new ways to motivate employees to eat in-house. By providing high-quality meals at reasonable prices, we can have a positive impact on the productivity of all parts of the business.

Section 3: Other Corporate Dining Services

CAROL C. WEISMAN

Procter & Gamble offers interesting lunch alternatives to its employees. If entertaining a client or hosting a meeting is the agenda for lunch, P&G employees may eat in the Tower Building Table Service Dining Room or in one of our five Dining Conference Rooms.

Table Service Dining

Overlooking the beautiful P&G Plaza gardens is our 100-seat Table Service Dining Room. Here our customers relax in pleasant surroundings of mahogany wood and starched table linens while a capable staff serves lunch to employees and their guests. The menu is a streamlined version of the one found in the cafeteria, with the addition of a few amenities: fresh flowers on the table, the passing of a tempting dessert tray, after-dinner mints, and a bottomless cup of Folger's coffee.

Table Service Dining is also unique because we accept only charge sales either to a customer's personal identification card or to a department code number. There is no tipping. A service charge is, however, added to the check to defray the costs of this labor-intensive operation. Business hours for this facility are the same as for the cafeteria.

Conference Dining

"Meeting and eating" is a way of combining work with pleasure in P&G's Tower Dining Conference Rooms. We offer our customers a variety of private dining conference rooms, ranging in capacity from 10–36, for the purpose of conducting business over a well-prepared meal. Our 102-seat operation employs its own talented chef who prepares meals from a select banquet-style menu. Luncheons are served between 12:00 P.M. and 1:00 P.M., allowing customers the opportunity to use the meeting space throughout the remainder of the day.

Customers include new recruits, executives, participants in training seminars, in-house manager meetings, and occasionally a civic leader or two. Only department charge codes are accepted as a method of payment because these rooms are booked strictly for business purposes.

Section 4: Special Events

PHILIP E. HAWKINS

At Procter & Gamble, most special events involve a business meeting in conjunction with a reception and dinner meeting. Other events create an interesting environment in which to give special recognition for outstanding volunteer efforts. Our special event strategy can be described in this way: When guests have left the event for the evening, they should have a clear vision in their minds that they have attended a first-class reception and dinner, that the service staff cared and demonstrated a high level of commitment and service, and that the facility was immaculately clean and well designed—*a truly outstanding evening from start to finish.*

One key to success of a special event is *detailed planning.* Detailed planning begins with special event team meetings (including the catering company) and continues with the creation of checklists covering every detail of the event.

As an integral part of planning a special event, we usually hold a test dinner for those responsible for the event in our department and the department hosting the event. At this dinner, the menu, beverage, service staff, and kitchen equipment are tested. The test dinner enables us to refine or change the menu and beverages, should this action be recommended by the group.

Special event checklists should be created to cover these considerations: budget, timing targets for the evening, parking, security, tour of facilities, scheduling of paramedics, invitations, guest place cards, decision about the most suitable location for the program, scheduling of a photographer, suitable entertainment if required, and flowers/decorations for the evening.

A checklist has been helpful to us in planning special events for groups as small as 100 people to groups of 5,000 to 34,000 guests. We have handled an employee open house for our new world headquarters and a recent birthday celebration where the company provided a festive picnic-style luncheon for nearly 6,000 guests outside in the P&G Plaza in honor of P&G's 150th anniversary.

Special event team meetings help "flesh out" the main ingredients necessary for a successful special event and determine how best to achieve that goal. The checklists enable us to define the total evening from start to finish. Together, the team meetings and checklists bring into focus specifically who will do what and how much it will cost. These tools help us be exact about expectations: what we expect from the catering company and what they expect from us.

Most of our special events have been a resounding success. Yet, as with quality control, the work is never done. With each special event, we are building and improving on past experiences to reach a higher level of success.

Section 5: Food Items

JACQUELINE M. SCHOFF

Five to ten years ago, the typical workday eating habits included a donut or roll for breakfast, a "hearty" hot meal for lunch in the dining room, and a soft drink plus a vending machine snack in the afternoon. Although the above daily menu is still chosen, two trends are changing the eating habits of employees and the structure of the cafeteria menu: *nutrition* and *fast food*.

Employees are very aware of the importance of a healthy diet, and so it has become necessary for us to offer nutritious selections to meet the demands of our health-conscious customers. Our biggest demand has been for low-calorie and low-cholesterol foods. Selections we offer include a daily salad bar, steamed cod, unseasoned vegetables, meat without gravy, fresh fruit salad, turkey products, and frozen yogurt. We also promote a nutritious meal called the "Fit and Trim Special." This is a low-calorie, low-cholesterol balanced meal. To market the "Fit and Trim," we post the daily special on a fluorescent board and list its calorie and cholesterol levels.

Another popular trend is fast food. The fast food generation, having entered the work force, demands fast food products, such as hamburgers, cheeseburgers, and French fries, in the workplace. Currently, with the healthy diet trend continuing to be strong, fried chicken and fish sandwiches outsell the hamburgers in our fast food grill.

Where are these food trends headed? There appear to be three directions: continued healthy eating, catering, and carry-out.

As nutritional awareness of employees increases, nutritious eating will increase. This will require altering menu items and offering more selections to meet the needs of all customers.

Catering is another growing trend. Business meetings are becoming very popular. To compete with the number of outside restaurants catering these meetings, it may be beneficial for the cafeteria to supply catered lunches for two reasons: convenience to the customers and profits for the cafeteria.

Because many employees like to eat their lunch at their desk, they buy carry-out food from nearby restaurants. The cafeteria providing carry-out service may again provide convenience to the customers and gain profits and competitiveness.

Whatever the future trends will be, it will be necessary for the cafeteria to evaluate them and evaluate the changes needed to fit the trend. Without the appropriate changes, the cafeteria will lose customers and profits to the plentiful competition.

PART C: BLUE COLLAR DINING

CLIFTON B. CHARLES

Clifton B. Charles launched his foodservice career as a manager trainee at Saga Corporation, a national foodservice management company. During his five years with Saga, he progressed through the ranks to become a director of foodservice. Cliff joined Steelcase in 1985 as a foodservice supervisor. In 1987, he was promoted to manager of foodservices, where he is responsible for the company's manufacturing feeding and vending operations in Grand Rapids, Toronto, Alabama, and North Carolina.

"People eat with their eyes" is an expression often used in terms of white collar workers. Yet, times are changing, and today many blue collar workers are adopting that same approach. The overcooked preformed hamburger, the undercooked thin French fries, and the watery soft drink are no longer the accepted norm in manufacturing feeding. Foodservice professionals are more than ever concerned about the blue collar worker receiving a quality product. With blue collar salaries in many of our major manufacturing corporations well up into the high twenties, the level of their tastebuds has risen accordingly.

In Grand Rapids, Michigan, at Steelcase, we are very concerned about meeting the quality expectations of our customers. There is a tremendous amount of restaurant competition surrounding our plants. Within a 5–7 minute ride a plant employee is able to patronize a Wendy's, McDonalds, or Burger King for lunch and now even breakfast. If we are going to keep customers coming back, we need to give them a reason to eat at the cafeteria: a quality food program at a reasonable price.

Providing quality to the customer is only one part of maintaining a good foodservice program. Making that person feel that he or she is important to your business is also essential. This extra care distinguishes a professionally managed operation from one that is run from the seat of the pants.

More often than not, the caliber of a restaurant's staff is dictated by the price of the food items on the menu. If you are paying $27.00 for prime rib, you expect the service staff to treat you like royalty. If they do not meet your standards then you might complain, but more often the restaurant will lose your repeat business.

At Steelcase, we try to give our customers that $27.00 service even if they only purchase a soft drink. You may ask yourself why make this effort—"They're only factory workers, they don't care." But in reality they do care. Without their support, our jobs will disappear. Some people will continue to eat here regardless of how they are treated. However, others are being attracted by our increasingly strong competition. In manufacturing feeding, if we are going to stay in the race then daily workouts to enhance service are necessary to remain competitive.

Meeting the need of our customers is very important, because it is their patronage that enables us to meet the foodservice's fiscal goals. Corporate management also has the same concern, but from a different perspective. Their need is to motivate employees so that they can increase productivity, which affects the fiscal health of the entire corporation.

That motivational impact is tied to the foodservice program. When production requires a plant to be operational longer than the normal 5-day work week, employees are often not receptive to the idea. To try to take some of the sting out of this decision, our foodservices department is asked to provide either a full foodservice or a limited meal during overtime hours. Many times it is not economical to do so. Sometimes we are able to convince management that providing this additional service is not cost effective, but more often than not we must open the cafeteria for service.

As a manager who is cost conscious and concerned about the corporation's well-being, you want, of course, to stay within your allotted budget. Being open during overtime and other similar situations makes it very hard to do so. However, you can begin taking some steps to explain your financial situation better. The first area to examine is food. Track the amount of food being prepared, the amount being served, the amount that is salvagable, and the amount thrown out. In some cases you will be surprised at the loss. Customer count is another means of determining if it is cost effective to open your doors. Participation is a major key to the success of any business. When tracking participation examine your register tapes and determine the number of beverages versus large ticket items sold (main entree, burger combinations). Determine if you sold enough meals to justify being open or whether your vending operation could have met management's need for foodservice.

Labor is an area that you can control but only with close monitoring. Reducing your staff too greatly will make it difficult for you to achieve your service objectives. Doing so will send a message to your customers that, by making them wait, you do not want them to be there. However, certain basic information—customer break times, customer counts at break times, popularity of items being served, and if additional help is required to serve a particular item—will help you better forecast your labor needs.

Dealing with customer complaints is as old as the business itself. Focus all your energy on pleasing that customer. When a customer has a problem in your cafeteria that requires you or one of your staff to handle, make sure that customer leaves talking about how well you resolved the concern.

There are no pat responses to customers' suggestions. As you notice, I used the word suggestion, which has a much more positive sound than complaint. Nobody likes to hear a complaint but you are much more receptive if you, in your mind, can look at it as a suggestion.

Realistically, the customer will more likely present a complaint than a suggestion, but it is your role as a professional to be receptive. For example, our foodservice operation ran a special on tacos. We normally sold tacos for 65 cents each or two for $1.30. We put the meat on the taco while the customer put on the cheese, tomatoes, lettuce (shredded), and sour cream. For the special, we bought a taco boat, which is considerably larger than a taco shell, put in twice as much meat, and let customers build their own taco. However, we sold this taco by the ounce.

Customers were very shocked when they got to the cash register. They were normally accustomed to paying $1.30 for two tacos and were now paying between $3.00 and $4.00 for one. Keep in mind they were receiving twice as much or even more per taco, but they could not see that. That day one out of every three customers suggested strongly that we review our pricing structure, which we did. We examined this special in detail and determined that neither the quality nor the quantity was inferior but that the concept of build your own was lost, and the perceived value was not apparent.

We quickly responded by going back to our old system for customers on the second shift and offering free beverages for our customers on the first shift who bought the special. Was it costly? Yes, when you consider there are about 5,950 employees in our plant. We kept the cost down because we limited the free beverage to lunch only. We also limited the complaints going any higher than my level (manager) because we responded quickly.

Employee turnover is a strong concern for our department. It all stems from one factor: pay. Our department acts as a feeder system to the plant. We bring in people to our department in a capacity known as on-call. When a full-time position is available we select people from our on-call staff to become full-time. After they have been in their position for 1 year, they are eligible to transfer into the plant. The majority of our staff has done that to receive higher wages. The foodservice industry is at the low end of the pay scale, although there have been great strides made in the past few years, especially in B&I foodservice. Still, the gap remains and our staff are very eager to make the transition into the plant. From all indications everyone who has transferred has been satisfied.

Our wage scale is not expected to be competitive with manufacturing, nor from a budgetary standpoint can it afford to be. So we must begin screening our current workforce in hopes of retaining people in foodservices. The majority of our workers who have transferred to the plant have been between the ages of 23 and 27 whose goals and objectives are shaped by their plant environment. These workers are looking to improve their economic standing. Since salaries are higher out in the plant, people tend to look at foodservice as a stepping stone rather than a permanent situation. As managers, our mandate is to learn from this environment and operate our department accordingly. We must examine that workforce and aim to attract those individuals who are truly committed to foodservice.

Establishing a successful B&I foodservice operation requires a sound base. The building blocks are commitment, quality, caring attitude, professionalism, and support. The dictionary definition of commitment is the state of being obligated or emotionally impelled. The important word here is *obligated* to making your food program the best it can be. Do not underestimate factory workers. They know the definition of quality. If you are committed to quality, you will clearly meet that challenge. If you are not genuinely concerned about providing them with a quality meal, they will quickly let you know both verbally and by not giving you repeat business.

Quality in a program is only as high as you want to make it. Many times we associate high quality with increased cost, but that is not necessarily the case. You have to achieve a balance between cost and quality by training the principal people who affect your program: your staff. The contact that your staff has with your customer on a regular basis represents your entire food program. Treating the customer well is probably one of the key components in maintaining a quality program. A simple "Good Morning" or "Thank You" means a lot.

A caring attitude must be evident from you, the manager, to your customer. This can best be expressed through your food presentation. A concern for detail can win you some points with your customer and also make your program one in which you can take pride.

Conformance to the technical and ethical standards of the foodservice industry is a sound basis for the continued growth of your food program. The corporation's commitment to the employee is reflected in the support it provides to the foodservice. Steelcase provides this support by allowing the foodservice program to be managed by professionals who are able to make decisions that have a long-range effect on the corporation and who are able to develop new concepts. Our food program is constantly growing, with many new challenges on the horizon. Are we ready to meet them? I believe so.

PART III

Promotion, Design, and Merchandising

7

Menu Development and Design: Creating a Corporation

SUSAN E. GUENTHER and DOLORES JUERGENS

Susan E. Guenther has been manager of food services at Wisconsin Electric Power Company in Milwaukee since 1981. She is responsible for the company's employee and executive dining operations, catering operations, as well as all vending operations in the power plants and service centers throughout the utility's large service territory in Wisconsin.

Since 1976, Dolores Juergens has held the position of foodservice manager at Northwestern Mutual Life Insurance Company in Milwaukee. She joined Northwestern in 1968 as a registered dietitian and in 1969 was named supervisor of operations and staff for the 624-seat employee restaurant, which serves 2,300 meals daily. She has direct responsibility for food planning, purchasing, and restaurant services, directing a staff of more than 90 full- and part-time employees.

The menu is the most important sales and merchandising tool for any foodservice operation. Every decision that is made during the menu writing process, whether it be related to pricing, design, creating, or merchandising, will have a direct effect on the bottom line. Strategies for menu development and design are so important that the first place to look in reviving an ailing restaurant is the menu.

Whether you are a new or existing manager or supervisor of a facility within the corporate world, a cookbook approach to menu planning is necessary. One of the ingredients of menu planning is an understanding of the corporate objectives or corporate cultures of your company. It is important to familiarize yourself with these objectives in order to run a successful operation that has menu planning as its core.

The corporate goal for foodservice might be to "provide the employee a nutritious, well-balanced meal at a reasonable cost, serving quality food and expedient service in a pleasant and sanitary environment." Once you understand that goal and quantify and qualify it with specific annual supporting objectives, you can proceed with menu planning. Too, be aware of unwritten customs or "sacred cows" that everyone knows exist, but are not documented. In other words, get to know your corporation by asking questions.

There are many different kinds of corporate foodservice. The operation can be partially or totally subsidized, a break-even operation, or a profit-making operation. The foodservice may be self-operated by the company or contracted out to a foodservice management firm. Foodservices also exist in many different environments. There are school lunch programs, corporate dining facilities, hospitals, airlines, hotels, fast food, and leisure dining places. The kind of foodservice and its unique environment will influence the development and design of the menu.

The menu planning and implementation process involves purchasing a raw product, storing it, processing it, merchandising it, selling it, and consuming it, all under the same roof and within severe time restraints. Few businesses can claim to be involved in such a complete process.

MENU WRITING PROCESS

To begin writing a menu, the following ingredients must be stirred, measured, and weighed carefully, and, in some cases, substituted without missing a beat.

Developing a menu requires an awareness of regional food habits, availability of food, seasonal changes, and various occupational types in the workplace. These factors vary menus for the employee cafeteria, the executive dining room, and catering on- or off-premises or for special occasions, such as board of directors', VIPs', or corporate guests' luncheons. Special promotions, such as a theme day, give-a-ways, or suggestive selling ideas, must also be coordinated with the existing menu.

After you have determined what or for whom you are writing the menu, give thought to variety, nutrition, popularity of each item, and customer acceptance. The items selected for the menu must be produced satisfactorily, given the equipment and talent available in your kitchen. Cost effectiveness of the menu should also be considered by determining which items contribute the most and least to the bottom line. Employees should be receiving value for their dollar, but the foodservice operator must be concerned with the bottom line. Being fiscally responsible takes every ounce of skill and ingenuity you can muster.

Careful recipe selection is necessary for ease of service and preparation. Track previously served menu items to give your customer what they like and keep your production on target for cost containment. After you have selected recipes for each menu item, standardize them for purposes of cost control and consistency of appearance and taste. One of the most cost-efficient methods of menu writing is the cycle menu because of efficient purchasing and use of leftovers.

Once the menu is written, supervise production carefully to ensure the desired quality of the end product. Constant monitoring and checking through taste testing of standardized recipes is required to ensure adherence to your standards. Taste testing should help the staff answer any questions asked by the customer. Quality control may be maintained by the manager's participation on a regular basis in taste testing. Deviations from established standardized recipes should be reported to management on a daily basis.

Promote food to the ultimate. Food should scream out to the customer, "Buy me, buy me." The better the food looks, the more you will sell.

Merchandising via word descriptors on the menus and menu board is an important element of promotion. Instead of merely listing barbecue beef on a bun, describe the food item as "a delightful blend of lean tender-sliced beef in a tangy barbecue sauce with fresh green peppers and onions served on bakery-fresh potato rolls." Rather than listing "a stuffed tomato with chicken salad and fresh fruit garnish," write "a large red tomato filled with homemade chicken salad and a mouth-watering mix of honeydew, cantaloupe, and strawberries." Do live up to your promises, however, and deliver the exact copy of the product you are describing. There are also important factors to consider in the appearance of the printed menu and menu boards that display the written descriptive copy. Consideration should be given to such details as the layout of the menu as well as the design. This is the vehicle that is used to sell your food and beverage product. Be sure that your menus are eye-catching, attractive, and clear. The menu boards should also be attractive, easy to read at a glance, and placed in suitable areas of the cafeteria. For example, in a scatter-style cafeteria, menu boards befitting the various food stations should be visible describing the menu and prices for the day. Paying attention to this kind of detail can increase your food-service sales significantly.

The food should be served to the customer at the proper temperatures, under the most sanitary conditions, and with the friendliest service. Customer acceptance is one of the final ingredients necessary to make the menu work.

REGIONAL FOOD HABITS

In some regions of the country, members of one or two ethnic groups predominate. The backgrounds of the residents of these regions dictate their food preferences, which have a great influence on menu selection. Therefore, be aware of the various ethnic groups in the region in which your corporation is located. Be familiar with the religious and social backgrounds of the residents of your area as well as the region's climatic, geographic and economic conditions.

In the South, for instance, collard greens, black-eyed peas, hush puppies, and sweet potato pie are common menu fare. In the eastern part of the country, fresh fish, clams, and oysters might be a regular part of the menu. In the southwest, Tex-Mex foods would be more appropriate.

A Midwestern menu would probably feature brats, German potato salad and deep dish pizza. Milwaukee would feature Friday fish frys of beer-battered deep-fried frozen cod, coleslaw, French fries, and rye bread. People in the Pacific Northwest would probably turn their noses up at the Friday fish fry and would be more apt to choose fresh salmon. Many of their foods are seasoned with an Oriental flavor. However, foods from other regions might be a treat or novelty if used for a special promotion.

A New England boiled dinner or spareribs and potato dumplings probably would not be very popular menu fare in Florida and certainly not at a pool party. Conversely, because of the shipping charges and special handling needed, it might be too costly to serve fresh abalone or mussels in an employee cafeteria in the Midwest.

In the warmer areas of the country fresh fruits and vegetables are in abundance year round. In colder climates fresh produce has limited availability, and usually only in season. Consider the availability and costs of putting off-season produce on the menu.

The menu should reflect the economic conditions of your audience. In corporations that draw employment from smaller areas or rural communities or that are located in depressed areas, extended dishes, such as casseroles, or economical foods might be added to the menu. In contrast, for a corporation in the heart of a large city that houses the corporate office, higher-tagged gourmet foods are appropriate and well accepted.

Certain religious restrictions may also need to be incorporated into your menu plan. Again, these vary from region to region.

You, as the menu writer, should be aware that you have your own food preferences and prejudices unique to your upbringing. Remember that you are writing the menu to feature the foods that are popular in your region as determined by the ethnic backgrounds and the socioeconomic levels of your market.

EMPLOYEE OCCUPATION

Menu writing is greatly influenced by the occupation of the employees you are feeding. For instance, the amount of physical exercise expended by employees determines their appetite. For workers in physically taxing jobs that require large expenditures of calories, meat-and-potato menu items are appealing. Employees in office jobs with more sedentary occupations might be more inclined to select salads and lighter fare.

FOOD AVAILABILITY

Most foods are readily available with today's modes of transportation and distribution.

There is no substitute for the quality of fresh foods, and to maximize quality and minimize cost, foods should be purchased when they are plentiful and prices are low.

Careful planning is necessary if you choose to put unseasonable or nonregional foods on the menu. For instance, if you put fresh seafood on a menu somewhere in the Midwest, you need to preplan its purchase. The quality of fresh fish will be lost if not served immediately. Because of the distance from its source, fresh fish requires special handling.

Many foods are abundant when they are in season. During these periods, incorporate the fresh, plentiful foods on your menu. Your rewards will be low costs, quality foods, and customer satisfaction. Use the bountiful harvests during these seasons for special promotions.

NUTRITION AND WELL-BALANCED MEALS IN CORPORATE DINING

Most corporations today have wellness programs, and employees are bombarded with nutritional information through the media on a daily basis. However, whether or not employees really understand what a balanced diet is, you as a menu planner must assume the responsibility of education through example in your daily menus.

A balanced diet means eating foods from each of the basic four food groups every day: the bread-cereal, milk, vegetable-fruit, and meat group. It is neither costly nor difficult to serve balanced meals because all the recommended foods include ones that are relatively inexpensive. With a little knowledge and judgment, regardless of budget limitations, it is within your power as menu writers to offer a balanced diet. It is a challenge to plan the kind of meals that nourish as well as tempt and satisfy your employees' appetites.

If you offer enough variety from the basic four groups every day, people will be able to select a well-balanced meal. Special diets should be referred to the medical department as the needs arise.

Even when nutritional foods are offered, they may not always be selected by the employee. Nutritional education becomes important if employees are to make wise food choices. There is an abundance of information available on cholesterol and sodium intakes, as well as on other nutrients, to assist you in providing as much information on the menu as desired.

You can do a lot to help your employees make good menu selections by publishing caloric values and other important nutritional information. Computer systems are now available to help you provide this data in as much detail as you or your corporate medical department feels is necessary. The degree of your involvement in disbursing nutritional information on the menu is unlimited.

Vegetable-Fruit Group

Citrus fruits, tomatoes, strawberries, cantaloupe, broccoli, cabbage, and bell peppers all provide vitamin C, which is necessary for healthy gums, body tissues, and blood vessels. Vitamin C also helps the body resist infection and aids in healing.

Carrots, winter squash, spinach, broccoli, apricots, cantaloupe, and sweet potatoes provide vitamin A, which is essential for normal vision and healthy skin. The clue in selecting foods rich in vitamin A is the color. The deeper the green or yellow, the more vitamin A.

These fruits and vegetables are good sources for fiber or roughage, which is necessary for normal digestion.

Milk Group

This group includes milk, cheese, ice cream, yogurt, and foods in which milk is a main ingredient, such as puddings and cream soups.

Without milk, it is difficult to obtain the calcium and phosphorus necessary for healthy bones and teeth. Milk also contains valuable protein, riboflavin, vitamin A, and fortified vitamin D. Vitamin D helps the body utilize calcium. Butter or margarine contains vitamin A.

Meat Group

Meats, fish, poultry, and eggs are the principal sources of protein that is vital for muscle building, growth and repair of tissues. Dried beans or peas, peanut butter, and nuts are also sources of protein. These foods also contribute good quantities of iron and B vitamins.

Bread-Cereal Group

Whole grain, enriched, or restored grain products make up this group. It includes bread and other baked goods, cereal, macaroni, noodles, rice, and cornmeal. These foods are excellent sources of food energy, also called calories; iron for blood building; and B vitamins for healthy nerves and skin and normal digestion and appetite.

Other Foods

Some foods do not fall into the four basic food groups. Such foods as salad dressings, gravies, fats, sugar, candies, desserts, and snacks are sources of energy. They also provide fun and variety in the diet and should not be discounted, even though they do not provide the essential nutrients of the basic four groups. The nutritious foods on the menu should help employees who participate in the corporate food program think about fitting their likes and dislikes into a daily pattern of healthful meals and good basic nutrition.

Proper Cooking Techniques

In addition to offering foods from the four food groups, preparation and proper cooking techniques are critical. For example, 90 percent of the nutrient content of food can be cooked away, peeled, or discarded thoughtlessly. Cooking foods at a high temperature diminishes the weight of the food, destroys nutrients, adds to food cost and, worse, decreases palatability.

Obtaining the maximum nutrients and eye appeal of food does not just happen. It has to be planned carefully. If you plan a perfect menu and cook the food improperly, all your effort is in vain. Vitamins and minerals are lost, food costs soar, and customers disappear. Cooking for maximum nutrient retention is a science and must be religiously enforced. Using standardized recipes is one way of achieving consistent results in cooking techniques. This is discussed in further detail in another section of this chapter.

Low-Calorie Foods

Along with offering basic nutritional selections on the menu, do not overlook those employees who wish to reduce their caloric intake. Because the customer in corporate dining eats in the cafeteria on a much more frequent basis than in the same local restaurant, low-calorie items that are high in nutritional value should be offered daily, perhaps in a special section of your cafeteria line.

It may be appropriate to dedicate a special section of the written menu to light fare items. They might be identified through such menu merchandising as calorie counters, weight worriers, etc. You might find that these are not the most popular items, but offering this type of menu fare is a must. "Eating to be thin" is a tremendous psychological struggle. Only the most disciplined customers will remain fans of this part of your menu for extended periods of time. Chocolate cake and "other goodies" will jump on their trays occasionally.

Because not all menu writers are dietitians, there are many publications and organizations that provide assistance to individuals interested in developing a nutritional, balanced menu. The American Heart Association offers a service to help designate heart-healthy items. There are weight loss organizations, both nationally and locally, that are more than willing to assist you. More and more cookbooks have calorie counts, as well as a nutritional breakdown for each recipe. As you build your cookbook library, make careful selections so that you have good sources of nutritional information, as well as good recipes.

Yet, do not completely eliminate the "fun" foods as you write the menu. By ensuring that there is something for everybody, you will have both variety and a nutritious menu.

CREATIVITY

Creativity is what distinguishes an outstanding menu from an average one. The expression of your creativity begins in the selection of menu ideas and continues in descriptive menu writing and the selling of menu items through merchandising and plate presentation.

You can use all your senses in writing, implementing, and selling the menu. You can hear, from many sources, new and different menu ideas that you might want to incorporate into the menu. These ideas can be gleaned from seminars, workshops, peers, or from your Aunt Matilda, for that matter. In return, employees hear what their peers have to say. Perhaps they are talking about that terrific new menu item you created that is taking the company by storm. Word of mouth is your best source of advertising if you give your customers something good to talk about. Hearing can be a powerful merchandising tool if employees are excited and enthusiastic about what you have done with the menu.

Smell could be like drawing a bear to honey. Recall how you react to the smell of fresh popped corn or the aroma of fresh baked goods. Do not be above buying fans to blow these smells around the building! Smell is an important part of merchandising. Retailers take advantage of this well-known fact.

The expression, "People eat with their eyes," is so true in the corporate world of dining. Given your choice of roast pork, mashed potatoes, and cauliflower or a plate of food where a picture has been painted with vividly colored foods to complement one another, which one would you choose? Crispy and browned is aesthetically more pleasing than soggy and pale. Every recipe should have a built-in chorus of garnishes to create a visual temptation. In fact, merchandising is such an important subject that an entire chapter of this book has been devoted to it.

You can pique the senses of hearing, sight, and smell, but if you do not satisfy the sense of taste, your efforts are in vain. Ultimately, fresh foods prepared properly taste best. However, with the improved scientific methods of flash-freezing, quality can still be achieved using good recipes, fresh seasonings that bring out the best possible taste, and the skills of your staff.

Creativity should also be used in the menu pricing structure. Touch can be related to your customers' touch of money—how much or how little has to be parted with upon reaching the cashier or receiving the bill from the waitress.

Another way that touch influences creativity is shown in the following example: a sandwich you have recently created looks appealing and tastes wonderful, but drips down the customer's arm while being eaten! Being touched this way may make the customer decide never to try this gourmet delight again.

Crunchy, crisp, smooth, and creamy are important sensations as food touches the mouth. The sense of touch, through a physical experience such as eating, can be satisfied by selecting appropriate food items for the menu.

Do not forget a "touch" basic. Serve hot food hot and cold food cold. China should be heated to serve hot food and chilled to serve cold food.

Variety is the spice of life. This is never truer than in foodservice. Planning variety in the menu is an expression of creativity. Be original and do not be afraid to experiment.

Descriptive menu writing should paint a visual picture of the menu. Become a master at this writing.

All of the expressions of creativity are meant to make the menu your own. Use as many resources as you can. Learn from your staff, your customers, and all the publications that are available. The person whom you least expect, if given the chance, may come up with one of the best ideas. Creativity prevents boredom of your staff, yourself, and your customers.

CYCLE MENUS

Each menu planner writes menus in a unique way. Some prefer to plan the menu on a daily basis. Others prefer to write on a weekly basis. The most efficient method is called a cycle menu, which is a pattern of repetitive food selections. It can be based on a 4-, 6- or 8-week rotation by season. There are many advantages to a well-planned cycle menu. First and foremost it saves time. You are able to track sales of individual menu items more easily and thus respond quickly to eliminate those that are not popular. Cyclical menus become a tool of management to simplify purchasing and food production.

Guesswork can be minimized for future menu items because there is predictability in repetition. There is an opportunity to take advantage of price promotions when it is known that a menu item will reappear.

The repetition and familiarity of menus promote the usage of standardized recipes. The staff becomes very skilled at preparing these recipes, and consistency is achieved.

A cycle menu provides an opportunity to maximize production of a menu item. For instance, if chili is on the menu and the forecast is to serve 300 portions today, and you as the operator know it will repeat four more times in the cycle, you may choose to produce 1,200 servings and flash-freeze the balance in three separate batches. The advantages of doing so would be to free your staff the next time that chili appears on the menu to do other tasks, such as cleaning those ovens that they always tell you they never have time to do.

The drawback of a cycle menu is its repetitiveness, which could become boring to the customer. Therefore, do not hesitate to interject new menu items that will keep the menu interesting. Doing so only requires a minimum amount of time on your part. It simply involves substituting one menu item for another. For example, baked cod amandine might be a menu item that you feel has been too repetitive and decreasing in popularity. There is an exciting new recipe that you have been dying to try—shrimp fajita stir fry—that you feel will create customer appeal and continued interest. Go ahead and substitute. The important thing to remember is not to let interest diminish to the point of losing customers.

Do not let a cycle menu inhibit promotions, theme days, or give-aways that generate enthusiasm from your participating audience.

STANDARDIZATION OF RECIPES

Standardized recipes use quantities of food that are precisely weighed and measured, thereby achieving a consistent and unifed product every time the item is served. This is every foodservice operator's dream; however, with independent and creative cooks, lack of consistency in raw materials, and spur-of-the-moment enthusiasm, it is a difficult goal to achieve. Checks should be made on the accurate preparation of menu items on a daily basis. Deviations should be recorded and corrected immediately. This is an ongoing challenge. If the chef or other production employees resist these checks because they feel creativity is being stifled, reply that creativity is actually being captured to ensure that, each and every time a menu item is served, the customer can depend on a consistently good quality product. Frequent checks remove the danger of having an item be a good experience one time and a bad experience the next.

Recipe instructions specify accurate weights and measured amounts of specific foods, cooking times and temperatures, proper cooking pan sizes and serving utensils, garnishing ideas, yields, and specific methods of preparation. The end result is that the customer will always have confidence in the menu.

TEAMWORK

It is not important how you structure a team. A team might include the foodservice management, staff, customers, and corporate representatives. Or it could be broken down into smaller groups, such as a cook's work group, a salad preparation work group, or a bakery work group. The important ingredient is to have an ongoing process in place where simple questions can be asked, such as What things are going well? What things need to be improved?

The benefits of this team evaluation process are total participation and communication by every foodservice employee involved in planning and creating the menu. Every employee comes to feel a sense of importance. They gain a feeling of pride in the quality of the product, which leads to employee satisfaction. Everyone loves a winner and to be part of a winning team. It challenges the creativity of every team member to achieve a singular goal—in this case, a winning menu.

Customers can be involved through customer surveys. Do not be afraid to ask for and listen to their ideas, suggestions, and constructive criticism reflecting their food preferences. Ideas offered by customers through these surveys might result in exciting menus.

Sponsor contests in which customers enter their favorite recipes. These recipes can be judged by a qualified panel and the winning recipes put on the cafeteria menu. The results are good public relations and customer involvement.

In a captive audience of corporate dining, the foodservice operator must be receptive to the challenge of change and be willing to meet this challenge with enthusiasm.

8

Anatomy of a Promotion

NEIL J. REYER

Neil J. Reyer is vice president of restaurant and travel management for Chemical Bank in New York. Neil joined the ranks of B&I foodservice in 1977 as director of foodservice at Chemical Bank. Later promoted to vice president, he established the bank's foodservice operations as among the finest in the country. Neil's awards and industry accolades include a 1984 Restaurants & Institutions *Ivy Award, a 1985* Metro Magazine *Award for outstanding foodservice industry accomplishment, a 1986 leadership award from the Marketing Agents to the Foodservice Industry (MAFSI), and a 1987 IFMA Silver Plate Award.*

As most of us in fast-paced service businesses, such as B&I foodservice, know, the one element that is constant in our jobs is change. The purpose of this chapter is to examine how foodservice directors and dietitians can fulfill successfully customers' and administrators' expectations for foodservice variety and change through the creation, development, and implementation of "special days." Any discussion of special-day promotions, however, must begin with an understanding of the B&I market.

Attracting corporate customers to corporate foodservice environments presents much the same challenge as that faced by commercial operators in attracting their customers. Today's corporate customer is almost always a voluntary (not a captive) customer and, as such, evaluates a corporate foodservice by all the same measures that commercial customers do when planning to dine "out." Discerning contemporary customers, whether by conscious design or some intuitive process, determine operations' cleanliness, prices, perceived value, food quality, decor, and level of service when making "go/no go" decisions on daily dining choices. Once this is understood, a foodservice operator can better appreciate the need to develop, merchandise, and market promotional programs that will indeed support efforts aimed at attracting and keeping target customers.

The foodservice business has more than once been compared to the theatre, where each day the curtain goes up on a new performance. In our

Note: Reprinted with permission from *Food Management Magazine*, Vol. 21, No. 12, Harcourt Brace Jovanovich, Inc., © December 1986.

business, however, we play to more or less the same audience daily. And because we cannot rebuild our operations each day to generate curiosity and renew interest, we must periodically offer appealing changes through effectively planned and implemented special-day programs.

By definition, special-day promotions are original, short-term foodservice programs that promote a particular theme, an ethnic cuisine, or a corporate objective to which a foodservice department is being asked to contribute. At Chemical Bank, we raise an imaginary curtain on a new show at least 12 times per year for a demanding and critical audience—our corporate customers.

Although special-day promotions are not new, increased competition and enhanced customer sophistication have added new importance to program development and implementation, along with a heightened awareness of the merchandising and marketing efforts we make within our foodservice environments.

The enormous effort that must be expended during the planning, development, and implementation of special-day promotions should result in the attainment of both quantifiable objectives and those that are not so easily measured but are important just the same. Such benefits include reducing customer complaints, increasing compliments and, in general, raising a special day's "comfort index."

At Chemical Bank Restaurant Services, there are a number of target objectives of special days. First and foremost, we look to increase overall participation, something our commercial colleagues call "traffic." We also want to increase our gross margins, revive and maintain customer interest in our current foodservice programs, promote our foodservice facilities, deinstitutionalize the institutional environments, and reduce our "bitch quotient."

Yet, although special days are important and can be fun to do, they also require a major resource commitment. Sadly, some of my colleagues consider the requisite effort unacceptably inconvenient, as it disrupts their daily production and service programs. Nothing we do is easy; why should special promotions be any different? As long as the objectives are met, any inconvenience you may have to endure is irrelevant.

INGREDIENTS OF SPECIAL-DAY PROMOTIONS

Special-day promotions, whether they are theme-oriented, ethnic, or highlight a particular program a corporation wants its foodservice department to support, have some key common ingredients.

Staff

It has become almost axiomatic that the success or failure of any food-service activity is tied directly to the performance of a foodservice staff. Well-groomed, well-trained, and enthusiastic foodservice personnel who are committed to the success of your special promotions will often provide the single most important means of communicating your program to customers.

Graphics

Printed materials—including menus, tip-ins, tent cards, and flyers—are an invitation to your customers to attend your special events. Poorly designed or executed printed media will be perceived by customers as a tout for an upcoming event that will also be poorly designed and executed. Therefore, high-quality graphics are a must. They convey a lot about you and the credibility of the program you are planning.

Promotion/Publicity

Any graphics program, no matter how well conceived or attractively presented, will have little impact if you fail to display your great graphics to customers in a timely fashion. Publicizing a promotion, therefore, is the process of getting the word out about a forthcoming special event. Our experience suggests that publicity that begins 2–3 weeks before a special day provides sufficient lead time to alert customers. Too much advance notice simply increases the probability of customers forgetting about an upcoming promotional event.

Food

Food should always be of high quality, no matter the type of occasion at which it is being served. Your customers should not have to wait for a special promotion to receive top-quality meal items. Nonetheless, during a promotion the menu, of course, will be special because enhancements in terms of portion sizes or basic ingredients add perceived value. An added benefit for operators is that customers tend to perceive special-day meal items as being fresher than usual bills of fare, as the nature of the menu precludes the use of leftovers from the day before.

Decor

Decor includes not only the physical modifications you may make to a foodservice facility in terms of decorations but also the provision of appropriate costumes or uniforms for employees. Decor, in fact, manifests the theme that holds an entire promotional program together, providing it with overall credibility. Nothing falls flatter after a major effort has been made on menu development and graphics for a Bastille Day special, for example, than letting customers see servers in their usual whites, rather than in French theme costumes.

Music

Music may be provided by live bands, combos, individual musicians, or prerecorded tapes. Whichever option is selected, music will certainly heighten the ambiance and authenticity of a special event. It is impossible to envision a successful St. Patrick's day promotion without bagpipes or a popular Mexican Fiesta celebration without a mariachi band. However, the expense of live bands or single musicians must be weighed against the overall cost of a promotional program and one's ability to recoup such costs through menu pricing. Certainly, records or tapes should not be overlooked because they offer an inexpensive way to enhance a promotion's overall ambiance.

Prices

Combining the above ingredients and knowing how much emphasis to give to each will, of course, determine any special day's effectiveness. Each ingredient is designed to add value to any promotion, and it is this value that must eventually be reflected in appropriate menu prices. Foodservice pricing is always important in a corporate environment, but on special days, it is even more critical. Prices that are too low or too high for your market spell disaster; hence, care must be taken to ensure that a favorable price-value relationship is created in the minds of customers in regard to your promotional program.

PLANNING FOR A YEAR, NOT A DAY

Once one has assembled all the ingredients for success, planning and implementation of special-day promotions now become an exercise in creativity, teamwork, and commitment. Because no one has a monopoly on creativity, we at Chemical Bank believe in involving as many people as possible in the development of promotional themes. In my experience, the more participation that one elicits from managers, supervisors, and food-service workers, the greater their commitment to the planning and implementation of the overall promotional program. Staff members who have a vested interest in creating a promotion also have a vested interest in solving any problems that may occur during its development and execution.

At Chemical Bank, promotional planning begins each November when our six unit foodservice directors participate in a marathon brainstorming session to create the ideas that will eventually develop into special- and/or ethnic-day events. In an industry where a long-range plan often refers only to the organization of a single day's activities, being able to sit down to plan and develop a year's supply of special promotions is little short of a miracle. Rather than using any number of books and pamphlets that offer canned programs or 365 reasons to throw a party, most often, we choose to create our own unique promotions. Of course, in so doing, we create the risk of failure that frequently dooms untested ideas. Yet, the element of risk and our acceptance of it probably foster a greater level of creativity among our managers.

So, each November that creative energy is released—hours of it! A listing of as many as 30 to 40 ideas is eventually distilled over a 6-hour period to 12 programs that everyone agrees will have the greatest chance for success in our market. There are, however, some time-saving procedures that facilitate our consideration process. First, we set aside those days for which we *must* create promotions; not necessarily because we want to but because to forget them would be to commit a cardinal sin. These days are St. Patrick's Day, Thanksgiving, and Christmas.

It is difficult to overrate the importance of tying your promotional schedule to your customers' expectations. For example, one year we decided to forego celebrating St. Valentine's Day in favor of a Leap Year Day promotion. However, this decision was a mistake we will not soon forget. To our customers, ignoring St. Valentine's Day was a sin equalled only by eating meat on Fridays during Lent or leavened bread on Passover. As a result, St. Valentine's is now a perennial fixture on our schedule of promotions.

Although there is no formula for picking those days that will work and work well, there are criteria against which all promotional ideas should be considered. Even an idea that seems to hold all the ingredients for success will likely die a miserable death if it is implemented on an employee payday, for example. Paydays are anathema to special days. So are Fridays and Mondays. If a special day is designed to feature items priced higher than normal, scheduling it on the day before a payday will also doom it to something less than success. Finally, if an idea passes all these tests, a fabulously beautiful day can destroy all our best-laid plans, as customers will undoubtedly flock outdoors.

Weather aside, no planning process would be complete without a thorough examination of data from prior years' special days. We not only review our failures but we also track our successes. Restaging successful promotions can be just as disastrous as repeating failures, especially when you consider that one of the reasons for having special days in the first place is to reduce customers' boredom. Remember, too, that the same customer who is just waiting for us to fail is also ready to offer us a chiding reminder, such as, "You did that last year. Can't you guys in foodservice be more original?"

Your first promotion planning session should be designed to accomplish the following basic tasks:

- Themes should be developed in brainstorming sessions.
- Agreement and commitment should be offered by all participants.
- Your objectives in developing the program should be clearly communicated.
- Pros/cons of the special day(s) under consideration—level of difficulty, production problems—should be evaluated.
- A date for implementation that will optimize sales should be established.
- Specific action guidelines, such as type and style of decorations, use and type of music, budget, and a system to obtain feedback data, should be developed.

A key element in the planning and development of special-day promotions is knowing how to come up with programs that are doable. Decorations, food, costumes, music, and other ingredients must all be brought together in support of a chosen theme. Program failure is almost assured if you do not develop an action plan for every last detail. If customers perceive a half-hearted promotion, rather than real commitment to a special day, they tend to reject the entire effort. If you cannot do it right or there is no hope of doing it right, then do not do it at all.

For example, in September 1982 we first staged our "Back to School Day" special promotion. For this program, it was critical that we be able to "transport" our customers back in time to their formative elementary school days. To do this, we had to create an environment that would be reminiscent of the month of September and all the appropriate nostalgic images that people associate with their early school years.

Fond memories of school crossing guards, apples for the teacher, brown bag lunches and, yes, even the small containers of milk were replicated in reality or image within our corporate dining environments. Simple peanut butter and jelly sandwiches were a formidable seller that day, outdone only by the ubiquitous cellophane-wrapped, cream-filled sponge snack cakes. Hand-written menus done by my daughter, 7 years old at the time, and reprinted on yellow lined paper promoted what turned out to be one of our most successful special-day programs. Similar to all our promotions, it was a "fun" effort taken seriously, with no details left to chance. On this occasion, the special-day program keyed on nostalgia, highlighting not only period food, but also objects and an environment with which everyone was familiar.

Then there are those unique occasions where style, form, and food combine to define a particular situation. A perfect illustration of this was our successful, "Happy Hour Buffet Day" promotion, where we chose to focus on the New York bar scene, a ritual replete with happy hour snacks. Although we did not serve liquor, we did replace the day's standard bill of fare with a multitude of bar-style hors d'oeuvres, everything from pigs-in-blankets to Swedish meatballs, all served from chafing dishes within the servery area. For one price, $2.75, customers were able to "graze" to their hearts' content, enjoying foods for lunch that one would expect to find only after 5 P.M. at a local pub. With only a minimum of decoration, such as lowered lights and displayed chafing dishes, and food planning, success on this occasion resulted from providing the unexpected.

Consider these other menu programming points.

- Augment the participation process by involving unit managers and chefs in the creation of menus.
- Create menus that are both appropriate to your market and, whenever possible, support your theme. If, for example, you have multi-unit operations, menus should not necessarily be the same at all locations, but rather targeted to each different audience.
- Experiment with table d'hote or blue plate specials that package appetizer, soup, entree, and dessert for one price.

HOW MUCH TO DO THE JOB RIGHT?

When planning special promotion days, attention should naturally be directed toward the overall implementation expense. Obviously, you must set a limit on the investment you wish to make for any such occasion.

Overspending or trying to get away cheap will not do. Instead, establish a budget for each unit under your management, based upon the physical size of the facility and number of staff. Never ignore your promotional budget-setting responsibilities by telling unit managers to exercise their own judgment, spend a "few dollars" and buy the decorations that they think will be needed to make a program work. A few dollars to you may mean hundreds, but to an overzealous manager, it may mean thousands! So set a cap on what you are willing to spend on environmental enhancements.

There are, of course, many ways to save money without decreasing program effectiveness. When it has been determined, for example, that to do the job right major decorations or stage sets will be required, consideration should then be given to renting materials, such as jukeboxes and old soda fountain counters, rather than buying them. When we at Chemical Bank have been faced with such a dilemma, acquisition costs have been reduced by "taking the show on the road." Normally, we provide special promotions at all our locations on the same day; that, of course, creates a burdensome expense due to the duplicate decorations and costumes required at each operation. However, by setting up a traveling roadshow and staggering our special events over several days at different facilities, initial acquisition costs are amortized over all facilities.

Some special days do not require an extraordinary effort or expense to be successful. Fantastic results can be achieved by "coat-tailing" onto a currently popular trend or fad. Our "Nifty-Fifties Day" was a perfect example. By mixing a little doo-wop music, trendy diner-style food, an old jukebox, and a couple of packs of cigarettes tucked into server's T-shirt sleeves, we created the popular ambiance of the 1950s. If you are lucky enough to have one of those old cafeterias awaiting budget approval for a major renovation, you will have a natural stage for an effective 1950s-era promotion. Of course, you do not really need an old cafeteria to make this special a great occasion. For us, success was achieved by offering low prices, big portions, and menu items that on any other day would have gone begging for customers. Old standards, such as open-faced hot turkey and roast beef sandwiches served with scooped mashed potatoes with crater gravy, sold out at $1.50, along with 10-ounce bottles of soda priced at a ridiculous 25 cents per pop.

PROMOTION BOOSTS SALES 22.8 PERCENT

One of the primary objectives in developing special-day promotions is to achieve a positive impact on bottom-line subsidy. Any increased sales volume gained through greater participation must be identified and recorded after each and every event. At Chemical Bank, detailed computer records, compiled through our point-of-sale polling systems, contain information on promotion sales, check average, and customer counts by location and in sum. This information is tracked and compared to typical or average day data. Typically, at Chemical Bank we experience sharp increases in all these key performance factors whenever we run a special promotion. For example, when we did our most recent promotion, the "Feast of San Gennaro," in September 1986, customer counts increased 15.6 percent, average checks rose a healthy 6.2 percent, and overall sales were up 22.8 percent. As noted, such favorable variances are not unusual. At Chemical Bank, key perform- ance factors, such as check average, customer counts, and sales volume generally reflect average increases of anywhere from 12 to 40 percent as a result of our promotional efforts. However, it may be unrealistic for other foodservice operators to expect similar returns. There are just too many variables inherent in B&I operations to establish standard performance objectives for all special-day promotions.

EXPERIMENTATION WITH NEW MENU CONCEPTS

Another most helpful characteristic of specials is the capacity they give us to experiment with new menu ideas or concepts. On occasion, a successful special menu can be translated into what we call "major" ongoing pro- motions, themed serving units that are either permanently set up as part of a facility's dining program or are moved from location to location on a rotating basis. For example, our highly successful "King Neptune Day" promotion provided the foundation for the development of a permanent fresh seafood station. Now known as "Billy Budd's Galley," this nautically decorated servery area allows us to feature and merchandise highly popular fresh seafood items, such as sole, scallops, swordfish, and brochettes of shrimp, which are prepared to order at the serving counter. A "Mexican Fiesta Week" promotion was later refined into the "MexiMart," a Mexican fast food shop, that was constructed and remained an average of 6 months at each of our operations.

SPECIALS—A PROFITABLE COMMITMENT

Special-day promotions and programs are profitable in a number of ways. They are fun for both foodservice staffs and customers and also provide managers with fabulous learning experiences and opportunities to test new products while developing a greater understanding of their target market—corporate customers. As long as our customers vote with their dollars and we have the ability to count those votes, we will always have the responsibility of meeting their needs and expectations. There is perhaps no better way for B&I executives to demonstrate their commitment to providing customers with high-quality dining experiences and caring service than to provide a well-planned and executed schedule of special days. If there is a design for foodservice success, it is found in the anatomy of a creative promotion.

9

Merchandising

BERYL J. YUHAS

Beryl J. Yuhas is principal of Beryl Yuhas Associates, which is located in San Rafael, California. Before forming her own foodservice consulting firm, Beryl was vice president of operations for Guckenheimer Enterprises, a large regional food management company. Beryl, a native of England, has over 30 years of experience in the foodservice industry.

When people in our industry are asked "What do you do for a living?", most answer, "I'm in the food business." How many say, "I'm in the business of selling food."? The most successful managers promote and merchandise their food programs, thus maximizing sales and minimizing the cost of operation. A well-thought out merchandising program can also result in other benefits, such as increased customer satisfaction, happy client liaisons, an edge over your competition, motivated employees, lower subsidies, and even fun.

Merchandising means different things to different people. Some managers feel that dressing up their cafeteria and employees a few times a year for a special promotion is what merchandising is all about. Special promotions are part of merchandising, of course. However, why not think about how your servery could look if you approached it from the perspective of every day being a special promotion (see Figure 9-1)?

You are responsible for generating excitement in your customers. If you are not excited about your presentations, why should your customers be? The description, "captive audience," is no longer true of our customers, yet you can captivate an audience with your food programs and creative merchandising.

For many years our segment of the industry was called "institutional." What does that word connote? Perhaps a workhouse in a Dickens novel, in which greasy gruel is slopped into a wooden bowl with a hunk of stale bread! Thank goodness, we have moved away from this image. Our industry and such organizations as the Society for Foodservice Management and its membership refer to us now as "corporate dining" or "B&I foodservice."

Figure 9-1 Self-service food bars, such as this make-your-own sundae bar, encourage customer participation, reduce labor, and afford the opportunity for everyday merchandising. (Photo provided by Trusthouse Forte Food Services, Inc.)

B&I foodservice has improved vastly in the past few years. Some of the most talented individuals in foodservice are now specializing in our segment of the industry. The majority of employee cafeterias are as good as and sometimes better than anything our customers can find in retail outlets across the street from our facilities.

Corporations are spending millions of dollars on new employee dining facilities. Many older ones are being remodeled and renovated. Today's cafeteria designs are enabling the operators to merchandise in ways that even the retail chains have started to emulate (see Figure 9-2). Both self-operators and foodservice management companies have upgraded and are continuing to upgrade their food programs, making the commitment to do it right.

The cafeteria setting is very rewarding because everything we have to sell can be displayed. Restaurants do not have the same visual opportunity to increase their sales as we do. They have to attract their customers' attention with their menu. Restaurant customers do not know what their choice will

Figure 9-2 Today's employee cafeteria is divided into stations for hot foods, sandwiches, deli, soups, salads, desserts, beverages, and merchandising for special theme days. (Photo provided by Corporate Public Affairs Department, ARA Services, Inc.)

look like until it arrives at the table. They hope that it will look and taste as good as the menu description.

Because people eat with their eyes, it is your responsibility to dazzle them, make them spend more than they intended to because everything looks so great. You need to make a statement with your food programs: "they should sit up and say hello."

My intention in this chapter is to excite you about merchandising and for you then to pass this excitement on to your employees to work as a merchandising team. You would be amazed by the good suggestions and ideas they can contribute when they are allowed to be creative. Let them share in your commitment to excellence.

Because merchandising affects all areas of the foodservice operation and ultimately its profitability, your efforts in this area will be instrumental in accomplishing and perhaps exceeding your clients' fiscal goals.

Your staff must be well trained, neat in appearance, cheerful, knowledgeable about your product and food programs, motivated, and encouraged to suggest new ideas and innovations that could enhance the overall performance of the operation. Remember both individually and collectively they can and will directly affect your sales and your ability to satisfy your clients' needs.

EVALUATE YOUR PROGRAM

You need to evaluate your programs and merchandising from the customers' perspective, from their side of the counter. What do they perceive when entering the cafeteria? Take a pad and pencil and walk the cafeteria as your customer does. Make notes of what you see, both good and bad.

Decor

First, consider the physical environment. Is it spotlessly clean? Is it warm? Is it friendly and relaxing? Will it encourage your customers to return? Keep in mind that the atmosphere you create should foster a pleasant and welcoming dining experience.

What kind of decor is presently being used? Is it in keeping with and is it an integral part of your merchandising program? Does it relate to the food you are selling; does it enhance or detract from your overall theme? With some careful thought you can achieve a total look that is consistent with your programs.

Many decorative items can be obtained from readily available sources. For example, supermarkets offer fresh flowering potted plants that will look great on the tops of your sneeze guards, utilizing space that is often a catch-all for a variety of items that give a cluttered appearance. The changing of these plants seasonally will add color.

Framed posters and/or food-related photographs may be used to cover large bare wall space. These are available from a variety of specialty shops located in most malls and city shopping centers. Discount book chains have a supply of cookbooks with colored photographs of the recipes. When opened at the appropriate page, these cookbooks can be put into see-through holders and placed over the salad bar, soup station, entree, dessert area, etc.

Your local import store sells a choice of artifacts to highlight your programs. They also stock a large supply of baskets and containers, which make a great alternative to stainless steel and plastic containers when used to accommodate many prewrapped and smaller items. These baskets may be set on and lined with some colorful material purchased from your local fabric store. Cut this material with pinking shears to eliminate the need to sew the edges. The use of this material will help warm the cold look of stainless steel counter tops.

Point-of-sale displays can attract attention, add color, highlight programs and special events, commemorate holidays, or advertise special menu items. POS menu boards placed at eye level help sell the product, and your customers will appreciate not having to search the large menu boards to see how much an item costs.

Remember you are in the business of selling food. Should you decide that your present decor package is a little tired or needs some changes, alter it to reflect your food programs and be sure that it is clean, crisp, and uncluttered.

Food Selection

Your merchandising program is aimed at increasing the sale of food. It is of the utmost importance that the food be fresh, of top quality, colorful, well presented, and pleasing to the eye and that it tastes as good as it looks.

Avoid long-term repetition of the same choices. Menus should not be set in concrete; people change, so should menus to keep up with the current tastes and trends. Many of your customers are trying to match their eating habits to a healthier life-style. However, we are not suggesting you cater only to the health enthusiasts. The goal is to satisfy as broad a customer base as possible.

Breakfast

At the breakfast period it is very easy to place most of the emphasis on grilled items, donuts, and danish. Although these items are popular, why not offer more choices?

Some excellent prepared bakery items are available from your purveyors, such as croissants; large muffins; banana nut, zucchini, and date nut specialty breads; and bagels. These could be displayed on footed cake stands or prewrapped in the material-lined baskets for grab-and-go.

Research where you can purchase frozen ready-to-bake products, such as cinnamon rolls, biscuits, coffee cake, etc. Display them in the baking pans, right out of the oven to the counter; your customers will be able to see and smell that they have been freshly baked. Perhaps have a crock of whipped butter available for these items.

The large cereal manufacturers have merchandising displays for their bulk cereals that are available to you upon request. Let your customers help themselves. Have available low-fat milk, a crock of brown sugar, and perhaps fresh berries in season.

Fill your salad bar ice bed, place a few palm fronds over the ice for color and display some bowls of bite-sized fresh fruit; the choices can change with the season. Fill in any gaps in the ice with whole fresh fruits and maybe sprigs of lemon leaves. This display can really make a statement.

Lunch

When planning your menus, think color, texture, and taste. Let the choices stand out instead of blending into one bland color. Use shallow pans for your entree selection whenever possible. Do not allow your cook to stack whole meat items, such as chops or roast beef, on top of each other. Use fresh vegetables when they are in season, but do not overcook them. Garnish the pans to give the food more appeal. Check what utensils are being used for dish-up. Use serving spoons with heat-resistant handles as much as possible, rather then ladles and dishers. Portion control is still possible without the use of institutional serving utensils.

At the grill station, offer an alternative to your regular menu. A grilled or broiled unbreaded chicken breast or fish filet served on a whole wheat bun or in a pita pocket garnished with a piece of fresh fruit or vegetable is an exciting choice. Calorie counts can be shown on point-of-sale material. What a great alternative to deep-fried or high-fat content items!

Rather then using stainless steel containers at the deli counter, use clear plastic storage pans for inserts; these are also available in white. Purchase a large basket for the breads and line it with material. Have available several choices of bread, such as whole grain, French, pita pockets, croissants, etc. Add more choices of cheese to include natural Swiss, cheddar, and Monterey Jack. Some great display items, such as large jars of pickles or peppers, are available for merchandising this area; check with your purveyor for availability.

At build-your-own sandwich bars, provide many choices of sliced meats and cheeses and chicken, ham, tuna, or egg spreads. Sliced tomatoes, shredded lettuce, avocados, fancy pickles, quality mustards and mayonnaise, and many bread choices should also be provided. As with the deli counter, do not use stainless steel containers. For example, meats, cheeses, lettuce, and tomatoes can be displayed on large china platters and the spreads, mustard, and mayonnaise placed in glass bowls or crocks. Fill in any bare ice with your next day's produce, such as whole vegetables, celery, heads of romaine lettuce, red cabbage, etc. Always keep the bar well stocked and colorful.

Use as many fresh vegetables as possible in your salad bar. Celery crescents, zucchini slices, and shredded carrots are great in the winter months. Again, rather than using stainless steel containers, use crocks or glass bowls for the ingredients. Do not place foods of a similar color next to each other. Provide low-calorie dressings. Place a large crock of freshly made croutons at the end of the line. Add height and color by using palm fronds and/or sprigs of lemon leaves in the center of the ice bed. Once more, fill in any gaps with fresh produce and fruits.

Why not try some new dessert choices, such as rich tortes, cheesecake, and some of the items that you may only use for catering. These desserts can be prescored and displayed on footed cake stands with see-through lids. Let your customers help themselves and charge a higher price for these new items. Most serveries have empty spaces on the counters just waiting to be filled with goodies. This is a good way to increase sales and encourage impulse buying.

The Basics

In closing, a word of caution. To ruin all the thought, effort, planning, and implementation of your merchandising program, you need only ignore the basics. Do not use tacky handwritten signs, such as "Out of Order," "Special of the Day," etc. Be sure that the tops of the sneeze guards are dust free, the tray rails are clean, the trays are dry, the floors are free from spills, and your employees are in uniform. Be assured, if any of these conditions are not met, sales will fall.

When you remember the basics and have fun with your merchandising, you, your staff and, most important, your client will have a foodservice of which you can all be proud.

10

Catering

WILLIAM C. LEMBACH

William C. Lembach has been with Eastman Kodak for 23 years; he began in the foodservice division as a summer employee working between semesters at college. Upon graduation from the Rochester Institute of Technology, he began permanent employment and the climb through the ranks from entry level to his present position as director of foodservices. Kodak is one of the largest noncommercial foodservice operations in the country, serving over 48,000 meals daily.

Why would a chapter on catering appear in a book about B&I food-service? Why would a B&I account want to investigate the subject of catering? The answer to both these questions is simple: financial rewards. Catering is a natural extension of the services provided at a B&I account.

At Eastman Kodak, where 48,000 meals are provided a day, catering represents an additional $2 million a year in revenue, a figure that is growing by 2–3 percent per year. Catering supplies special needs both on-site in the physical plant and in areas in the surrounding community. Catering can be as simple as preparing a pot of coffee for a small meeting or as complex as a prime rib dinner for 2,000 or a wedding reception for someone's very special day.

The bottom line is that, whatever services the customer is looking for, catering allows the B&I foodservice manager to provide those services. Yet, every B&I account is different and has different restrictions on what can or cannot be done. The serving of liquor is probably the most controversial issue surrounding catering. As a result of strict liquor liability laws and the moral stances of corporate management, the serving of alcoholic beverages may not be allowed during a catering activity. Needless to say, this fact will certainly limit your competitiveness with the commercial segment. However, even without a liquor license, there is still a good deal of catering business available, but it must be developed by the B&I manager.

The first step in planning a catering service is to define your objectives. It is important to look at your present operation to determine the type of catering you want to be involved in and how best it fits your customer's needs. You may want to provide a full range of catering services or specialize in certain areas with which you feel comfortable. The present size, scope, and management philosophy of your organization are key variables in determining what you will be able to accomplish. These questions will help you clarify your objectives.

- What is the best equipment to have and how best to transport it?
- Do we have the staff?
- Do we have the proper facilities, such as equipment, space, and personnel?
- What type of food and menu should we offer?
- How cost effective can we be?
- Will we be able to deliver a quality product?

EQUIPMENT

There is no readily available guide to equipment selection. Your choices depend on you and your customer's needs. Once you have decided on the direction you are going to take, go out and look, listen, and experience what is going on in that segment of the business. Restaurant and equipment shows at local, regional, and national levels are an excellent start. For example, the National Association of Food Equipment Manufacturers convention (NAFEM) and National Restaurant Association (NRA) offer excellent exhibits. Restaurant equipment wholesalers can show you many items and supply catalogues and make pertinent suggestions. Trade journals and magazines also feature many relevant articles and carry many manufacturer advertisements. Direct discussion with manufacturer representatives is also important. Such trade organizations as the National Restaurant Association or the Society for Foodservice Management encourage the exchange of information. You may want to attend tours and seminars when possible. Also, there is no substitute for experiencing, when possible, the very services you wish to offer. Go to events or functions that most clearly duplicate the catering activities that you wish to provide. Finally, your key personnel, if you have chosen them well, can be an important source of information in your equipment selection process.

The spectrum and variety of equipment are as great as the possible occasions for their use. This section examines a few of the many options in catering that are open to you and some of the equipment you will require.

Whenever there is good weather, people like to have gatherings outside. Picnics, clambakes, and barbecues are traditional outdoor gatherings. On the increase, however, are requests for outdoor weddings, reunions, bar mitzvahs, ethnic festivals, dinner meetings, and seminars, all requiring more formal wear. Important cooking equipment includes grills (gas or charcoal), steamers, and holding units (hot and cold). For serving, chafing dishes (sterno or electric) or portable steamtables are necessary. Folding tables and chairs, condiment units, and a large array of serving utensils and dishes are needed. Beverage containers and serving stations are also required. You may even consider tents if no shelters are available. Much of your outside equipment can be adapted for indoor gatherings. It is now popular to use carts to merchandise food products. These carts could be interchangeable and part of your catering line.

Catering equipment, as with any other equipment in your operation, should be functional and cost effective. For example, equipment for a coffee and snack break can range from informal insulated coffee pots or thermos containers with plastic trays and paper products to fancy silver tea service with elegant trays, fine china, silverware, and carts. When selecting catering equipment, one of the first considerations should be customers' needs and frequency of use. Consider whether it is even necessary to buy the equipment; it may prove more cost effective to rent it. If you only use the equipment once or twice a year, why use valuable space to store it and tie up your money in inventory? If you plan ahead when you schedule events, you can take advantage of the many rental supply companies in business today.

If the decision to purchase is made, consider the equipment's durability. Catering equipment is frequently moved about and takes a lot of abuse; yet, it must still look good and function properly. Adaptability, function, and versatility are other important qualities. Can it be easily used? Can it be used for a number of purposes? For example, do you buy electric chafing dishes, sterno, or the type that you can use either way? Does the equipment break down for easy storage, transport, and cleaning? It is important that equipment be the least complicated as possible.

For some situations you will need custom equipment made for your particular needs. There are some interesting outdoor cookers, spits, steamers, and grills that have been custom made and do an excellent job.

Finally, depending on how much and what type of catering you become involved in, you may have to consider purchasing a vehicle for transport and set-up. Such vehicles are usually custom designed for specific needs and can include refrigeration and preparation equipment, holding units, generators, and hydraulic lifts. Some vehicles are as simple as any empty cargo van. Companies providing these vehicles are listed in the Yellow Pages of your telephone book.

One important rule of thumb to remember is that you usually get what you pay for. That means in effort as well as money. If you spend the time to educate yourself, ask enough questions, and make a concerted attempt to define your use and needs, you will be able to make the wise decisions that will give you the most value and profit from the catering equipment you purchase.

STAFF

A catered function's success and how it is perceived by your client will be influenced by the quality of food products, personnel, service, and total presentation of the function. In all instances, the quality of the food and the presentation or level of service is totally within your control. You should choose personnel in accordance with the requirements of each function. It is important to know your client's needs.

A catering staff person may be chosen on the basis of an interview and submitted resumé, with follow-up of references. Staff caterers must be neat in appearance and have a pleasant personality. They must be flexible and able to adapt to continuously changing situations and to have an "in control" ability. A self-motivated, quality-conscious person, with a flair for creativity, is crucial to a catering staff.

In catering, participative management is a very necessary mode of operation. Through group meetings and input of staff, you will be able to develop the individual skills of each person to bring about as a group the effect you want. Every facet of the presentation will fall into place with little need for direction. The client has placed a trust in you, the provider of this service. This trust must be carried through to the ultimate. Your reputation and your financial solvency are at stake. If everything is right but the people serving the event are wrong, your catering future will be bleak.

PARTICIPATION OF CLIENT IN PLANNING

In preparing a proposal for a requested function, you must brainstorm with your client. The hows, whens, wheres, and whys of each event must be addressed and mutually understood. Being able to coordinate either a backyard paper service picnic or a corporate executive sterling, china, and crystal service for cocktails, hors d'oeuvres, and dinner requires a total understanding of your client's needs.

FACILITIES

The choice of facilities is determined by the catering functions that you intend to provide. In many cases, your client will specify the catering location to be used, and it will be your responsibility to make the location fit your services. Sometimes the area selected by the client may not be suitable and you may have to make some creative recommendations on how to best use the facility to do a quality job. The ability to look at an area and analyze its potential for meeting your needs and those of your client is a skill that takes time to learn. Catering often requires the skills of a magician in order to make the room appear larger than it really is or to create something special out of a facility that is considerably less than special.

For example, in an industrial setting, you may be asked to present an elegant dinner in the middle of a chemical production area located on the fifth floor. However, the elevator only serves four floors, and to reach the area, you must navigate a series of twisting corridors and two separate flights of stairs. In addition, the client wants the event held at 6:00 A.M. for 250 people. Sounds like a case for a textbook—not a real-life situation—but in fact, it really happened. With a good staff, some creative thinking, and a lot of planning and hard work, the event was a huge success. It was videotaped and is now a part of a film on quality.

Not all events are as challenging as the one just described, but serving a conference room, office, or large meeting area from a central kitchen will always be difficult. Throughout the entire process you must always remember that you need to present a quality product. In catering, you have only one chance. If clients are satisfied, they can send you more business from their companies and those who attend the event. However, if the event is not successful from the client's point of view, then you have lost that continued business and that of the other guests.

ADVERTISING

Advertising is very important to the success of catering because most B&I customers only consider foodservice to be available during the meal periods and are unaware of the wide range of services that can be provided. Therefore, publish a catering booklet in which some or all of these suggested services could be listed.

- coffee break packages
- beverages and bakery
- appetizers
- box lunches
- cold luncheons
- hot luncheons
- buffet

- evening dinners and accompaniments
- picnics and clambakes
- party accompaniments
- special services

Your booklet should also include both general information and specific details on event planning, ordering deadlines, how to make changes, guaranteed attendance, and minimum lead times.

In addition to the booklet, you may want to print a separate price list. Keeping the price list separate allows you to change prices without having to reproduce the entire catering booklet. On the price list, provide a brief description of the food items available in each category as listed in your "services provided" section. Try to be creative in your descriptions. Instead of a vegetable tray, write a "vegetable mountain," or describe an assortment of muffins and sweet rolls as "muffin mania." Renaming your catering selections to arouse the interest of your customers can be an important first step in gaining their business.

Catering can entail a great amount of work for the foodservice group, but the personal rewards from doing the impossible and beating all the obstacles that stand in your way make it all worthwhile. When your customer tells you how great everything was and says, "I didn't know foodservice could do these things," it gives you a sense of pride and reassures you that you have made the right decision in choosing your career. B&I foodservice is a challenge and catering is just one of its many challenges.

11
Retail in a Nonretail Environment

CHARLES SPELLER

Since joining Marriott Corporation in 1987, Charles Speller has been general manager of business foodservice operations at the Northern Trust Bank in Chicago. In that position he has implemented a variety of new marketing and merchandising programs to generate additional revenue, cut costs, and help reduce the bank's foodservice subsidy. Before assuming his present position, he was the Marriott district manager at the First National Bank of Chicago. Charles also worked for Motorola Food Works in several capacities before assignment to the company's world headquarters in Chicago, where he was responsible for all catering, vending, and foodservice operations.

We continue to hear that the B&I segment of foodservice operates in a noncommercial and nonretail environment. However, current trends and practices by B&I contractors and self-operators are slowly changing this perception. The industries' leaders are beginning to realize that there are fewer and fewer "captive audiences" (prisons and hospitals are the exceptions). We are discovering that, to compete with outside businesses and to capture our share of the market, we must constantly seek new and innovative ways of designing our facilities, merchandising our products, and convincing our customers to spend more of their discretionary income within our operations. Two methods of capturing market share that have emerged recently are "retail" merchandising and take-out food.

Operators are finding that to capture additional revenues we must do more than provide the standard cafeteria menu cycle to our customers, who have become extremely sophisticated in terms of their perceptions of price/value and quality and their management of personal time. This increased food consciousness of our customers and their desire for increasingly upscale menus have developed partially due to the following social and economic trends:

- an increase in the number of working women, single parents, and dual-career households
- an increase in the consumption of meals that feature ethnic and gourmet items

- employer-sponsored van, carpool, and babysitting services for its employees
- a desire by clients to seek additional ways to reduce operating costs associated with their foodservice programs
- increasing demands on personal and work time

Because of these changing societal and demographic trends, the take-out food-market is becoming an increasingly important part of the foodservice industry. According to the Gallup Organization's 1988 *Annual Report on Eating Out*, take-out food is a major part of the diet of many Americans. In fact, 10 percent (1 out of 10) of all adults purchased take-out food on any given day during 1987 (Gallup, 1988).

TAKE-OUT PROGRAMS

One response to these changing market trends has been the development of various versions of take-home programs within B&I foodservices. Most of these programs feature a wide range of take-home food items offered to employees at the end of the business day. A sampling of take-home items is given below.

- assorted sliced or bulk-serve cold meats and cheeses
- salads, such as seafood, pasta, potato, and coleslaw
- baked goods, such as breads, rolls, pies, Danish, sweet rolls, muffins, and such seasonal items as fruitcakes
- ready-to-eat items, such as hoagie sandwiches, lasagna, baked chickens, and Chinese egg rolls
- ready-to-cook items, such as steaks, hamburgers, bratwursts, shrimp, chicken Kiev, and other frozen foods, including precooked and packaged entrees, desserts, and side dishes

Freshly ground coffees by the pound, imported candies, teas, oil, and other upscale products normally associated with grocery stores have also been sold for take-out.

Factors that must be considered when establishing a take-out program are described below.

Contract Type

Obviously, any thing that the contractor can do to raise sales and reduce the foodservice subsidy will be beneficial to both the client and the contractor. How the profits derived from these activities will be split up is determined by the contract type. In a profit and loss operation, the contractor accepts all profit and all losses if the take-out program is not a success. In contrast, a "fee" account sometimes results in increased contractor profitability if sales are increased. Additional profits are given only if the subsidy is also reduced. This is known as an "incentive" or bonus fee.

Staff Capability

Management skills—talent, knowledge, and tenacity—or the lack thereof can either make or break a program. The same program could be implemented in two similar facilities; one could fail and the other succeed simply because of the one manager's ability to execute the program. Another factor related to staff capability is, of course, the number of employees and managers assigned to a facility. It is much easier to implement additional facets in a foodservice program where the unit has more than two or three nonexempt employees. This relates directly to the concept known as "economics of scale."

Physical Plant

Any equipment or space needs must be addressed before starting a take-out program. Counter space, glass-enclosed deli counters, scales, and cold pans all have to be available to enable proper sanitation and operational procedures.

The manager should first outline the menu of take-out items to be offered. From this menu a diagram and equipment list should be developed to ensure that all areas—product display, packaging, cashiers, etc.—are planned before beginning the program. This mental exercise will eliminate problems and answer questions *before* they are encountered, thus minimizing customer dissatisfaction and employee frustration.

Customer Spending Threshold

This threshold depends on such variables as demographics, locality, and pay scales. On-site management will be able to determine what sells, but several methods may be used to give you some idea of the price/value relationships relative to your customer base. One that I have found to be effective is the *area price survey*, which is simply comparative shopping. Everyone loves a bargain, and most people will be tempted to buy if you can price your merchandise lower than the competition, especially if you can be more *convenient* to your customers. Prepare a grid-style spread sheet with the items on one axis and your cost/selling price versus your competitor's selling price on the other (Table 11-1).

When doing the survey, be sure that you are comparing similar items. Before you start, you may need to purchase some of the items to compare product quality. You can also inquire as to brand and specifications from the salespeople at the market or convenience store, e.g., Danish ham, 80/20 hamburger, Hormel, etc. Finally, update your comparison often as meat and other perishable commodities fluctuate in price frequently. From this research you can then determine your selling prices, keeping in mind the mark-up or the percentage of profit you would like and/or need to make.

You should also consider *sales mix/profitability* of the items before setting the prices. In other words, are you selling many items at low profit or a few items at a high profit? This is an important factor in pricing your program.

Management Commitment

As mentioned earlier, the manager can make or break your program. It often takes a lot of the manager's time to plan and implement a take-home program. If the manager is not committed to the program and to overcome the obstacles as they come up, your take-out program will be short-lived.

Time

Consider when during the shift the program will be offered and whether time spent by employees is focused to control activities as they occur (proactive—not reactive). Be sure that time spent by the customers in selecting items and paying for them is kept to a minimum. Remember that convenience is extremely important to the customers.

Client Attitude

The client's attitude must be positive before you can even consider a take-out program. If the proper client approval is not granted before going through the planning processes outlined here, the client could stop you at any point during the planning process. The client may stop your efforts out of concerns for building security (especially true of federal/government

Table 11-1 Area Price Survey

Item	Our Cost	Selling Price	Dominicks	Jewel	7-11
N. Y. Strips #1180	$5.25 lb.				
Ribeyes					
Shrimp, 21/26					
Hamburgers 4/1 (80-20)					
Ham, sliced					
Turkey, sliced					
Cheese/Swiss-sliced					
Stouffers—Lean Cuisines					
Potato Salad—lb.					

suppliers), aesthetics of the operation, or compatibility with existing goals. After all, we as contractors are guests in the client facility and we must abide by the client's wishes regarding the type of program that can be offered to its employees.

Available Support

The contractor's company and vendor support is essential to the success of a take-home program. Purchasing/procurement support and distributor assistance facilitate obtaining both favorable pricing and the kind of products that you wish to offer.

Packaging

Disposable packaging for take-out must be functional, as well as aesthetically pleasing. The product must reach the customer's home at the desired temperature. Many of the manufacturers of these products have "stock" merchandise available, but most operators prefer to have their logo or trademark imprinted on the items. Labels have a more professional appearance if they are preprinted with an overall graphic theme that is carried over from the other packaging.

Some of the major manufacturers of paper/disposable packaging are Sweetheart, Solo, Dixie, Hoffmaster, and Duro. They will be happy to work with you in developing a program to package and merchandise your take-out program.

Merchandising

Merchandising the program is probably the most important key to setting up a take-out program. It is the standard by which the other facets of the program are judged. Merchandising covers nearly all areas of the program concept—from packaging to advertising to actual product displays.

This is the area that also allows for the most creativity on the part of the operator. Any experience that the unit manager has in the area of graphics, window or product display, and marketing will be extremely beneficial to the selling of the total program to the client and to potential customers.

Convenience to the Customer

Imagine working hard all day, commuting to your home, and then having to prepare your evening meal once you get there. By the time you eat and clean up the dishes, the time to get ready for bed is fast approaching. This is the scenario being faced by more and more Americans every day, which explains the attractiveness of a take-out program to many of our customers. They can pick up their meal either partially or completely prepared and then have more time at home to do the things that they would like to do. Because convenience is the major factor in the success of a take-out program, the operator should concentrate on making it as convenient as possible. Have entrees and salads prepackaged, preweighed, and even presold so that all the customer has to do is walk in and pick up the order. Provide a convenient way of getting the product home. If possible, have large grocery bags with handles, delivery programs, and similar options available to customers so that it will be easy to get the product home.

The results of a successful take-out program are two-fold. The price perception to our customers is significant, which makes the take-out program a meaningful and popular benefit of the foodservice program to the host company and its employees. Second, the contractor is able to reduce operating costs associated with the foodservice without seeking selling price adjustments for breakfast and lunch items, as is usually the customary procedure.

Types of Take-Out Programs

Deli/C-Store

Several variations currently exist on this theme. The primary items sold are sliced meats, cheeses, and prepackaged salads/entrees. We as contractors seeking to increase our market share need simply to copy or modify existing programs at local grocery and convenience stores to our own in-house operations.

Candy Sale

In this program, we purchase candy at wholesale and act as a fresh frozen distributor of boxed candy. This is especially popular during holiday periods and is very convenient for our customers who need to buy last-minute gifts for family gatherings.

Meat Sale

Another area in which you can benefit your customers and increase sales is by selling cuts of meat, hamburgers, hot dogs, and seafood items at near wholesale prices. Limit your selections and have your vendors prebox the items. Frozen delivery to your customers is preferred for proper temperature retention during transportation by your customers to their homes. You should also provide dry ice and shopping bags for long-distance commuters. It is preferable to have customers preorder and prepay for the product. This saves them time and enables you to forecast usage closely. To do this presale successfully, you must send out flyers/order forms well in advance of your delivery date (Exhibit 11-1).

RETAIL

Another trend which has been sweeping our segment of the industry is the perception that we are finally becoming "retail." The B&I foodservice segment of the industry has traditionally been known as nonretail and noncommercial primarily because of the *nonpublic* nature of our operations. However, that is changing, as is the very way in which we operate. Even our own perceptions of cafeterias as what we knew in grammar school—long tables, lousy food, and a staff that resembled our grandmothers—are no longer valid. In fact, some very sophisticated foodservice programs are in place throughout the country's schools, businesses, and hospitals and with those programs comes the "retail" marketing traditionally associated with public segments of our industry (restaurants, hotels, etc.) The level of services to be provided is determined by the goals and commitment of each individual company. They may want to offer a small retail shop similar to a hotel or airport gift shop, featuring high-impulse items, or implement a convenience store concept with a full range of snack foods.

Exhibit 11-1 Flyer/Order Form for Holiday Sale

HOLIDAY SALE

HAPPY THANKSGIVING!
...YE OLDE MEAT AND BAKE SALE
FOR THE HOLIDAY S

Place your order prior to Friday, Nov. 20th for the pick-up on Tuesday, Nov. 24th and Wednesday, Nov. 25th. Prepayment is requested on all orders. Cash or personal checks will be accepted for this sale.....

ORDER FORM: (Return to cashier)   (circle one)
NAME _____ Exten. _____ PICKUP: 11/24
                                                                    (or) 11/25

*WHOLE TURKEY/frozen 10-11 lb.	$10.00ea. x	@	=	_____
HAM/whole, boneless 10 lb.	$24.00ea. x	@	=	_____
DUCKLINGS/long island 3-4 lb.	$5.25ea. x	@	=	_____
PRIME RIB ROAST/choice, BONE—IN	$3.75lb. x	lb.	=	_____
RIB—EYE STEAKS, choice 8 oz.	$6.25lb. x	lb.	=	_____

*PLEASE HAVE TURKEY ORDERS IN BY NOV.17th.... (ADD 8% TAX)

WHOLE PIES @ $3.50 EACH!!! (ADD 8% TAX)

APPLE _____   MINCEMEAT _____
PUMPKIN _____   DUTCH APPLE _____

Take-home baked goods such as breads, rolls, cakes, pies, danish, and cookies, have been well-received at many of Marriott's accounts. Non-food items that lend themselves well to retail in a corporate setting are high-impulse items such as greeting cards, small gift items, stuffed animals, selected magazines and paperbacks, jewelry, and company-logoed merchandise (sportswear and athletic bags). Other services popular in a corporate setting include film developing and video rentals. How we decorate our service areas, set up our food displays, and use other related merchandising techniques is important in capturing these sales that for years went to retail segments. Once we understand the importance of merchandising a product, we can develop a sense in the customer that this product is a bargain that is worth the extra effort of getting it home from their place of work.

Display materials, props, and untraditional signage have been used with particular success in the grocery and department store trades. The Hubert Company provides the grocery and convenience store industry with everything from European-style deli cases and counter displays to window signs and video rental forms. Another company that provides decorative display materials for the department store industry is Neidermyer Displays.

Merchandising our products is the challenge all operators face as we move into an era in which we must constantly seek new ways to increase sales, reduce subsidies, and improve profits.

REFERENCE

The Gallup Organization. *The 1988 Gallup Annual Report on Eating Out.* Princeton, NJ, 1988.

12

Designing for the Repeat Customer

BILL BABCOCK

For over 25 years, Bill Babcock has been principal of the nationally acclaimed design firm of Babcock & Schmid Associates located in Bath, Ohio. During that time, he has directed projects for a wide spectrum of domestic and foreign foodservice chains, including Pizza Hut, Kentucky Fried Chicken, Chick-fil-A, Carl's Jr., Grisanti's, Saga, Hospitality Inns, and Playboy Enterprises. Babcock & Schmid Associates has also received numerous design awards, including Restaurant Hospitality *magazine's award for "the Best Chain Restaurant Design," a Clio award for "the Best Retail Packaging," the Packaging Institute of America's "Best in Category," and the Iron & Steel Institute's Award for the best design of an industrial product during a 2-year period. The following chapter is based upon an interview with Bill Babcock on winning with design in noncommercial foodservice operations.*

DO WE DESIGN DIFFERENTLY BECAUSE WE HAVE THE SAME CUSTOMERS EVERY DAY?

Designing for a noncommercial foodservice is no different from designing for a commercial foodservice. One should create the space so that it allows for different experiences over an extended period of time. Customers want different experiences from a restaurant, depending on their particular mood.

Some spaces have natural attributes, such as windows. Rather than designing the area by the windows exactly the same as the area away from the windows, design it a little differently so as to offer a different experience. If the person wants a different experience than is offered near the windows, he or she would eat in another area.

The same holds true for the area near the serving line. One could assume that the area by the serving line would be a bad area to sit in, so you would try to make it secluded or design it so the serving activity is not intrusive for the people who are sitting there. On the other hand, when people are in a more interested, interactive, or outgoing state of mind, they might prefer to sit by the serving line and watch the activity and at least be psychologically involved in the activity.

The first approach—of trying to make the serving area secluded—is along the line of "let's try to make the whole environment the same," whereas the second approach capitalizes on and features the natural attributes or characteristics of the environment. The second approach accommodates different states of mind.

In terms of seating, the commercial segment of the market provides many different seating types, which again appeal to the different states of mind or the different attitudinal segments of customers in restaurants. There are tables for four, two, and six, as well as booths and banquettes. More tables of two are used, which provides the facility the flexibility to group them. These seating types not only accommodate different size groups but they also accommodate different attitudes. Sitting at a table is a more formal experience than sitting in a booth. Sitting in a banquette tends to be a little more intimate experience. Different seating types offer variety, which is the most important element of design.

WHAT ARE THE DESIGN CRITERIA FOR THE COMMERCIAL MARKET?

Design criteria relate primarily to marketing, operations, and cost. Your marketing goal is to get the most number of people into the establishment the most number of times and sell them the most food you can sell them. You achieve this goal by instilling the idea that the B&I foodservice is a benefit to the employee. In other words, it is so good that it is a perk of employment.

Design should make the people look good and make the food look good. It should provide a total experience, rather than merely "eating." Make the experience memorable and enjoyable.

It is important to acknowledge that B&I operators are in competition—with brown bagging, the commercial outlets on the streets, and internal competition, such as vending machines. To succeed, the B&I foodservice must differentiate itself from the competition.

HOW DO WE GET CLOSER TO THE DESIGN ON THE STREET?

B&I operators are studying what is going on in the fast food segment and trying to bring the successful elements into their foodservice operations. If people want hamburgers and French fries, we cannot give them roast beef and mashed potatoes. How does that affect design? Do you bring the street look into the cafeteria as well?

That is a double-edged sword. One must assume that B&I operators are not able to duplicate the fast-food operation. So then, the question is, "Do you do a bad duplication of fast food, or do you try to do something different?" I recommend the approach of doing something different. Look at your strengths, whatever they are, and try to capitalize on those strengths to accomplish something different from the fast-food operators, rather than just trying to beat them at their own game.

One strength is that B&I foodservices have larger facilities to work with, both in the front of the house and in the kitchen. This means that they can prepare more complex menus, with more variety. Presumably, the speed urgency of your customers is not as great as in fast food. If the speed urgency is not quite as great, you do not have to hustle the people through the selection process.

Fast food offers a very standardized approach to ordering. The customer walks up to the counter, looks at the menu board, gives the order, gets it, and sits down. Compare this with a cafeteria set-up or a steak-house-type line where the menu can be merchandised at several different points to involve the customers and perhaps change their minds. In a steak-house line, there are four menu presentations, and we have found that people change their mind about what they want to eat at each one of those points.

In B&I foodservice, the selection of food process can be more interesting than in a fast-food situation. Rather than say, "We need to be more like fast food," and try to compete with the chains, we should take advantage of our opportunities to merchandise the food. Fast food operators have a problem with merchandising, and they are going to continue to have a problem with it because of their space limitations.

B&I is more similar to a single-unit operation than a chain with 5,000 stores. A single-unit operator can outspend a multi-unit operator on each unit just because of the economics of the situation. Big chains cannot spend large amounts of money revamping the interiors of each unit simply because there are so many units. The single-unit operator who can prove that there is a payback for remodeling can actually afford to spend more money on an individual unit than the chains.

Develop some design strategies based on that fact. For example, remodel the B&I facility frequently. You could do a major revamping every so often or do small changes very frequently. Many hotel operators follow the strategy of doing improvements all the time; changes always look like they had just happened or are about to happen. Do the same thing with your B&I foodservice operations. You can make it look like some change is always occurring, that the foodservice is keeping abreast of the latest trends.

The key question becomes, "Where can you best spend your money on facility improvements." If the goal is to make yourself look different from the chains, concentrate on those areas where you are already strong. Take advantage of your bigger facility, or do better food merchandising, or give it a "new look" more frequently.

Another strength of B&I operators is that they are much more flexible than the chains and they ought to take advantage of that. Chains are locked into using the equipment that they already have because the costs of implementing changes in all the units would be prohibitive. B&I foodservice managers ought to be operating like the single entrepreneur, but with the financial backing of the big company for which they work. They have the best of both worlds: the flexibility of the single entrepreneur but with the financial clout of the chains.

The problem is that most operators do not take advantage of their flexibility. They are merely operators, not marketers. They leave facility improvements to the architect who designed the building and the consultant who installed the equipment.

DO YOU HAVE TO DESIGN TO YOUR CUSTOMER? DO EMPLOYEES WANT STYLE? DO THEY APPRECIATE IT?

The most important point to remember is that your employees are human beings who are exposed to other foodservice operations. They are making comparisons, and they have reference points as to what is good dining and what is bad dining. Now, how do you want them to refer to your operation? Do you want them to think it is good or bad?

Some employees really are a captive market because their plant is located far from any restaurants and they only have a half-hour for lunch. Yet, do you want them to think this is a good experience or a bad experience? It is very simple. If they perceive your foodservice to be bad, they may think, "Hey, my company is trying to stick it to me, because I'm a captive market, and they know it, and I'm overpaying for it."

Shopping at the mall is a very educational experience in terms of foodservice. All of the fast food chains are in the mall environments, as well as a mix of small entrepreneurs doing what I call product development for the fast food industry. Even if your employees only shop and do not eat at the mall, they are still going to be knowledgeable about foodservice.

If I were not committed to doing the best possible job in foodservice, I would not offer it. I might have vending, but I would make sure that it was the best possible vending experience.

HOW DO YOU KNOW WHEN TO REDESIGN A FACILITY, AND WHAT CAN A REDESIGN DO FOR YOU AND YOUR EMPLOYEES?

There are a number of signals that tell you when a redesign is necessary. The most obvious signal is that the facility looks like it is falling apart. The carpet is threadbare, and the like. Another obvious signal is that the employees are not using the facility. Another one is your boss telling you that a redesign is necessary, for whatever reason.

The subtle signals are more difficult to spot. One is the feeling of misgivings you have about the facility. You know in your heart that there is something wrong now, or you know in your heart that unless you do something now, there is going to be something wrong in the foreseeable future. Even if everything seems to be fine at your operation, you see changes going on around you to which you should respond. You can wait a long time and try to implement major changes all at once, or you can keep up with the trends by doing a number of small changes more frequently.

To keep up with change, you need to monitor the competition, making sure you look at what is happening in all segments of the foodservice industry, including fast-food and full-service chains, healthcare, schools and universities and hotels. Take advantage of such associations as the SFM (Society for Foodservice Management) by talking to your peers who attend the meetings about what they are doing. Eat out at your competitors. Do not just make foodservice management an 8–5 job, leaving it behind when you leave for the day. Be aware. Attend conferences, read magazines, and take advantage of all the other opportunities available to enhance your knowledge.

If you look at foodservice as a benefit to the employees, then you ought to be managing it like a benefit to the employees. Ask yourself how you can improve the communication about this benefit to increase employee awareness of it. The opportunity is to do it at the personal level by communicating this concept— "Our company is in there working for you guys all the time." Make it look like you are spending money to improve the dining experience instead of just spending money for the sake of it.

Your goal is to give your employees a sense of camaraderie or of being part of an elite. They should feel like they belong to a certain group of people who have the opportunity to eat at this great place. So, try to do everything you can to reinforce that this is a great place to eat. Whether that means you are merchandising from a quality standpoint (you have sought out all these great items that you have brought in for the employees) or whether you have made a great purchasing deal so that the employees can have the best price on all of these items, reinforce that concept.

Have your employees tell you when there is the need to change the food-service. Conduct some type of in-house research to find out what the employees feel. Monitor the employees' attitude continuously about the foodservice. Doing so will surely create the impression that you cared and that something creative was going on.

HOW DOES MODIFYING A SPACE COMPARE TO COMPLETE REDESIGN?

Modifying a facility may not involve changing the food, service style, or the entire foodservice operation. Rather, cosmetic changes to the interior are put into place. To do this decorating job, I recommend that you hire professional help. Picking the right colors does not cost any more than picking the wrong colors, so you might as well pick the right ones. Depending on the job and your budget, you will begin by treating the floors, walls, and windows. Furniture is the next level of improvement and lighting the next. Take advantage of any natural attributes in your redecorating process. For example, I once redesigned a small area inside a plant. With little trouble, a wall was opened to make an outside court, enabling employees to eat in a room with natural light.

More major changes begin with changing the menu and service style and then letting the environment evolve from the new menu and service style. Commercial restaurants are designed this way, with the menu developed first. Such changes are possible in the noncommercial setting, but they take a different level of expenditure than just a minor fix-up.

Graphics are important when looking at redesign. Graphics can convey the message that the foodservice is not merely a sideline of the corporation. Through research we have found that airport and hotel food operations are viewed as sidelines. This perception causes the consumer to think, "There isn't really any commitment here to food. Therefore, the product isn't going to be as good as it would be if I went somewhere where there is a real commitment." Anything that can be done to exhibit a commitment to food-service and make it appear as if it were not a sideline is very important. Hotels exhibit that commitment by giving a personal name, such as "Hugo's," to the restaurant. Such a name implies that there is a person named Hugo, who is running the operation. In the consumer's mind, "We're going to Hugo's," is a great deal different than "Let's go up to the cafeteria."

Graphics are a good way to convey your commitment to foodservice. Yet, if you are a company in the business of making fender stampings, how does that give you the credibility of doing a good job in foodservice? By using the company logo but with added elements of a unique foodservice design, graphics can show that this operation has the company blessing, but it is somehow different from the company. Another way to gain credibility is for the foodservice to have different management from the overall corporation.

HOW DO THE ELEMENTS OF DESIGN—LIGHTING AND COLOR, ETC.—CREATE A TOTAL IMAGE?

When you design, you are using applied psychology. All of these physical elements in a space that you are manipulating affect the behavior of the people in the space. For example, if you put a barrier in a space, that is going to change the user's perception of the use of that space.

Colors exert effects in the most primitive sense. If you want a space to be relaxing so that people stay and relax, do not use bright colors. Bright colors increase the pace. Traditionally, fast food operations have used these colors because they want rapid turnover. In contrast, in bars and lounges where you want people to stay and spend money on drinks, soft and restful colors, such as soft blues and greens, are used.

In the last few years, foodservice designers are developing more creative space plans. These plans are conceived not only in a horizontal plane, but also vertically. Some commercial restaurants use different levels of seating to stimulate eye contact and to make strangers feel comfortable with each other.

In a commercial space, the separation between the dining space and a kitchen area is manipulated so that a customer does not necessarily lose complete contact with the food. For example, food merchandising goes on as plates of food are being brought in to other people. This merchandising says, "I have already made my menu choice, but the next time I come in, I'm going to have that."

WHAT IS THE DIFFERENCE BETWEEN A DECORATING APPROACH AND A DESIGN APPROACH?

The interior decorators and interior designers make a great deal out of the distinction. With the first level of expenditure mentioned above, which only involves cosmetic changes, a decorating approach is needed. Such an approach does not require a master plan. When you become involved in major renovations, you start with virtually a clean slate. You are designing the space to accomplish your objectives. You need a plan to determine how the renovations should proceed in order to accomplish all of your desired objectives.

Today's decorating trend now is very much part of the postmodern movement, which uses mauve, taupe, plum, and similar colors. It is plushy and full. I do not know how long that trend will continue. The fern bars and the macrame plant hangers were popular for 10–15 years, starting in the 1970's and just faded 3 or 4 years ago. Theoretically, trends are popular for that length of time; the trends of today will probably be popular for another 10 years. I feel that the postmodern movement will be popular for at least the next 5 or 6 years, but that the New York deli approach—that black and white tile look—will not be. I might have given that "look" a design award 2 or 3 years ago, but I do not think it will sustain itself for a long period of time.

When choosing materials, you are constantly making trade-offs between operations, maintenance, and the kind of effect you are trying to achieve with your customers. For example, to achieve the greatest ease in maintenance, you would put in tile floors, formica tabletops, stainless steel, and a big drain in the center of the floor so at night the maintenance staff could hose down this "cattle-feeding pit." What you have created then is a low-maintenance, but hostile environment. On the other side, you can use all soft materials that control acoustics and create a warm and friendly feeling. Yet, wood and carpet are hard to maintain and need frequent replacement. Good design tries to balance those two dimensions, achieving a compromise between maintenance, operations, and customer comfort. There is no easy way to do that.

For example, consider whether tablecloths should be used. The operations department would certainly urge that tablecloths not be used. Yet, highlighting the tablecloth or tabletop would be a good way to design an environment that would be changing more frequently than normal. I might design the space as a more neutral envelope and then place added emphasis on the tabletops through lighting and what is happening on the tabletop. Then, when I changed the tabletops, it would be very obvious.

Your choice of materials greatly influences how your space is perceived. Marble versus wood versus formica makes very different statements about whether the foodservice is an expensive or inexpensive place. Your choice of wallcoverings—whether paint or wood or silk—will make a similar statement. Too, materials dramatically influence the cost of design. The same amount of space can cost you $50.00 per foot or $500.00 per foot, depending on the materials you select.

The chair is the customer's most intimate contact with the environment. You probably spend more time trying to pick out the right chair than you do on any other design element. You are looking for a chair that expresses the character of what you are trying to create, that does not fall apart, and that is comfortable.

HOW CAN IMPULSE SALES BE MAXIMIZED?

The time to sell merchandise is when people are "hot" to have it, not after that desire has gone. I would try to sell the impulse items as add-ons both before and after the meal. Those two places are not necessarily mutually exclusive, although the cashier area could be confusing unless you had two stations for pay. You want to sell the people the add-ons when their juices are running, not after they have eaten a meal. That is why the desserts are always put at the front of the line.

It is all a matter of allocating space to sell the impulse items. For example, truck stops have a merchandise area separate from the food. If B&I wants to do a good job with these sales, I think that a separate area, similar to a store, is needed. However, the store should not be the only place for add-on sales. There might be a transition area between the food area and the store, with a cashier between the two areas. Or combinations of both of those two elements could be placed in the middle around the cashier. The farther away from that centralized area, the more specific the activity becomes.

Positioning of add-on sales items is important. Supermarkets use the old ploy of placing staples, such as bread and milk, in the back of the store so that the customer has to walk through all of the other aisles to get to them. As they pass the other merchandise and they are hungry, they buy it.

People are coming to your foodservice facility to buy lunch. As they do that, you want to walk them through the merchandise. Therefore, add-on items must be located at an entrance or an exit. The chances of catching impulse sales as customers exit are slight. Your only opportunity to merchandise some product as the customer exits is at the cashier station. Your chances of getting someone to make an impulse purchase decrease dramatically if they have already paid for their meal. They are unlikely to pay twice, so, your best opportunity for sales occurs before the customer has paid for the meal.

One way to increase sales after the initial sale of food is to have a separate cash point. For example, after the customer has eaten lunch, he or she has a few minutes to spare. The customer is more likely to purchase some items from the retail section if there is a separate cashier for that purpose; he or she would not pick up an item and stand in line with others who are purchasing lunch.

You have to develop a strategy for this kind of retail—deciding what you are going to sell and what items can make money. The project should be product-driven. If you decide you are going to open a small shop just to sell "stuff," it is not going to work. What you are going to do should dictate how you are going to do it, rather than reverse.

Giving another name to the retail area might help establish an identity for it and give it credibility. Why would you buy something in the company store? Most likely, for convenience. Therefore, I recommend a convenience-type operation, such as a mini-convenience mart, that would feature convenience-oriented merchandise, rather than items that require a purchase decision. Anything that requires a purchase decision will probably be a problem in this type of retail situation because you would not have the credibility to sell it. Unless it was a well-known brand item, people probably would not buy it.

Another possibility for the retail outlet could be to sell signature items that are made in the foodservice operation.

Like all impulse retailing, the merchandise should be highly visible, with floor-to-ceiling displays. It is a simple case of "If you don't see it you're not going to buy it."

The ideal situation would be to have a retailer running the shop. I think there is an opportunity for retailers to go into corporations, set up the retail operations, and run them, similar to the way that contractors do the foodservice.

WHAT IS THE ROLE OF THE EXECUTIVE DINING ROOM?

The executive dining room should convey to executives that they have "made it." It is a symbol of their success. Such executives are most likely running multi-million dollar corporations, and the executive dining room can be nothing less than the best. They may be inviting their counterparts from another company or national or international dignitaries that they are trying to impress.

Because this area has to be of superior quality, you should hire a professional to help in the design. Do not have the building architect do it or try to do it internally. Corporate dining is a world of its own. Attention to detail, from table service to decor, is very important to achieve the right feel.

It is important to ensure that the process of developing the executive dining room is done correctly. Starting from the first step, it is important to combine representatives from operations, marketing, finance, and administration into a project team. The team then has to formally develop your criteria for design. A formal statement of criteria is good because it forces trade-offs between departments and ordering of priorities. Those criteria are then used to develop the project and to evaluate the various proposals that are made for that project. The preplanning and the programming and analysis phases of development involve representatives from each one of the facets of the project.

IF YOU ARE A FOODSERVICE OPERATOR, HOW DO YOU IMPLEMENT THE PROGRAM? DO YOU BRING IN A CONSULTANT? DO YOU BRING IN A DESIGNER?

To implement a foodservice program, analyze those skills that are required to complete the task. Certainly, you need implementation skills. Implementation involves menu development and the planning, purchasing, and installation of equipment. Who has these skills of planning, purchasing, and installation in both the front and back of the house? They could be architects, foodservice consultants, interior designers, etc. Make a list of those needed to complete the project and then decide if they are internal or external.

The design steps involve preprogramming, analysis, and establishment of criteria. The end result is a project brief against which concepts and ideas are evaluated. One concept or method of design will meet the criteria better than the other ones; that is the one that you develop further into a presentation package. That package really allows you to look at this project and decide if this is what you want to do. Then specifications must be generated.

The five basic phases are preprogramming, concept, refinement, specification, and implementation. Whether you are designing for a B&I facility or a restaurant, the phases of the project are the same. The only difference is that the B&I facility should be perceived as an employee benefit, and that fact should be reflected in the quality of the operation from design to service to the food.

PART IV

Nuts and Bolts of Operating a Foodservice

13

Purchasing

MARTIN CHERNEFF

With over 30 years of experience in the foodservice industry, Martin Cherneff is principal of M.H. Cherneff & Associates. Before forming his own company, he was vice president and marketing director of a large foodservice consulting firm. During his 14 years with Interstate United Corporation, Marty had total responsibility for the company's foodservice operating procedures. Before assuming his position at Interstate United, Marty worked for ARA Services, where he served as director of operations of its hospital food management group and as director of operations of its Mexican subsidiary.

Purchasing is a vital, dynamic function of all foodservice operations. As in any manufacturing process, ensuring that the right raw materials of a defined quality are available when needed, in the right quantities is an important part of the food production/service process. This chapter provides an overview of purchasing procedures, how they fit into the total foodservice process, and the key elements of purchasing so that the function may be observed and properly supervised. It examines the elements of food and supplies specifications, various purchasing techniques and systems, the use of automation, and the purchasing process from production planning through receiving/storing.

The purchasing process for a foodservice operation is very similar to the purchasing function in a production plant of any kind. Raw materials of all descriptions are purchased in the needed quantity and quality to manufacture a finished product or line of products. Depending upon the end product, production may be either continuous—making the same line of products every day in the same order and in the same fashion—or by "batch process." In the batch process, as the name implies, all production energies are directed toward making a limited number of products in a comparatively short time frame. At the end of the "batch run," production efforts turn to making a planned amount of other products, models, or styles. In the retail environment, especially in corporate foodservice where the "product line" (menu) changes daily, most production is batch process. Therefore, the discussion in this chapter focuses primarily on the batch process mode, producing for immediate use. Such techniques as sous-vide, cook-chill, or cook-freeze are not discussed. These techniques, although part of batch process, produce and process food items for inventory to be used as needed in the near future.

PURCHASING PLANNING

As in any production program, the acquisition of the raw material needed to produce a planned number of "widgets" (menu items) should be carefully planned. Information essential to the planning process includes the identification and understanding of purchasing specifications, complete descriptions of the quality of the raw material needed, the amount of material needed, the established sources that can supply the needs, and when the material must be delivered to be available for production. Purchasing is complicated by the fact that during any production period as many as 50 to 60 items may make up the product line (menu).

The purchasing program in any foodservice establishment must conform to the overall configuration of the foodservice program. The defined quality level, the menu, and the physical facility (i.e., the adequacy of storage; the amount, type, and condition of the kitchen equipment; and the size of the servery) all influence what, when, and how material is purchased. For example, raw, prepeeled, and cut potatoes for French fries are useless if the kitchen or servery does not have deep-fat frying equipment. Whole fresh fish should not be purchased if no one on the staff knows how to process the fish further for preparation and if the head and other parts are not to be used as in a "Court-Bouillon."

FOOD PURCHASING

The classification "food" has a number of subclassifications—raw both fresh and frozen, processed, fresh, frozen, dehydrated, and canned food. A standard corporate foodservice program normally uses all of these types of food in its kitchens. Corporate foodservice programs with high quality standards have always preferred to use only the freshest, best-quality raw materials. However, this is not always possible or practical or economical. Many raw fruits and vegetables are not always the best quality when purchased "fresh." Fresh can mean as long as 2 weeks have elapsed from harvest until the product is delivered to the foodservice receiving platform.

Foodservice operations that are not within easy delivery distance of major distribution centers may obtain a consistently better quality product by purchasing some items frozen or even processed (cooked). Some raw food products deteriorate very quickly and need to be used very shortly after harvesting. These products are generally shipped to market by air express, adding considerable cost to the purchase price. Fresh fish is an example of this kind of food. For the most part, however, raw food, even that grown in other countries, is available to the foodservice industry in good supply and in good fresh quality. (Good in this reference is not a definition of a quality range, such as "USDA Good," but rather a description—the opposite of "not-so-good.")

As a general rule, raw food should be purchased as close to the time of need as possible. Purchasing in this fashion leaves little room for error. Delivery must be on time and the product must be right and in the needed amounts. Because purchasing close to time of need leaves little time to replace any product that falls short of quality specifications, such purchasing requires a dependable supplier who can consistently meet the specifications of quality, quantity, and delivery.

Time of delivery must be defined. "As close to the time of need as possible" refers to the start of preparation, not the time of service. Bringing a frozen product in on the day of service when at least 48 hours are needed to temper (defrost under proper conditions) and cook it is not close to the time but is too late.

The decisions of what to buy, when to buy, and how much to buy are usually influenced by a number of factors. Price is a major factor, but not the only factor in purchasing. Vendor reliability is another important consideration in making purchasing decisions. If the vendor cannot deliver quality or quantity on time, the price is meaningless.

Two purchasing processes are purchasing for inventory and purchasing for need. Each of these techniques has its attributes and drawbacks. Nor are they mutually exclusive. Many purchasing programs use both processes.

Purchasing for Inventory

In this process, as its name implies, production material (food) and other items are purchased to be put into inventory to be available when needed. These items are usually used frequently and continually, have a longer shelf-life, or have such high use that they will not be in inventory long enough to deteriorate. Many of these items have such a high level of predictable use that they can be set up on standard delivery schedule under contract (discussed later in this chapter). Many fall into the category identified as staples, i.e., those items that are the basic ingredients for a number of menu items (recipes), such as flour, salt, pepper, ketchup, mustard, tomato sauce, tomato paste, cooking oils, soup bases, eggs, onions, potatoes, celery, parsley, pastas, napkins, straws, and disposable ware, including cups, take-out items, bags, paper products, and detergents. Notice that all the foods in this list of staples do not have a long shelf-life; some are highly perishable, but are used frequently. In a later section of this chapter are discussed ways of lowering the quantities needed to maintain inventories at the level that carefully balances need, usage, use of assets, inventory turnover, and space.

Purchasing to Need

Purchasing to need (or use) requires close coordination and information from a number of functions within the foodservice department. To ensure that the raw material is on hand, on time, in the proper amounts, and of the proper quality and configuration requires, first, good communication; second, good planning; and third, good coordination. The production manager must communicate the number of portions of each item to be produced, when the material will be needed, and, if there is no recipe (plan) for the items, what raw material and in what quantity is needed. In later sections, this chapter discusses ways of automating not only the aspect of production planning but also many aspects of the purchasing function.

If planning and communications are accomplished effectively, there will be sufficient and correct raw material (food) on hand at the proper time to produce the planned number of finished products (portions) with little or no raw material left over.

PURCHASING SPECIFICATIONS

Purchasing specifications, sometimes referred to as food specifications, dictate the "what to buy" part of the purchasing function. Food, the raw material used in the production process, comes in various sizes, shapes, grades (quality identification), packaging, and production techniques (for those items that are processed in whole or part). Classifications of food and some of the applicable specifications are presented below.

Meats

Meats are graded according to a strict grade identification process from the U.S. Department of Agriculture (USDA). Most meats in the marketplace today have been inspected and graded by USDA inspectors stationed at the processing plant. Not only do they inspect and grade meat but they also inspect processing methods and sanitation. In order to qualify as a federally inspected USDA processing plant the physical facility must also meet minimum construction and equipment specifications. All meat processed in a USDA inspected plant has two stamps on it. One stamp indicates that the meat has been inspected by the USDA and the product is wholesome and fit for human consumption. The other stamp is a quality stamp that indicates the grade. The stamps should be clearly evident in all raw primal and secondary cuts of meat.

Meats cut into component parts usually conform to a set of specifications developed by the National Association of Meat Purveyors (NAMP) and the USDA. These specifications describe the various cuts of meat, how they should be cut from the carcass, the weight range, amount of fat cover, the nomenclature of the muscles and bones, if any, and an NAMP number. Most standard specifications for meat use these NAMP descriptions. Therefore, a strip loin NAMP #180, Weight Range B Grade Prime is a clear, complete specification that is understood by the purveyor and the purchaser.

The availability of meat not only broken down into specified primal cuts but also processed further in a number of different ways, including cooked and portioned, complicates the purchasing process further. An example of a processed meat is veal cutlet. Strictly speaking, the term "veal cutlet" is a purchasing specification that is close to complete in its own right. The only thing missing is the portion size. True veal cutlet means a portioned, whole piece of meat cut from a veal leg, containing no sinew or connective tissue that has not been processed further, such as tenderized. Unfortunately, the strict specification of veal cutlet as defined by USDA has been diluted and bastardized. Veal cutlet can be purchased cut from other than veal leg, fabricated, cooked, breaded, tenderized, etc.

As mentioned above, a form of processing is known as "fabrication." As the name implies when referring to meats, fabrication is the mechanical processing of pieces of meat into something that resembles or can be substituted for a more expensive meat product or that answers a specific market need. There are many "steaks" on the market today that are labeled enigmatically with such names as "Philly Steak," "Processed Steak," "Cheese Steak," etc. These products are sold to meet a certain market demand and could have their place in a corporate foodservice environment, although not as a substitute for the higher-quality product they emulate.

Chopped meat, more accurately named "ground meat," is another example of a processed meat. The specifications for this product are also varied and numerous. The most often-used specification is the ratio of fat content to lean meat (solid muscle). The specification 85/15 indicates that 15 percent of the total weight is fat, or roughly 2.5 ounces in every pound. Chopped meat used for Steak Tartar (ground beef served raw) should be very different from the chopped meat purchased for use in spaghetti sauce. The chopped meat destined to be served as Steak Tartar should have a minimum of fat, probably no more than 5 percent, and should be processed from the more tender, better-quality parts of the carcass, such as tenderloin pieces, trimmings from sirloin strips, or the rib sections. Chopped meat (ground) for meat sauce can be from any part of the carcass as long as it is composed of muscle and fat in the desired ratio with no other ingredient, such as bone, sinew, or additive, unless specified. Chopped meat in today's market is available in many configurations and with some additives, such as ground processed soybean protein, an inexpensive protein additive that increases volume, reduces cost and affects the size, look, and taste of the finished product.

Chopped meat can also be purchased already formed into a variety of both raw and cooked products. Hamburger patties are available in a number of sizes and shapes with various other ingredients added. They can be either cooked, seared, or raw. The same variety can be found in lamb and pork.

The processing of chickens continues to expand in varieties and techniques. It is difficult to tell the grade of a processed chicken or even inspect for grade at the receiving dock. However, packaging and labeling regulations require that sufficient information be displayed to define the product, its quality, any additives, its weight, and any processing that has been part of its production. Chickens can be purchased dressed whole; by various parts—breast, drumstick, wings—or pulled, breaded, cooked, rolled, etc. The end use (menu items) determines the way it should be purchased.

Such specialty meats as salami, bologna, sausage, bacon and corned beef should be tested and tasted for yield and flavor in order to determine which should be purchased. A word of caution. Such items as sausages, wursts, and hot dogs should be purchased from a reputable USDA-inspected vendor and handled safely when purchased fresh. Improperly processed and/or handled products in this group can be dangerous.

Cheeses

Purchasing decisions for cheese are determined by taste and the end use of the product. Cheeses are made from cow's milk, goat's milk, and a variety of other dairy products. Processed cheeses are manufactured and handled differently than natural cheeses. Ingredient labels provide sufficient information to identify the process and the ingredients, as well as USDA inspection.

Milk and Eggs

Most milks and eggs are purchased fresh when they are to be used in their "natural" form; that is, milk for direct consumption by the customer and eggs used for scrambled, fried, boiled, or poached egg dishes. Milk and eggs used for baking or other cooking that lose their identity in the process can be purchased in a number of forms. The recipe specification and preference of kitchen management (chef, pastry chef, production manager) will dictate the form of these products. Milk is available condensed, dried, and processed to remove fat content and lactates. Eggs can be powdered whole, yellows only, cooked in tubes for slicing, cracked (shelled), frozen, and prepared by other processing methods for special uses in baking.

Fruits and Vegetables

The growing customer preference for fruits and vegetables is to purchase them fresh. Improved transportation and fresh "processes" have made this possible for a wide variety of fresh fruits and vegetables.

A whole chapter could be devoted to the specifications of superior quality in fresh fruits and vegetables. Some terms, such as firm, unblemished, smooth, and crisp, can apply to a number of different fruits or vegetables. However, specifics defined by the USDA apply for many vegetables, such as fresh corn, tomatoes, lettuces of each variety, asparagus, string beans, broccoli, and pea pods.

Specifications for processed fruits and frozen vegetables can be more easily identified because of labeling regulations. The grade of the raw fruit or vegetable at the time of processing into the frozen product is marked on the package. Canned fruits and vegetables are also marked as to grade, size, weight, and cut, as well as packing medium. The cut indicates how the vegetable was prepared, such as diced, julienne, chunks, whole, etc. The packing medium depends in large measure on the product packed. Water pack, brine, light or heavy syrup, and oil of various types are all regularly used packing environments. Usually, canned fruits and vegetables are canned as Extra Fancy, Fancy, and Standard, indicating the quality of the raw fresh item. The use of preservatives and/or spices or flavorings is also clearly labeled. Fruits have an added dimension of the medium in which they are canned, which in most instances is referred to as syrup. Syrup is usually simple syrup and can be extra heavy, heavy, regular, in its own juice, or water packed. The extra heavy syrup contains the most sugar.

Coffees, Teas, and Other Beverages

The quality of coffee is based on the source of the "green" beans (coffee beans freshly harvested before roasting), the grade of the green beans, the roast method, and the blend of the different beans. The term "100% Columbian" coffee only means that all of the beans were grown in Columbia. There could be several grades of Columbian green beans in various ratios in a 100% Columbian coffee blend. It is important to understand that one of the main methods that vendors use to maintain the price of coffee is to adjust the blend. Most of the flavor and aroma of coffee are contained in its highly volatile oils. Because the oils and the attendant aroma and taste dissipate rapidly once exposed to air, coffee should be vacuum packed where possible and opened in only the quantities to be used immediately.

The growth in popularity of freshly brewed decaffeinated coffee has made it a close second in consumption to regular coffee in some situations. The use of water in the decaffeinating process to remove the caffeine is the preferred method, producing a better quality and more natural product. The other decaffeinating method uses chemicals that dissolve the caffeine.

Teas are growing in popularity. Various blends of teas, mainly in tea bags, are available in the marketplace. The availability of flavored teas and coffees and brewed iced teas makes the purchasing of teas and coffees more complicated.

Another variable is packaging, especially of coffee. Most coffee is now ground and packed in accordance with the way it will be brewed and the size of the brewing equipment. Coffee for pour-over equipment is packaged differently than coffee to be urn brewed and urn-brewed coffee comes in different packaging sizes for different-sized urns. Grinding coffee beans immediately before brewing in front of the customers is a merchandising technique that is growing in popularity, making it necessary to purchase coffee beans unground. All of these variables must be identified and clearly stated in the purchasing specifications.

Spices, Herbs, Pastes, Sauces, and Bases

As a general rule, spices and herbs should be purchased in small quantities. In reality, however, and all too often in my opinion, spices and herbs are purchased in large quantities to economize on the unit cost and because it is easier for purchasing and production to have these on hand in relatively large quantities so as not to have to purchase them frequently or run short. Even though the unit cost of the better, fresher, and smaller quantities of herbs and spices may be significantly higher, the cost per portion is usually very small, thereby making the fresher and better quality the better choice. Spices and herbs deteriorate in potency and flavor when exposed to air and allowed to grow old. This is true even of the water- and oil-soluble varieties.

The choice of sauces, pastes, and bases for soups and gravies is a matter of preference based on their reaction in various recipes. The grade and quality, as well as brand name, should be decided on by testing in advance and the use adhered to until changed by mutual consent among management, food production management, and purchasing. Pastes and sauces are usually graded by the amount of solids in the sauce, such as tomatoes in tomato sauce. Recipes are usually developed based on a specific sauce or paste or puree and should not be deviated from without reviewing the effect on the quality and quantity of the recipe item.

Paper Supplies

Paper supplies fall into two categories: (1) disposable serviceware and packaging and (2) sanitation paper supplies.

Disposable serviceware refers to single-use throw-away dishware, flatware, and cups that are manufactured either from paper or plastic. Packaging/sanitation paper supplies include paper napkins, paper, and plastic used for wrapping, storing, and take-out use (other than service disposables). Plastic wrap, aluminum foil, wax paper, and paper bags fall into this category. Disposable kitchen towels, plastic aprons, plastic gloves, toilet paper, and paper hand towels are other sanitation paper supplies.

The purchasing of these items is based primarily on the need and type of use. Plastic clamshell-form containers are used for heat retention take-out items, such as hamburgers. Clear, plastic-covered larger containers are suitable for cold items, such as salads. The type and size of the napkins to be used depend largely on personal preference, cost, and the method (equipment) used to dispense them.

The growing concern for biodegradability and the handling of solid waste will increasingly affect the use of plastic in kitchen, servery, and in packaging.

Cleaning Supplies

There are three categories of cleaning supplies: (1) dishwashing detergents and sanitizing agents, (2) pot and pan washing detergents, and (3) general cleaning and sanitizing agents, including polishing chemicals and cleansing powders. The equipment used in cleaning and sanitizing, such as mops and mop buckets, griddle stones, scrapers, squeegies, brooms, electrical scrubbers, polishers, and flexible shaft brushes for pot scrubbing, are also included under cleaning supplies.

The companies that supply the chemicals for the dishwashing, pot scrubbing, and other cleaning activities also supply ancillary services and detergent dispensing equipment. Most of the equipment is in the form of electronic dispensing and monitoring devices that feed detergent, rinsing agents, and sanitizing chemicals in the proper concentrations to clean and sanitize the china, glassware, silverware in the dishwasher, and the pots and pans in the pot sink or pot washing machines. These companies also provide maintenance inspections on warewashing equipment to maximize its efficiency and effectiveness. Most of them also offer sophisticated training programs and aids to instruct employees in the proper methods of operating dish machines, sanitizing pots and pans, and general cleaning activities.

It is difficult to compare the products of these companies with each other. Most often, the purchasing decision is influenced by a combination of results (i.e., cleaner pots and pans and dishware), and the services and training assistance that are offered by each company. The purchase of dishwashing and sanitizing chemicals and dispensing equipment is usually done on contract and is only changed when some dissatisfaction of one kind or another becomes evident.

China, Glassware, Flatware

The selection of these items is usually based on very subjective factors. Color and pattern are usually specified based on design criteria and individual preference and taste. However, there are purchasing considerations in the area of handling, especially warewashing, that should be specified. Obviously, china, glassware, and flatware for high-volume cafeterias will receive harder wear than those items used in an executive dining room or private dining room environment. Yet, even fine china, glassware, and silverware are subject to the chemicals present in commercial detergents, rinse agents, and sanitizers and may fade or crack due to the exposure to chemicals and the heat of final rinse water.

Another consideration in the selection of china and glassware relates to the use of lowerators for plates (both heated and unheated) and racks to wash, store, and dispense cups and glasses. The height of footed glassware must be coordinated with the ware washing and storage racks that will hold them.

If silverplate is being used for fine dining, the routine use of a silver burnishing machine will keep the silver flatware polished and shining. There are silver burnishing machines available that also polish serving trays and platters.

PURCHASING TECHNIQUES

There are two basic techniques of purchasing: contract purchasing and quotation purchasing.

Contract Purchasing

Purchasing contracts come in several forms. One form is the contract for periodic delivery of a predetermined and anticipated total volume of merchandise at an agreed-upon price or price determinator. The price determinator usually is determined by the acquisition cost from the wholesaler or manufacturer. The final price is often expressed as a percentage above that cost, commonly referred to as "cost plus" contracts. In order for this type of purchasing to be effective a number of variables must be identified.

- the approximate amount of the product(s) to be used during the contract period
- the contract length (period)
- the delivery schedule, i.e., daily, weekly, as needed, etc.
- the specifications of the product; for example, milk homogenized, Grade A, packed in half-pint peak packages, with the "pull" date clearly marked on the package closure
- the price, either a fixed price for the length of the contract, a cost-plus agreed-upon mark-up, or a series of prices that change at an agreed-upon interval
- the terms, either prompt payment terms or additional discounts or rebates based on achieving certain benchmarks, such as volume (exceeding certain volumes of pieces, pounds, units, gallons, etc. within certain time schedules)
- service, such as that offered by chemical companies that sell dish machine and other cleaning compounds and who also service the dishwashing and pot washing equipment or the servicing of coffee and tea urns offered by some coffee suppliers
- the pack size in which products are packaged

Packs and packaging to fit a specific use or method of use of a product are a significant factor that needs to be clearly specified. Portion-packaged items obviously differ greatly from bulk pack; in addition, in the category of portion packaging there is a wide variety of packaging. As an example, fountain syrups packed in plastic gallon containers will not work in a soda "factory" that requires boxed fountain syrups. Therefore, the specification must state that the syrup is to be packaged in boxes to be connected to (manufacturer's name) postmix dispensing equipment.

The advantages of contract purchases are

- known sources that can provide the service and quality of products needed
- known or controlled prices
- ease of purchasing and ordering
- other services are available because of quantity of purchases

Contract purchasing is a technique used by many foodservice management companies for many products. One of the services offered by these companies is the opportunity for small user clients to purchase food and supplies at quantity price schedules that reflect the purchasing volumes of all of the purchasing done by the food management company.

Most of the food management companies now have contracts with national and local suppliers to purchase bread, dairy products, meats, vegetables, canned and frozen foods, paper supplies, cleaning chemicals and ware washing detergents, and fountain syrups—virtually every item needed by a foodservice operation. Most of these contracts clearly define the specifications of every item in the contract, as well as a pricing procedure that allows for fluctuations in the marketplace, either up or down. In addition, many of the food management companies enjoy additional discounts or rebates based on their volume of purchases.

Individual self-operated foodservice programs can also purchase on a contract basis. Purchase contracts are of value because they facilitate the purchasing function and getting known quality merchandise at a negotiated price. Contract purchasing at set prices can protect the foodservice program from rising prices, but can also lock the purchaser into prices that are not advantageous in a falling market.

Quotation Purchasing

The most common form of purchasing, especially for items with prices that are driven directly by supply and demand and that fluctuate from day to day or week to week, is quotation purchasing. It is also used for items for which the need is not continuous but is dependent upon menu use.

The purchaser requests quotations for the specified foods from two to four reputable suppliers who are known to the purchaser and who have demonstrated quality, service, and fair prices. After receiving quotations from these firms for delivery within a week to 10 days, the purchaser can then select the items from the firm with the best price. This can be the best price for each item or the aggregate best price after applying the amount of each product needed to arrive at the total cost. At times, the consistently higher quality of merchandise within a specification available from one supplier will make it a "better buy" to purchase on the basis of quality, rather than price. Quotation purchasing is generally most effective when purchasing fresh food, meat, fish, poultry, fruit, and vegetables.

Quotation purchasing requires clearly defined and understood product specifications. This is especially true with foods that are sold "as grown" and are graded by quality and size, such as fresh vegetables and fruits and meat items that are processed from whole carcasses and/or are sold whole but graded by government inspectors. When purchasing meats in standard cuts and in portion cuts, the National Association of Meat Purveyors' Meat Buyers Guide (available from NAMP, 8365B Greensboro Drive, McLean, VA 22102) clearly defines grades, primal cut processing specifications, and weight classifications. Reference to a NAMP specification from the Meat Buyers Guide cannot be misunderstood.

Quotation purchasing is also the more prudent method when purchasing equipment, utensils, china, glassware, and flatware. With these goods, the manufacturer, model or pattern number, and size specifications are clear. The suppliers are quoting prices on exactly the same merchandise. Price, delivery, and reputation are the deciding factors.

AUTOMATED PURCHASING

The rapid development of the computer and accompanying telecommunication techniques has given rise to automatic purchasing systems. Computer-assisted foodservice management systems can now automatically identify purchase requirements based on recipe ingredients and planned production quantities for any defined production period, translate that into purchase orders, and electronically transmit the orders (following a purchasing review) to the contract vendors. These systems use a recipe file, a food item file, and a contribution analysis menu planning and menu item process that (1) indicate the proper number of portions and the sizes of all the recipes needed for a given production period, (2) combine all like ingredients, (3) produce a purchase list sorted by contract purveyor, and (4) automatically transmit the order via data phone to the vendor. Less sophisticated systems only produce the purchase list, but even this level of automation adds a new dimension to foodservice management. These systems not only provide specific and detailed purchasing information but also vital data in food production and control.

14

Financial Systems

CANDACE ANN YORK

A native of Dallas, Candace York has been involved in the foodservice oper-ations for Texas Instruments for the past 15 years. During her tenure with the company, she has seen the company grow from 7 employee foodservice facilities in Dallas to 44 across the United States. Her background includes a degree in nutrition from the University of Texas and an MBA in Management from East Texas State University.

DEFINITIONS

In order to understand the various options possible in financing an em-ployee foodservice operation, we must first examine the "game plan" for the corporation. Some corporations wish to provide in-house foodservice as a part of their benefits package to their employees. This usually implies the operation will run at a discounted cost to the employee and be subsidized or supported from corporate funding.

If foodservice is viewed by the corporation as a "convenience" or "serv-ice" to its employees, then it is often self-supporting and operates at prices comparable to that of an outside restaurant. A finer tuning of the financial situation may demand a profit-and-loss type of accounting whereby the sales from foodservice pays the costs involved in providing the service.

In-house foodservice may be required because of limited break periods in a highly regulated production company where assembly lines must run on a schedule. These services may be subsidized, break-even, or run for profit, at the discretion of the company.

Direct costs of food, labor, and supplies are usually considered to be costs to be covered through food sales. Supplies can include uniforms, paper goods, cleaning supplies, printing costs, office materials, dinnerware re-placements, glassware, silverware, small utensils, vehicle rentals, linens, other rentals, and miscellaneous expenditures to provide foodservice, such as signage, promotional materials, etc. Indirect costs, such as management fees, taxes, licenses, permits, utilities, depreciation costs, maintenance, and occupancy (space rental), may or may not be counted as expenses to the foodservice operation. The indirect costs may be absorbed at a different operational level within the corporation. It is imperative to have well-defined guidelines specifying the direct and indirect costs to be used in establishing an in-house program.

The decision whether the operation should be self-operated or contracted to a foodservice management company must be a corporate decision. However, self-operation may result in higher labor costs and less flexibility in being able to move or remove personnel from the operation.

If the corporation feels it is unprepared to handle a "specialty"-type service, then it may elect to hire a management company to provide the service for it. The management company then performs all the required functions of operating a foodservice, such as hiring and training personnel, food preparation and ordering, sanitation, menu planning and pricing, special promotions, cashiering and money collections, maintenance, and equipment specifications. Financial arrangements between the food management company and the corporation are either fee-based on a percentage of sales, on a commission structure, or a flat rate based on sales volumes. Another negotiable option is whether the corporation or the management company owns the inventories. If the corporation owns the inventories, par levels can be established and monitored so that a great deal of money is not tied up at any time in products sitting in costly square footages of storage space. In the other option, the management company carries the inventories and charges the corporation for *usage only* on a regularly reviewed basis. The management company will, of course, also police its inventory levels in order to minimize cash flow problems, should it own the inventory. In either case, it is important to monitor and control inventory levels to prevent tying up large amounts of dollars in capital and space to provide in-house foodservice.

Exhibit 14-1 Self-Operated Foodservice

NET CASH SALES (WITHOUT TAX) + CHARGE SALES[1] + VENDING SALES = NET TOTAL SALES

NET TOTAL SALES − LABOR COSTS (INCLUDING BENEFITS) − FOOD COSTS − SUPPLIES COSTS = 0 = BREAK-EVEN

This exhibit assumes that only direct costs are covered and the foodservice is self-operated.

[1] "Charge sales" may be an internal corporate decision that allows employees to charge foodservices rendered within the company to their particular group or division in the organization.

Exhibit 14-2 Foodservice Contractor

NET CASH SALES (WITHOUT TAX) + CHARGE SALES + VENDING SALES =
NET TOTAL SALES

NET TOTAL SALES − LABOR COSTS (INCLUDING BENEFITS) − FOOD COSTS
− SUPPLIES COSTS − MANAGEMENT FEE = 0 = BREAK-EVEN

This exhibit assumes that only direct costs are covered and the foodservice is managed by a contractor.

Break-even is the final term that merits discussion. Again, guidelines for costs must be determined first. If direct costs only are to be covered by the profits made from sales, then the financial statement for a self-operated foodservice would look like Exhibit 14-1. Should the operations be run by a foodservice contractor, then the financial analysis would look like Exhibit 14-2. Vending sales and costs are included in the discussion of the total foodservice program because they have a significant impact on sales volumes and profits and losses.

GOAL SETTING

In varying degrees, all corporations that provide an in-house foodservice program for their employees wish to make it as satisfying as possible. However, the goals set for the foodservice are often in opposition to one another. Satisfying to whom becomes the issue. The financial analysts view foodservice as an expensive overhead cost when the corporation's business is not concerned with the food industry, yet personnel departments and benefits administrators realize the positive effect that in-house foodservice can have on the overall satisfaction of the employees with the work environment. When the costs to provide the service outweigh the benefits derived, difficult situations result.

Therefore, it is *most* important to recognize that foodservice is a volatile, ever-changing operation dealing with very personal preferences on an individual scale of judgment and that it can be a viable, positive benefit or a strongly negative influence upon a company's workers. Setting the goals to attain maximum results is the primary responsibility of the corporation, either for its own self-op structure or for a management company. If the corporation decides to operate its foodservices at a subsidy, then it must determine what subsidy level it wishes to maintain. For different types of B&I services, there are different "acceptable" subsidy levels (Fig. 14-1) that appear to be trends in today's market.

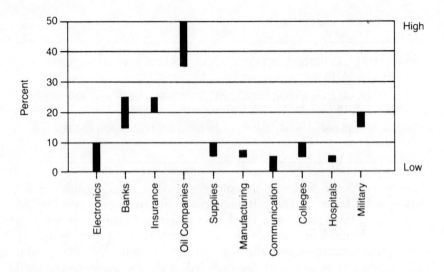

Figure 14-1 Subsidy Ranges for B&I Service Industries

Goal setting must also take into account such measurements as raw food costs as a percentage of the sales dollar, labor costs (including benefits), replacement costs, and fees. Participation levels as target goals have to be established, as well as types of services to be offered (off-shifts, executive dining, breakfast, break periods, lunch), hours of service, and the amount of variety to be offered. Participation levels seem to hover around the 50 percentile mark. Participation may fluctuate due to the weather, hours of meal service, ease of access to "outside" food establishments, payday schedules, holidays and vacation schedules, amount of variety offered, and corporate attitude toward in-house dining. For example, the corporation must determine whether it wants to compete with the fast food market, the commercial cafeterias in the area, the full-service restaurant business, or a combination of any of these in order to achieve customer satisfaction (Fig. 14-2). *Perception* of the in-house foodservice operation must be a predetermined goal, too. The corporation must decide how it wishes to communicate its foodservice message to its employees. Is it "first-class," a high school cafeteria atmosphere, or just a "meets requirements" attitude?

Pricing strategies are the last of the systems goals to be established. Pricing may be done at the competitive outside market level, below market level, or by inclusion or exclusion of sales taxes. Pricing may be determined by the corporation itself or by its foodservice contractor. A corporation wishing to run a subsidy operation usually prices its food items below outside market levels. The percentage points below the outside market at which food shall be offered for sale must be decided beforehand as well.

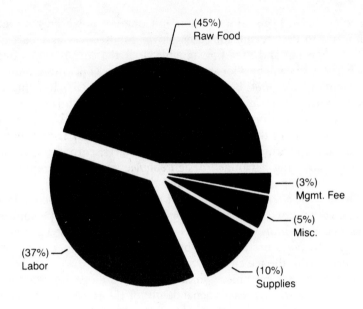

This assumes a Mgmt. Fee Operation.

Figure 14-2 Direct Cost as a Percentage of Net Sales Dollar

It is a fairly standard practice in the industry to price vending items comparable to the outside market and price manually served items below the competition. The logic to this is that margins generated from vending items, which are more easily controlled by portion and item cost, will offset the costs involved in producing a daily menu in the kitchen, which fluctuate because of market cycles and availability, waste, and variable portion controls.

Whether sales tax should be included or excluded from the advertised selling price of an item is at the discretion of the management. In comparing outside facilities with in-house services, customers often do not recognize the tax added at the register when the "advertised" price does not include the tax. They therefore perceive their employee foodservice prices as higher. If management fees paid to contractors are based on sales dollars, then the sales tax must be deducted before computing the fee for services provided.

For whatever pricing system is selected, however, it is advisable to make price adjustments at the "grassroots" level of the operation in order to respond quickly to market changes as they occur.

Goal setting for controlling overhead costs is a much more complex issue. The corporation may or may not want to highlight its costs for the foodservice operations. Legislation pending in Congress, however, may require corporations to declare subsidized employee foodservices as a part of the employee's income and therefore taxable. It is the corporation's duty to decide which costs will be allocated to the foodservice operations and which will not, but the costs must be covered, one way or another. The contractor's overhead expenses include support management costs, both by district or region and at the corporate levels; special expertise used to market the goods and services of the contractor's organization, such as registered dietitians on staff, executive chefs, training managers, corporate accounting personnel, marketing personnel, design engineers, etc.; and computer systems or other equipment investment and the related depreciation costs required to provide a complete package of foodservices to its clients. In some instances, contractors also pay rent for the space that their personnel and services occupy within the corporation's walls. Operating licenses, fees, insurance, and taxes are also paid by the contractor, which may or may not be included in the fee charged to the corporation.

Self-operators face even more "hidden costs." Utilities, for example, can be metered for kitchen areas independently of the rest of the facilities or can be allocated as costs based on square footage occupied. Because there are different utility rates based on the type of business in which the corporation is engaged, rates can be appallingly high in some instances for foodservice space. If the corporation elects to provide some of the services normally offered by the contractor, then costs will rise accordingly. For instance, some companies may collect, count, and deposit cash collections made from cafeteria registers and vending machine coin boxes in order to keep all the profits themselves. This usually entails duplicate labor efforts and dual supervisory functions, as well as an investment in equipment and vehicles. Maintenance and cleaning services are often provided by the corporation for foodservice operations too. A larger and more highly paid and trained maintenance staff is required to know how to repair all types of kitchen and vending equipment than is needed to provide only general building maintenance.

The single biggest factor in overhead costs to the corporation is the cost of depreciation on capital equipment. Most corporations provide the physical plant and the equipment needed to produce an in-house food program. Kitchen and/or vending equipment is very costly as both an initial investment and an ongoing expense. Depending upon the levels of service required and the estimated production needs of a facility, capital costs to outfit a kitchen can range from $25,000 to $1 million. It is therefore wise to invest carefully.

In addition, the corporation's overhead costs include specialized management personnel to work with the contractor, bookkeeping and accounting services to audit the contractor on a periodic basis, and administrative personnel costs to process incoming or outgoing contract employees.

For the self-operator, some of these costs may be inseparable from the rest of the corporate organization. Labor costs, however, with its corresponding benefits, still loom large as a cost to be managed in such a situation. Depreciation, utilities, maintenance, bookkeeping, accounting, and cash handling are other costs. Occupancy or rental of the space occupied by the foodservices group may be another overhead cost.

The final factor in goal setting is to determine service levels. Although a separate executive dining facility is often considered desirable for image, it is costly to provide, staff, and maintain. It also tends to draw an invisible line between the general employees and the management levels within the corporation. If that is the corporate aim, however, then the cost implications

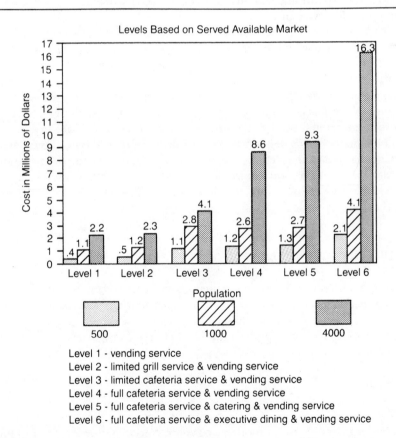

Level 1 - vending service
Level 2 - limited grill service & vending service
Level 3 - limited cafeteria service & vending service
Level 4 - full cafeteria service & vending service
Level 5 - full cafeteria service & catering & vending service
Level 6 - full cafeteria service & executive dining & vending service

Figure 14-3 Annualized Direct Costs versus Service

must be handled. At the very least, more staff are required to serve both an executive dining room and an employee area. More supervision is needed as well. Service costs for such sundries as linens, dinnerware, fresh flowers daily, etc., increase by at least 50 percent. Food costs rise proportionately due to a greater variety of prepared items, dual menus, and increased waste. Whether a corporation elects to have executive dining or simpler, catered functions to conference rooms, there are still costs in providing these services.

Employee feeding can be done elaborately or simply, depending upon the desires of the corporation. There are fixed costs of providing manual foodservice, whether to 5 or 5,000 customers. Employee foodservice becomes expensive when the company demands off-shift service, service to very small pockets of people, or service during holiday periods. Multiples of fixed costs occur with expansion of the menu, points of service, length of service time, and types of service offered.

Vending service, on the other hand, can be provided fairly economically, because of the controls inherent to the program. Portions are controlled, inventories are not as perishable as manual foodservice, and waste is minimal. Vending services can adequately meet the needs of off-shifts and small populations if well presented and large enough to handle the necessary volumes. The margins returned on vending items are usually greater than those from manual service. Labor costs for vending service are lower, and maintenance is more defined and controlled. Vending service, however, is impersonal and cannot replace the human touch of the foodservice program.

Although there are some measures of cost for services versus service levels provided, there are so many variables in the relationship between the two that analysis is difficult. As an example, see Figure 14-3.

INDUSTRY EXAMPLES

To define costs and their consequences more clearly, it is helpful to examine specific operations and the financial accounting methods used. Companies A, B, and C are all major corporations in the United States that provide their employees with in-house foodservice programs.

Company A

Company A is a management fee-based account with break-even as its operating target. It uses a foodservice contractor to perform primary functions. Break-even, at Company A, means that all direct and indirect costs must be covered by revenues received through vended and manual food-services. The corporation provides maintenance, space, cleaning staff, utilities, and equipment. Its personnel collect and count all cash monies received through case registers and vending machines. Company A sets all selling prices for food items and dictates target cost percentages to its contractor. Menus are approved by the corporation, as well as promotional plans before their execution.

The contractor provides the personnel to prepare and serve the food items and to service vending machines. Their responsibilities also include kitchen sanitation, menu planning, and specialty catering functions, as well as payroll, bookkeeping, and inventories. The contractor owns all inventories and charges out weekly usages to the corporation. Levels of service provided include manual services at breakfast, lunch, and break periods; second-shift meal service at particular locations, snack bars, and grill operations; catering services both on-site and off-site; and full vending services.

This method of operation is somewhat unique to the industry because design planning, equipment specification and purchase, money collection, and financial accountabilities are all done by the corporation, rather than by the contractor. This method creates duplicate expenses for administrative overhead because both sides of the foodservice operation are doing financial reporting and analysis, as well as supervising employees.

A new foodservice facility is particularly taxing for the first 3 years of operation due to the tremendous cost of depreciation and facilities on a double-declining balance base of 7 years, rather than the usual 9 years that most other corporations recognize. Pricing for vended service is based on a par with outside competition, but manual service is priced at 10 to 15 percent below the outside market, and these prices include sales tax. All of these factors contribute to an in-house food program image of "service," rather than "benefit." If a location cannot support the costs of a manual foodservice because of the smallness of the population, then only vending service is provided. There is no executive dining room for Company A's employees, and all manual service is operated "cafeteria" style, either through a single line or a scramble system. Participation levels average 56 percent of the population.

Company B

Company B is a self-op facility based on a profit/(loss) financial arrangement. All inventories, of course, are owned by the corporation. Pricing policies are set by the corporation and reflect a slightly below market target. Breakfast, lunch, off-shift, carry-out, on- and off-site catering, and executive dining services are all provided by the corporation. Vending services are provided by an outside contractor, but none of the revenues received from vending sales is returned to the Company B operations. Beverage machines are turned on "free play" twice per day throughout the facilities. Under a separate vending contract, the outside contractor purchases and owns its vending equipment, but Company B specifies and purchases kitchen equipment itself. Straight-line depreciation spread over a 10-year term is paid by the foodservice group within the corporation as a part of its operating cost. Additional indirect operating expenses include outside maintenance, management staff salaries, and benefits. Direct costs charged to the operation include direct labor, food, laundry, travel expense, cleaning services, business forms, and dishwasher, cleaning, and paper supplies. No rent or utilities are charged to the operation. Inventory levels are regulated according to space and need. Using a completely computerized system creates built-in controls on production, usage, leftovers, inventory needs, and menu planning. In addition to an ingredient room where production is monitored and controlled, Company B also uses programmable registers and large-scale computerized reporting systems to maintain a close watch over the services it provides. Money collections and accountabilities are done for the manual service by Company B. The vending contractor collects and counts its own revenues. Company B enjoys a 65 percent participation level from its employees.

Company C

Company C operates as a self-operated subsidy account, using its own employees to provide meal service for breakfast, lunch, off-shifts, break periods, catering, and executive dining on a 24-hour-per-day, 7-day-per-week cycle. Pricing is equal to or less than the outside competition, based on overall food cost target percentages.

This corporation uses an outside contractor for vending service, but it receives a commission from the sales of coffee, cold drinks, candy, and cigarettes. All machines are owned by the outside contractor, except the cold food machines, which are purchased by the corporation. Those revenues are kept in-house.

Company C purchases and provides all kitchen equipment and is charged depreciation on its purchases on the straight-line method over a period of 7 years. Additional indirect costs charged to the corporation include rent, utilities, administrative management salaries, and benefits. The operating policy for foodservices is to recover all direct costs of food, labor, and supplies through vending revenues. The balance of the operating costs is to be covered by the corporate subsidy. Inventories are ordered against par levels and inventory investments of boxcar load lots are often used to take advantage of discounted prices. Vending inventories, of course, are owned by the outside contractor. Both the outside contractor and Company C's employees collect and count cash monies. Company C has an 80 percent participation rate for its population on a three-shift basis.

SYSTEMS PROS AND CONS

There are as many financial combinations for running in-house foodservice programs as there are operations in existence. The pros and cons of each type of accounting system vary according to the viewpoint and perception of the service received. In break-even accounting, all of the costs of the operation are highlighted, but the costs of large-scale expansion, upgrading, or improvement are imposed only on those who pay for the service through their participation in the program. This usually makes selling prices comparable to outside market levels and creates a friction that becomes difficult to overcome. If your employees perceive in-house foodservice as a corporate benefit rather than a service, they will automatically expect to pay less in-house than at a commercial restaurant even for the exact same product. A constant comparison is made between in-house services and outside competition, yet services provided by each may not be equal, i.e., liquor may be served in an outside restaurant yet not be allowed on company premises. The price of the hamburger may be identical in both establishments, however.

Contractor-operated foodservices offer financial advantages over self-operation because minimum wage personnel are usually recruited by foodservice contractors, whereas corporate pay scales may be significantly higher. In contrast, however, an "us" and "them" relationship is avoided by using company employees in the cafeteria. An attitude of corporate involvement may be instilled more readily in a self-operated environment than in a contractor-operated one.

Profit and loss accounting becomes very clouded very quickly. A "true" P&L would charge all direct and indirect costs to the foodservice operation, treating it as a separate company functioning within the corporation's walls. It would subtract all expenses from total revenues to determine the foodservice's bottom-line performance. Because of the nature of in-house feeding, however, the corporation usually places stipulations or performance requirements upon such an operation, either restricting access to the establishment to its employees only or by hours of service, or menu items to be offered, or prices to be charged. All of these regulations cost money. If a

P&L account is contractor-operated, a corporation may also run the risk of seeing poorer service, less menu variety, or lower quality when profit levels begin to decline or participation levels change unfavorably.

Subsidized operations are the "easiest" to run financially, as long as the corporation has an open checkbook attitude toward expenses. However, even subsidy accounts can be regulated and financial discipline maintained. The most obvious benefit of a subsidy is a lower selling price to the customer on products consumed. Most corporations set a subsidy level for foodservice operations that they consider "acceptable." Any subsidy over that agreed-to cost support requires corrective action, similar to the P&L accounts. The perceived value to the customer is usually higher with subsidized accounting systems, which generally leads to higher morale and a more favorable attitude toward the corporation's foodservice operations. In lean times, however, corporations may be forced to eliminate or reduce subsidy levels, thereby quickly destroying the goodwill built toward the foodservice group.

INCENTIVES

Incentives can play either an important or minor role in the costs of doing business. Some corporations offer a bonus package to management-level foodservice personnel based upon sales-volume improvements during the fiscal year or upon expansion of participation levels. Bonus packages may be in the form of cash, extra vacation accruals, or gifts of a predetermined dollar value. A percentage share of the profits above the established goals is sometimes offered and may be disbursed to management- and operational-level personnel. With self-op companies, stock options may be offered for outstanding performance or for exceptional promotional skills. Attendance incentives are most commonly used at operational levels to encourage a stable, dependable workforce. They can be as simple as a special meal served to those whose attendance records are noteworthy or as elaborate as extra days of pay, gift certificates, coupons, and discounts at local department stores, or additional employee benefits. In fee-operated accounts, additional sales automatically provide additional incentives to the contract company because fees are based on volume.

CONCLUSION

It is very difficult to make generalizations about foodservice programs and the financial variables in running them. Each operation is highly individual, based primarily upon the corporate need of keeping employees in-house during their meal breaks during the day. Whether the service is provided in a pleasant, attractive atmosphere, with a large variety of services offered, and with prices that are lower than retail competition is strictly a decision to be made by those who pay the bills. Whatever the choices, costs to perform this operation remain similar; *accounting* for these costs runs the gamut of alternative choices. Whether operated by company employees or contractor employees, there are advantages and disadvantages to all methods. The choice of break-even, profit and loss, or subsidy accounting tends to be more a matter of interpretation than function, and the unmeasurable benefits of employee satisfaction, morale, and perception of their company's foodservice program weigh heavier in the balance than the costs necessary to maintain it.

The degree to which a corporation will provide a subsidy is based upon the image it wishes to create, both internally and externally. Emphasis should be placed on the quality, wholesomeness and nutritional value of the food served and on employee well-being. Controls are established to keep the foodservice operational costs in line with other "overhead" corporation expenditures not related to the business in which the corporation participates, i.e., the costs of providing employee fitness facilities or day-care centers, for example.

Is one method or system better than another? It depends upon what the corporation wants or expects from the foodservices group. It is the responsibility of the organization that provides funding to determine the direction its in-house foodservice program will follow.

15

Computers in Foodservice Management

BOB KILGORE

Bob Kilgore is the director of marketing of The CBORD Group, a leading computer software company headquartered in Ithaca, New York. In this capacity, he provides marketing direction, services, and support to the company's foodservice management systems and communicating systems division, as well as to value-added resellers associated with CBORD products and the markets in which they are sold. He is also responsible for support, communication, and organizational activities for CBORD's formal User Group.

It would be hard to imagine a bank, an insurance company, or a manufacturing plant that could operate competitively today without computers. We have become comfortable with the idea of computers performing analysis, calculation, record keeping, scheduling, and a wide range of other activities for the institutions we serve. Generally, we accept the fact that they perform many activities faster, more accurately, and less expensively than we could perform them manually. Yet, most foodservices have not been computerized to any great extent. Some foodservice managers perceive their profession as an art and see their primary professional tools as experience and intuition. Although we accept the indispensable role of computers in our organization's operations, many of us are resistant to the idea that they can contribute significantly to foodservice management. Many of us fail to understand that food production is a manufacturing process, and the professional skills and experience that managers apply to their work are basically engineering skills.

Our list of food ingredients is a parts list that we use to build our products, which are standard recipes. Our menus are product catalogues, which are intended to create demand and satisfy clients in our various markets. The basic principles, procedures, and controls are identical for all foodservice applications from vending to fine dining. The variable factors are menu quality and mix, costs, and pricing, which may differ widely in various parts of a single B&I foodservice operation.

A small minority of B&I foodservices are now using computers on a large scale as management tools. These foodservices are typically producing better, more consistent products at significantly less cost than their manually operated counterparts. Pioneers in computerized food cost and production control, such as Hallmark Cards, Inc. in Kansas City, Missouri; the Upjohn Company in Kalamazoo, Michigan; and the Eastman Kodak Company in Rochester, New York, have paved the way for their colleagues in B&I foodservice. They have proven the value of computer controls in quality foodservice settings—implementing, operating, and, in some cases, developing several generations of computer systems, each generation surpassing its predecessors in power, sophistication, ease of use, and economy.

Food production is not only a manufacturing process; it is a *very complex* manufacturing process. Hundreds of recipes must be constructed from over a thousand different ingredients. Vendor bids for raw ingredients must be evaluated strategically on the basis of a number of complex criteria. Demand must be forecast for recipes in the menu mix. Costs must be calculated in advance of service and pricing determined to comply with financial constraints. Cooks and chefs must be told how much of what to prepare and when. Food must be ordered and inventories maintained. In the end, performance must be evaluated and compared to forecasts. This is important not only from an accounting or profit and loss point of view but also as a means of evaluating menus and production forecasts with an eye toward continually improving future performance.

Foodservice managers have performed surprisingly well using manual means for hundreds of years. Yet, the sheer volume of calculation, scheduling, and coordination necessary to analyze, plan, and execute a large-scale, quantity food production process as well as it theoretically *could* be done is beyond human capabilities. Various aspects of the process are performed incompletely or skipped altogether. As a result, estimates and a degree of "padding" are facts of life in even the best-run foodservices. The results are overordering, overproduction, waste, pilferage, and fairly limited menus. Human beings can handle only a relatively limited number of variables with accuracy and control.

The best of today's computer systems take full advantage of the skills of experienced managers. They do not replace people, but rather provide management tools that maximize the effectiveness of skill and experience. They provide managers with information to plan effectively and accurately. Computers can analyze and compare buying strategies for least-cost purchasing. They can predict customer counts and preferences among menu items. They can forecast costs and margins in advance of service.

When the plan is decided upon, computer systems can make it work by ensuring that precise quantities of food are ordered and prepared. Standard recipes ensure consistent, quality products. Computer power can also handle more variables, permitting more varied and interesting menus. The result is a more satisfied clientele and minimum costs, waste, spoilage, and shrinkage. And of course computers can compare actual results effectively with the plan immediately, allowing managers to improve the planning process on a continual basis.

In order to understand how these results are obtained, it is important to understand computers, what they can and cannot do, how computers are used in foodservice, and, most important, how to evaluate and install a computer system in your operation.

THE COMPUTER EXPLOSION

There has been a recent explosion in computer technology. Computers' processing speed, information storage capacity, and ability to communicate with other computers have increased dramatically. At the same time, hardware costs have decreased, the physical size of computers has been greatly reduced, and most current models are capable of operating in any physical environment suitable for humans.

Traditionally, computers fall in three general categories: mainframes, minicomputers, and microcomputers. At one time these categories were differentiated by meaningful differences in information capacity, speed of operation, and communication ability. Over time, those distinctions have become blurred. In the future they will become even more so.

Mainframe Computers

For practical purposes, a mainframe computer is a large machine with virtually unlimited storage capacity. It can run many tasks or *programs* simultaneously. It is very fast, with the capability of processing 64 *bits* of information at one time. Mainframes were originally intended to serve the total, centralized data processing needs of large organizations, with a network of *terminals* (or keyboard and display stations) by which many users could use the machine at one time. Mainframe systems usually require a large and stable professional computer staff. Often "end users," such as the foodservice staff, merely submit information on coding forms and receive printed reports in return, never personally interacting with the computer.

Minicomputers

Minicomputers were originally developed to satisfy the needs of organizations unable to justify costly mainframe computers but that still required a centralized computer capability. They were smaller and slower, able to process 16 or 32 bits of information at one time. They could accommodate a limited number of users simultaneously. Minicomputers required a well-trained, but not necessarily professional computer staff, often limited to a single individual. They were also significantly less expensive than mainframes.

Microcomputers

Microcomputers caught the computer industry by surprise. They were originally intended as toys for home entertainment and as specialized research computers for scientists and engineers. They were small, capable of processing only 8 or 16 bits of information at one time, and had very limited storage capacity. They were also extremely limited in their ability to communicate with other computers. Yet, they were very inexpensive.

Small businesses and entrepreneurial computer programmers were quick to take advantage of their low cost. General-purpose software, such as accounting spreadsheets and word processing systems, were perfected quickly, creating a growing demand for the "personal computer." Hardware suppliers quickly reacted with faster, more powerful hardware with greater storage capacity. A snowball effect was created, which almost daily offered less expensive, better computers and a great variety of good, affordable programs for special applications in business, science, education, and entertainment.

The only element missing was a lack of standardization. Systems differed greatly and were not compatible with each other. Programs could run on only one type of microcomputer. Different microcomputers could not talk—or communicate—with each other.

IBM standardized the microcomputer industry with the introduction of its Personal Computer in 1982. Recognizing IBM's dominance in the computer industry, most hardware manufacturers and software suppliers began developing equipment and programs that were compatible with IBM systems. The result has been a new age for computer users. Microcomputers have changed everyone's notions of computers and how they can be used. Small, inexpensive computers now have more speed, storage capacity, and communications ability than many mainframes of 20 years ago. They are also extremely simple to operate. No longer are all of an organization's computer applications put on a large centralized computer. Computer applications are becoming increasingly decentralized, putting control directly into the hands of the end user. Information that must be shared among the organization's computers is transmitted over cables or telephone lines.

The Computer Environment Today

The result of the microcomputer explosion has been reduced cost, more user control, faster turnaround of information (the time between entering information and obtaining reports), and generally greater efficiency.

The distinctions between mainframes, minicomputers, and microcomputers have become almost meaningless. Computer hardware decisions are currently being made almost exclusively on what applications are needed by the individual user department. Many departments, including foodservice, devote several inexpensive "micros" to different purposes. Placing all of one's "computer eggs" in one basket is no longer desirable or economically necessary in most cases.

WHAT A COMPUTER IS

Regardless of what type or size of computer you are considering, it is important to understand what a computer is, how it works, and what its limitations are.

At best, a computer is a mindless calculator. It can do only what it is instructed to do by the software, another name for the programs written by computer programmers. Yet, computers are incredibly fast and accurate and very reliable. They seldom make mistakes. In contrast, computer programmers often make mistakes. Despite the best testing procedures, computer programs of even moderate complexity *all* contain bugs, or errors. As the software industry matures, the number of errors will be reduced. However, in terms of cost-benefit relationships in testing (for both developers and users who must pay for development), there is a level of diminishing returns. "Bugs" will always exist.

Computers are not a substitute for human judgment. The judgment of the individuals who design the programs is reflected in what the system can do and how it does it. The judgment of the managers who use the system determines how well the system serves the real-life needs of the foodservice. Used properly, the computer is an enormous resource for gathering, processing, scheduling, and routing information to help manage the foodservice.

WHAT A COMPUTER IS NOT

Human beings have an extraordinary ability to solve problems and make decisions. To an extent, computers can be taught to duplicate the standard decision-making process we use, to solve repetitive problems. Yet, the value of the experienced foodservice manager is judgment, which computers do not have at all. They merely analyze and present information that managers then use to plan and to evaluate the probable effects of various planning alternatives. When managers select an acceptable plan, computers can carry it out in precise detail, identifying potential problems to resolve.

New developments in computer science are creating software that has a much more sophisticated ability to make complex decisions. This field is called *artificial intelligence* (AI). In the future, the use of AI strategies will enable applications systems to "learn" from experience. An example would be a system that recognizes that a certain unit manager consistently over-estimates census forecasts. The system could quickly detect this pattern and adjust future forecasts by this individual accordingly.

However, even the best artificial intelligence techniques merely mimic fairly simple sets of prearranged decisions. Human control and judgment are, and always will be, the critical elements in every computer system.

COMPUTER SOFTWARE

Computer software is simply a detailed set of instructions that tells the computer what to do under all of the conditions it will reasonably encounter. Your software determines precisely what can and cannot be done with the computer. It is also the *interface* with the computer. It determines how the computer is told what to do and how the results of computer operations are reported. How well and easily the software allows this two-way interchange of information to occur determine how *user-friendly* the system is.

Computer software comes in several levels. The *operating system* controls the housekeeping of the system. It allows the user to bring *application programs* into action. These are the programs that perform the specific work or applications of the system. Applications programs can be written in any one of literally hundreds of languages.

Programming languages are shorthand systems that allow programmers to code complex activities with a minimum of instructions. All are designed to simplify programming for specialized purposes, such as business, scientific calculations, etc. A good, well-supported application program will require no user knowledge of programming languages and very little knowledge of operating systems. The point of all good computer software is to accomplish the desired activities of the system with as little complexity for the users as possible.

Which Comes First?

It is important to realize that without software, the computer is an empty box. It can do nothing.

A common error among prospective computer users is the selection of computer hardware without the assurance that applications software exists that will operate on that equipment. Even when an organization's programmers intend to develop foodservice software in-house, it is prudent to select a computer that will operate commercially available software as well. Most organizations correctly select applications software first. Typically, this selection limits the hardware alternatives available. Usually, however, a range of cost-effective alternatives are still available from which to choose. Without prior selection of software, there is no assurance that any given computer will provide any software alternatives whatsoever.

Hardware can usually be purchased "off the shelf" in relatively short order. Software can take years to develop, should that option become necessary.

BECOMING COMPUTERIZED

When correctly selected, installed, and managed, computer systems can change the complexion of the foodservice management function considerably. The results are less pencil pushing, fewer crises, and more time to plan and innovate. Initially, however, management will encounter major overhead costs in time and money required to plan for and select a system, install it, and establish operating policies.

The time dedicated to these activities is worthwhile. Computer systems are expensive in terms of hardware and software costs and staffing commitments. Without sufficient planning, computerization can be an expensive mistake. The planning process will also result in a better understanding of the foodservice, where it excels, and where it needs help. Independently of the system selection, this process is always worthwhile.

Before Acquisition

Before acquiring a computer system, it is always necessary to follow these ten steps.

1. Analyze your foodservice thoroughly; know where you are weak and where you are strong.

2. Determine the proposed role of the computer in your foodservice.
3. Locate prospective computer software and hardware suppliers.
4. Evaluate the software alternatives in view of your needs.
5. Select appropriate software that will grow with you.
6. Evaluate and select compatible hardware.
7. Define the prospective roles and responsibilities of each key individual in the foodservice. Make these individuals *accountable* for their roles.
8. Establish measurable goals and checkpoints.
9. Document expected costs and reasonable benefits.
10. Sell the plan to your management.

At this point, the benefits, costs, and potential risks of computerization should be clear to the manager. It is also at this point that the manager should consider whether or not the foodservice is ready for computers. If it is not, nothing has been lost. The process of evaluating the foodservice itself will usually result in practical ideas for improvement.

Installation

The installation of a major computer system is a difficult period for the foodservice department. It is a one-time process, with individuals playing new roles in the foodservice and adjusting to new ways of doing things. Entering massive amounts of critical information—the *database*—into the new system is also necessary during this period, regardless of the specific applications being installed.

From a human resource point of view, it is important that all employees are completely familiar with what they must contribute to the system and what the system will provide them in return. Sample reports and forms should be used where possible in this education and training process.

The steps in installing systems vary somewhat, but usually involve the following elements:

- scheduling of all activities
- training employees in both hardware and software use
- building the database; for instance, food ingredients and standard recipes
- implementing the system step-by-step (unit-by-unit, in multiple-unit operations), accommodating the experience and background of the staff
- assigning and enforcing clear accountability, distinguishing between "start-up" and continuing responsibilities

- documenting procedures and performance standards
- shaking out the bugs

Things inevitably go wrong during the installation of a computer system. It is wise to anticipate this and maintain manual back-up procedures until confidence is established. In any event, do not panic. Establish contingency plans so that panic is unnecessary. Hope for the best but plan for the worst.

Operational Control

Once in place, tested, and familiar, computer systems can create a very favorable environment for both management and the foodservice staff.

Traditional foodservice management operates in a climate of educated approximation. Roles, expectations, and performance standards are often ambiguous. A disproportionate amount of time is spent fighting fires. In contrast, computer-aided management tolerates very little ambiguity. Responsibility must be clear-cut. A single individual must be responsible for each piece of information that goes into the system. By the same token, individuals must act on the basis of information produced by the computer, exactly and precisely. Management must enforce the accurate and consistent use of the system. In this environment of *correct* information, problems and successes become glaringly evident through *exception reports*. This standard computer management technique identifies results in summary form for management *except* when those results are abnormal. By this means, detailed management intervention is restricted to areas where it is necessary. Unnecessary paper work is largely eliminated.

Results are relatively easy to measure. Persistent problems are relatively easy to identify and resolve. Standards are measurable and roles are clear. Successfully computerized operations are generally less stressful than their traditional counterparts. Employee evaluation is meaningful and constructive.

Over time, the control loop—planning, performing, reviewing, and revising the plan—becomes tighter for the foodservice as a whole and the individuals in it.

The Traditional Role of Foodservice in the Organization

In many organizations, foodservice has been considered a necessary, but low-priority service function. Fortunately, enlightened management is increasingly understanding the major role that foodservice can play in employee job satisfaction. Employees induced to eat on the premises also work more productive hours than employees who eat off-premises.

Proper nutrition is also being linked to on-the-job productivity. Corporations are finding that they can provide nutritious, attractive menus in a pleasant environment and enhance profits in the process. Employee foodservice subsidization is common and increasing.

Computers can achieve the goals of providing nutritious meals to more employees by allowing expanded menus, reduced costs, and nutritionally analyzed menus.

Uninformed corporate managements, and unfortunately some foodservice managers themselves, often assume foodservice to be an entirely intuitive process. They have difficulty understanding food production as a complex manufacturing process involving thousands of variables and dynamic costing. They consequently find it hard to believe that computer management tools have a place in foodservice. In reality, food production is an ideal application for sophisticated management information and control systems. Their cost-effective performance has been successfully demonstrated in a wide variety of foodservice types and sizes. Any area of foodservice may be enhanced by computer controls.

COMPUTER APPLICATIONS IN
FOODSERVICE MANAGEMENT

There is almost no limit to what computer systems can accomplish for a foodservice. Any process or procedure that can be completely defined can be programmed for computer control. The key questions regarding which applications (functions to be controlled) should be computerized are related to costs and benefits. Careful analysis can accurately identify the costs of computerization. Benefits are sometimes harder to measure. Food cost savings are fairly predictable. Improved labor productivity is harder to forecast, but can be approximated. Other factors, such as improved menu quality and service, can be difficult to assess in terms of dollar value. Planning for computer controls should concentrate first on those areas most likely to yield a clear *payback* or those areas identified as trouble spots for management.

Implementation should be conservative. Rather than attempting to computerize the entire operation at once, it is usually wise to adopt a flexible, *phased* implementation approach. Key applications should be installed, tested, and perfected in sequence. Planning, however, should be done on a long-range basis. This is particularly important in the selection of hardware that can accommodate systems applications for several years.

This section briefly describes applications that are currently being successfully managed with computer controls. Technological developments are proceeding so rapidly that this list will likely be incomplete before it is published.

Food Production Control

The heart of food production control is two large and complex databases—food ingredients and standard recipes. The food ingredient database, commonly referred to as the food ingredient file or inventory file, comprises basic information about each ingredient used by the foodservice operation, including the name of the item, preferred vendors, costs, purchase units, inventory units, issue units, and conversion factors. Many of today's computer systems for foodservice management come with a large and fairly complete food inventory file, eliminating much of the data entry burden of getting started.

This database and the ability to update, add to, and delete items from it easily are critical to both food production control and inventory management. Standard recipes are the key to effective production and cost controls. The accuracy and degree of control provided by computer systems are proportional to the accuracy of the information provided to them. Recipes must be formulated precisely and adhered to in the kitchen. Failure to enforce this policy in a computerized operation will result in overproduction, waste, inconsistent product, inventory shortages (when a cook estimates, it is almost never an underestimate), and meaningless costing projections. Enforcing standard recipe use will yield the payoffs of greatly reduced food costs, minimum waste, accurate accounting, and streamlined, efficient inventory control.

Building a database of standard recipes is the most tedious and difficult chore in implementing a cost and production control system. It can and usually does take months of dedicated data entry and recipe formulation. Some suppliers can provide "precoded" standard recipe files, including some of the best-known quantity cookbooks. With minimal adjustments, these databases can be used almost immediately. The foodservice can then add its own recipes in a relatively leisurely fashion.

Recipe Costing

Recipe portion costs—the key to effective menu planning—can be calculated in minutes for all of a large institution's recipes. Most systems provide a simple means of changing portion sizes as well. Some provide automatic cash-pricing calculations, complete with profit margins, based on current ingredient costs and the foodservice's own mark-up criteria.

Recipe Extensions

Many computer systems are available that automatically extend recipes from whatever portion count is indicated in the "standard" recipe to whatever portion count is needed for kitchen production forecasts. These systems can be very simple or elegant. A point of controversy in all recipe extension programs is how units of measure are presented for cooks. Cooks normally approximate amounts when ingredient amounts are presented in decimals or in units not normally used in the kitchen. The only sure way to determine how effective these conversions are is to examine a random sampling of extended recipes. The best systems allow great flexibility in units of measure.

Systems should operate the way that foodservices do. Some recipes are either not tested or are not valid above or below a specific yield. Kitchen equipment constraints may also limit the amount that can be prepared at one time. Some recipe extension programs automatically "batch" recipes. These systems indicate the recipe for a main batch, as well as how many times it should be prepared. They also provide the recipe for the "remainder" batch.

Some spices and ingredients do not extend in linear fashion. That is, doubling the recipe may not require doubling the spicing. A small number of current systems have formulas for "nonlinear" ingredients that do not extend at the same rate as other ingredients. An alternative method of dealing with this problem is to "batch" the recipe extension in sizes for which "linear" spicing is valid.

Centralized Production

Recipe extensions in a centralized production environment can be dealt with very efficiently through computer controls. Centralized production falls into two basic categories: (1) a single kitchen producing food for more than one service area and (2) multiple kitchens in which some food preparation is always handled in a specific kitchen or food preparation area.

Sophisticated systems aggregate or combine recipes for the same items into a single larger recipe and print a distribution report, indicating the serving location(s) or other kitchen(s) to which finished products will be delivered and how much will go to each. In some cases, interdepartment or transfer costing mark-ups may be automatically applied to items produced in one kitchen for use in another.

Advanced systems also produce itemized production summaries, listing all items to be prepared and their quantity, and "picklists," indicating in issue units precisely how much food must be retrieved from storage locations to satisfy production requirements for the meal or day.

Cook-Chill

The emergence of cook-chill and cook-freeze strategies for food preparation has added a new level of complexity to the management of centralized food production. Yet, the potential benefits of these types of production are enormous.

By preparing food in large quantities and holding it in a nearly finished state for rethermalization, the utilization of production facilities is maximized. Labor and energy costs are dramatically reduced. Mandates for cost consciousness in the noncommercial sector of the foodservice industry suggest that the use of cook-chill and cook-freeze strategies will increase.

From a management perspective, inventories of perishable finished product with a limited shelf-life must be monitored and controlled. In addition to managing "external" (from a production point of view) inventories of ingredients, "internal" inventories must be monitored and controlled.

Production forecasts must evaluate chilled or frozen product on hand against total needs and production straight from the kitchen. Finished product must be used within its shelf-life or discarded as waste. Because of the typically large scale of these operations and the number of service operations they supply, the complexity of distribution is greatly increased.

Generally, the complexity of large-scale cook-chill and cook-freeze operations requires computer controls for optimal performance and maximized cost savings.

Menu Planning: Analytical Information

Planning effective menus, whether for cash operations or cost-oriented operations, requires information. This aspect of foodservice management, more than any other, requires the judgment that only experience can bring. Yet, computers can provide several categories of information that can effectively assist the experienced manager.

Menu Item Analysis

Most systems require that users organize all items that will appear on menus into *menu planning groups*. These contain items with similar characteristics in terms of their place in menu planning. "Green vegetables" or "beef entrees" are examples of menu planning groups. The items within any group are, to a degree, interchangeable on the menu. Factors that dictate whether they should be interchanged are relative client preferences and item cost (in a subsidized or cost-oriented operation) or margin (in a cash or margin-oriented operation).

Computers can list all of the items in any menu-planning group in order of increasing current portion cost, or, for cash operations, in order of decreasing portion margin. Using these reports, the menu planner moves up the list from an item whose cost is too high or whose margin is too small until a suitable replacement is located, either with a lower cost or higher margin. Computers can also automatically list all recipes using a specific ingredient, the cost of which may have risen significantly, in order to evaluate the overall effect of an ingredient substitution. Some systems automatically make that substitution in all recipes on request.

Customer Count Forecasting

For many types of foodservices, the computer can automatically forecast expected customer counts based on past trends. Care must be taken to be sure that managers at least review this information before the system is permitted to act on it. In some cases, human judgment can determine that today is not a typical day and the trend will not hold.

Although computers can be "taught" (if they are programmed to do so) the implications of special conditions, such as weather, competing events, etc., it is in most cases more cost effective to rely on the skill and judgment of experienced managers for these decisions, at least at the current state of technology.

Preference Forecasting

There are many ways to predict the relative preferences for various menu items. As with census forecasting, predictions reflect trends. The larger the customer base and the more "fixed" or unchanging the menu, the more accurate forecasts are likely to be. Again, manager experience should mediate the analysis of the computer.

Interactive Menu Planning

Interactive menu planning is a fairly new concept. Advanced foodservice management systems permit the creation and *precosting* of menus on-screen.

As the planner enters the menu item, the computer displays its name, portion size, selling price, and current portion cost. The planner need only indicate the total customer count anticipated and the portion count forecast for each menu item. The computer instantly calculates and displays the total cost, sales, and margin the menu will generate, as well as the cost, sales, and margin per customer. The effect of each menu addition is known immediately. Changes can be made until the menu meets all of the financial criteria of the specific serving unit, using the analytical tools discussed previously. Obviously, this form of menu planning has applicability beyond standard production planning. Catering operations, for instance, can construct and accurately cost and price menus for clients during a short telephone conversation.

Advanced systems allow a virtually unlimited number of menus to be created and stored for reference and action. Each menu may be broken down into several *meal zones* per day and may be extended for a cycle length of up to several weeks. Some systems even permit word processing-type "cut and paste" features for copying all or part of existing menus and/or recipes to speed the planning process. Some costed menus may be stored for comparison with future menus to examine the overall effects of food cost changes over time. Completed menus may be reported in detailed daily printed consolidations that analyze the financial implications of the planned menu in great depth. Menus can be strategically created in a short period of time, with very accurate cost analysis in advance of service.

The accuracy of the menu-planning process with management tools of this power increases over time. Experienced managers operating in a tightly controlled cost environment can consistently meet financial goals within 1/2 or 1 percent on a monthly basis and immediately accommodate revised financial constraints.

Fully featured systems use selected menus for a number of automated procedures. They analyze the planned menus for all serving units and automatically schedule and print kitchen production summaries, extended recipes, storeroom picklists, and advance preparation and withdrawal lists. They also analyze vendor order and delivery schedules and report how much of which food ingredients to order from which vendor on which day to ensure that precisely the correct amount of food is on hand to satisfy the food production demands of all kitchens. Systems with perpetual inventory management capabilities use order requirements to generate purchase orders automatically, and use picklists to generate issues, both with manager review.

Menu Engineering

Menu engineering is a term created by Michael Kassavanas at Michigan State University and Don Smith at Washington State University. It identifies menu items based on their financial contributions to the foodservice and their popularity to customers. Obviously, the ideal menu consists of nothing but high margin, popular items. Real life, as every experienced foodservice manager is aware, is a good deal more complicated. B&I foodservice management has increasingly moved toward commercial foodservice techniques in terms of providing exciting, attractively presented menus in a pleasant environment. The goal, of course, is to attract employees to the foodservice and to enhance the quality of the work environment. At the same time, financial criteria provide constraints to operation, whether on a break-even, subsidized, or income-producing basis.

In a commercial environment with a relatively fixed and modest menu, menu engineering can be practiced manually with a high level of success. In a large and varied B&I environment, with cycle menus and multiple-serving locations and styles of service, the process is prohibitively complex.

Computer systems, with their ability to analyze and present large numbers of complex variables based on criteria of preference, cost, and margin, can provide B&I foodservice managers with the tools to use these techniques effectively. The bottom line is effective foodservice, with a menu that both serves patron satisfaction and financial accountability well.

Postcosting

In postcost analysis actual customer counts and menu items prepared and used are entered into the computer. The computer then provides detailed consolidations and summaries of daily production results, including food usage. It also compares forecasted to actual results as a means of making timely refinements to planned menus. This continuing feedback results in continually improving performance. For users of preference and customer-census forecasting, this postservice input also provides the database that the system uses to make future forecasts. The best of today's computer systems put control of the foodservice directly into the hands of management. Planned, precosted menus form the basis of a tightly controlled, efficient, and predictable foodservice.

Point-of-Sale Systems

Electronic cash registers differ widely in their capabilities and the manner in which they operate. Some are "intelligent," with a degree of built-in computer processing ability and memory. Others are "dumb," performing only clearly defined activities. Most intelligent point-of-sale registers have some ability to communicate with computers.

Communicating registers can be connected to a central computer to provide valuable management information immediately after a meal period. A centrally located manager can produce an analysis of menu sales mix for any meal period for any serving unit. Reports and summaries traditionally extracted from register tapes can also be collected, analyzed, and reported in meaningful format by the computer. This information includes much of the data required for postcosting purposes as well and can be communicated directly to some food cost and production control systems without data re-entry. Where this type of system is feasible, it represents the ultimate in immediate feedback.

Perpetual Inventory Management

Systems are available that are specifically designed to manage foodservice inventories. They can be used as *stand-alone* systems, with the sole purpose of managing inventories, or they can be used as an integrated part of a larger foodservice management system. Computers can greatly simplify inventory management and reduce the time necessary to perform and extend physical inventories.

Computer systems can print *inventory tally sheets* sorted in the order that the inventory is stored. Inventory takers need only fill in quantities; the computer then automatically extends them, based on any of a number of cost criteria. The computer also analyzes and reports the variance between actual and calculated inventories.

In the near future, physical inventories may become paperless, with inventory takers keying product codes and quantities into a hand-held terminal that will transmit the information to the computer via FM radio or by plugging the terminal into the host computer. For organizations requiring parstocking, the computer can monitor inventory levels and automatically generate purchase order indicators in specified reorder quantities, coordinating these with stocks committed to food production.

Warehouse management is analogous to centralized food production in terms of inventory systems. Basically, the computer system treats warehouses as master inventories or vendors for other foodservice storage locations, tracking the movement of inventories from warehouse to production storage areas. They can even be instructed to apply user-defined mark-ups to items moved from the warehouse to local storage locations.

The increasing power of full-featured foodservice management systems is bringing the entire philosophy of perpetual inventory management into question. In traditional foodservice, inventories are necessarily overstocked to a degree to accommodate approximations in meeting production demands. For this reason, turnover factors, the number of times in a given period that the average value of food on hand is replaced, are relatively low. The precision of today's computer systems, the degree of control they provide, and their sophisticated scheduling abilities allow inventory on hand to be reduced to an absolute minimum. Turnovers may increase by a factor of four or more as food is delivered on the loading dock and processed to the serving area in the least time possible. In this environment, the costs of maintaining a total perpetual inventory usually outweigh the benefits. Maintaining tight inventory controls on selected high-ticket items may be a cost-effective compromise to traditional inventory management practices. With the ability to postcost the food production process that computer systems provide, the primary accounting justification for maintaining unwieldy perpetual management systems may also be obsolete.

For operations maintaining complex warehouse operations in which perpetual inventory management is a necessary control practice, computers can dramatically reduce the labor and clerical requirements of maintaining them.

Bid Analysis

A recent development in foodservice management systems technology is the introduction of programs to evaluate various purchasing strategies. There are many different purchasing styles and strategies: prime vendor, brand preference, limited numbers of vendors, "cherry picking" (choosing least-cost items individually), etc.

The problem of optimum mix—what overall strategy will result in least cost—is beyond human abilities to calculate. Computers can simulate the results of differing strategies quickly, helping managers evaluate their implications. The effectiveness of these systems in reducing costs has surprised even their designers, introducing a major new area of control for foodservice.

Trend Analysis

All foodservices are intimately interested in food cost trends. Very large organizations even practice "hedging" or securing the rights to buy food in the future at a specified price. The aim of hedging for most organizations is not so much to gamble on windfalls as it is to ensure that food prices will be predictable.

Trend analysis of various types can be performed quite easily by computers. Many organizations store "costed" menus at various points in time to study the long-range effects of overall price changes. Others cost out a "market basket" of representative foods for recurrent study. The process is certainly not a crystal ball but, combined with experience, can be a significant aid in planning, particularly in pricing for cash operations.

Corporate Wellness Programs

Nutritionally adequate menus are a necessity in B&I foodservice operations. Many inexpensive computer systems are on the market that provide perfectly adequate nutritional analyses of recipes and even menus.

Nutritional analysis is an affordable computer application for nearly every foodservice. It is valuable, not only in helping guide and improve the health of the customer but also as an inexpensive public relations gesture that will contribute to the image of the corporation as a whole and the foodservice specifically.

Yet, corporate foodservice is beginning to extend beyond nutritional adequacy. Increasingly, special menus are being offered that cater to a health-conscious clientele and to executives, employees, and staff on a nutritionally balanced weight reduction or maintenance diet. Some systems are so flexible and easy to use that they encourage diet counseling as a service or simply as an employee benefit; these systems maintain dietary goals for individuals and compare them to the employees' average dietary intake. At the very least, these programs can print a nutritional analysis of food being served for customer review.

Accounting Applications

Foodservice has the same accounting requirements as any other business enterprise, with few substantial differences. Some full-featured foodservice management systems have integrated accounting features, such as operating and financial statements, accounts payable and receivable, etc. However, most organizations have firmly established computer applications that perform these services, as well as payroll activities.

For foodservices without these resources that want to run these applications, there are software packages suitable for nearly every variety of computer hardware. A number of very flexible and reliable general-purpose spreadsheet systems are available as well at a relatively low cost.

Labor Productivity

Foodservice, with its large pool of labor resources and irregular scheduling demands, has distinct labor management problems. Computer systems can automate and analyze labor requirements, identifying least-cost staffing strategies and ensuring complete coverage.

Systems are in development that allow "intelligent" timeclocks to communicate with computers in integrated time and attendance control systems. Eventually, these systems will allow labor scheduling and analysis, control and monitoring of clocking in and clocking out, and payroll processing in a single system. In large operations, this type of control will more than pay for itself in time measurement accuracy of fractions of minutes. The benefits of computer analysis of labor utilization in this environment will result in even more significant savings.

Other System Applications

There is no limit to the efficiencies that computer systems can provide to foodservice management. Other related applications are numerous.

Room and event scheduling can be a major problem, particularly for foodservices maximizing resources and other income by exploring catering opportunities. Systems are available that do room and event scheduling, including generating lists of particular arrangements and reminders to perform scheduled activities. Generally, they control all of the details of physical facilities used for meetings, private dining, and related activities.

Access Control Systems are used not only to permit or deny access to restricted areas but can also verify dining privileges and automatically monitor, control, and provide billing for foodservice charge programs. Such systems, often with automatically applied payroll deductions, will become an increasingly effective means of encouraging patronage in the B&I foodservice environment.

SELECTING SYSTEMS

The availability of affordable microcomputer hardware has created a market for software systems serving foodservice applications. The foodservice software industry has become very competitive. As a result, the quality and usefulness of systems currently available are now very high.

The prospective buyer can afford to be critical. When examining any type of software, ask these questions of the supplier.

• How easy is the software to use? Does it require instructions or can activities be selected from lists of options or *menus*? Does it have a "Help" feature in which a keystroke will display an explanation of what is being done and how to do it? How complete is the documentation? Is it in clear, plain English?
• How useful and clear are reports and display screens?
• Is the software flexible? Are methods built into the system to "customize" it to the way you operate without additional programming? Will it allow growth and change in methods of operation?
• Are various systems functions integrated? That is, do individual programs share databases automatically, or must data be re-entered?
• How comprehensive is the software? It may not be intended to handle a broad range of activities, but how completely does it serve its intended purpose?
• How secure is the system? Does it provide password security? Does it allow management to provide different systems privileges to different categories of users or even individual users?
• How well supported is it? What happens when something goes wrong and under what conditions? Is there a trial period?

For relatively simple, inexpensive software systems, the answers to these questions should provide sufficient information to make a buying decision. For systems being considered for "self-development," either by the organization's own computer department or a custom programming organization, the same basic questions apply.

With more complex, expensive systems, the stakes for foodservice management are much higher and the evaluation much more complex. See Appendix 15-A for a checklist of elements to evaluate in major software systems.

THE HUMAN FACTOR

No discussion of computers in foodservice is complete without some consideration of people—*all* levels of people in the foodservice.

From the point of view of enlightened management theory, people are the most valuable asset of any enterprise. They need to be informed, nurtured, motivated, and encouraged. From a purely pragmatic point of view, dissatisfied, insecure employees, at even the lowest levels, can and *have* destroyed the effectiveness of computer systems.

It is important that managers responsible for installing computer systems understand fully the roles and relationships of people and computers. The first important point to understand, believe, and pass along to employees is that COMPUTERS DO NOT REPLACE PEOPLE. Rather, computer systems provide people with the resources to do their jobs better. Properly used, they will make those jobs more rewarding, less ambiguous, and less stressful. A foodservice staff that fully understands these points well in advance of implementation will usually contribute enthusiastically to the project. There are proven methods for gaining this acceptance.

Employee Orientation: Conditioning

"Conditioning" employees to operations in a computer-assisted environment is a delicate matter. Because it is natural for employees to feel some insecurity and ambiguity about their roles in the postcomputer phase of operations, it is important to solicit their advice and consultation at every step of the planning process: spring no surprises. Define clearly to all employees what the computer will mean to their jobs. What information must they provide for the system and in what form? What information will they get back? What will it look like? What will they do with it? How will it make their jobs easier? Emphasize the importance of each individual to the total system operation. Although it is valuable to explain the general operation of the entire system so that employees can appreciate their role in the process, it is generally best to keep detailed explanations limited to each individual's assigned function. Too much detail can be intimidating.

One effective sequence of orientation events begins with a general presentation of the proposed system to all affected personnel. At this meeting, individuals can be shown where they fit into the process. Next, working sessions are held with individuals, or with small groups holding similar responsibilities, to go over appropriate reports, forms, and responsibilities in detail. Finally, the group as a whole meets to integrate their individual areas of responsibility into a total system management and control team. These sessions are especially valuable for identifying "holes" in the organization and revising responsibilities. In practice, several meetings, formal and informal, are needed before responsibilities are completely identified and workloads are evenly distributed.

One major result of this educational process, in addition to accomplishing the reorganization, will be a sense of ownership by the employees on the "computer team." It will become their project, and they will make it work. They will hold a set of realistic expectations about responsibilities, accountability, interdepartmental relationships, benefits and, just as important, anticipated problems.

Good computer systems result in more manageable, satisfying jobs in foodservice. Consultative planning, such as involving cooks in the recipe standardization process, can transform a potentially traumatic experience into enthusiastic acceptance.

Phased Implementation

Most large computer systems consist of several parts. Regardless of how motivated employees are, too much new responsibility at one time can overwhelm and discourage them. It is best to keep scheduling flexible and plan to have one aspect of the computer operation running smoothly before attempting the next step. Good managers have a good understanding of their employees' capabilities. Involve the best people in the foodservice first. Earn and nurture their enthusiasm. Listen to their feedback and be flexible. Let them help sell the system to their peers.

Management can install a computer system. However, employees will determine how well it performs its function.

SUMMARY

Computer technology can be a servant or a master. It is evolving so rapidly that it is no longer enough to know the state-of-the-art. It is also necessary to know where computer technology is headed. Foodservice managers who have done their homework will benefit enormously from computer-assisted management. The process boils down to a few simple points of understanding.

- Know what is needed.
- Know what is available.
- Know what *will* be needed.
- Know what *will* be available.
- Know the potential financial and psychological effects on the organization as a whole and the foodservice specifically.

Finally, after having investigated foodservice management systems thoroughly, do not be afraid to say "no." Some foodservices—even *good* ones—are not ready for computers. Through the process of investigation, the foodservice will have a greater understanding of itself and how it can be improved, with or without computers. The basic groundwork will have been done when the time *is* right.

Appendix 15-A

Selecting Computer Systems for Foodservice Management

The acquisition of a complex and expensive computer system is a major long-range project. These systems, depending on their complexity and the hardware necessary to operate them, may cost anywhere from $3,000 to $250,000 or more.

The right computer system in the right foodservice can have dramatic effects in terms of cost savings, improved and expanded service, and increased employee productivity. A poor or ill-considered choice could impair the effectiveness of the organization. Choosing a computer system is sometimes known as a "career decision" for foodservice managers for obvious reasons. The appropriate amount of time to allocate to the project depends entirely on the stakes: the potential benefits and the real costs. Caveat emptor.

Use this outline in guiding your way through the decision-making process.
I. Know *your* organization well.
   A. Review your structure, organization, and people critically.
      1. What do you do well?
      2. What do you *not* do well?
      3. Where are you slipping? Why?
      4. Where do you need help?
      5. Are your procedures standardized?
      6. What quality of people do you employ in what positions?
   B. Prioritize your needs.
      1. Determine short-term versus long-term.

    2. Determine probability of high returns versus marginal gains.
    3. Determine realistic versus "blue sky."
    4. Determine "needs" versus "wants."

II. Get your house in order.

  A. A poorly organized and/or managed foodservice is not a good candidate for computer-based management controls.

  B. Computer applications magnify the problems of an out-of-control foodservice.

  C. If tangible gains cannot be reasonably expected by installing computer controls—either in the short run or near future—hold off. Don't fix it if it ain't broke.

III. Analyze your needs and your goals.

  A. Write up your ideal plan for technologically assisted management control.

  B. Do not publicize the plan at first. Your understanding of what is possible, and even what is *desirable*, will change during the course of your investigations.

IV. Investigate what is available.

  A. Locate software suppliers.
    1. Inquire among colleagues.
    2. Contact the various foodservice associations in your own and related industries.

  B. Request and evaluate the product literature, including report samples.

  C. Ask for and attend a system demonstration at a client site if possible.
    1. *Perform* some simple computer activities if it can be arranged.
    2. Review the client's documentation.
    3. Take a systems operator or unit manager to lunch.

  D. Obtain a list of system users you can contact.
    1. Create a checklist of questions.
    2. Call the users and take notes.
    3. Determine which features are in use and which are not and why.
    4. Call back if necessary; you will have more and better questions after speaking to a few users.

  E. Ask if you can attend a user group meeting or client training session at your cost.

  F. Evaluate the following.
    1. What are the real software costs and capabilities—initial and continuing?
    2. What are the benefits indicated by suppliers and users?
    3. What are the features that are standard or "custom" or additional?

4. What are the hardware requirements, capabilities, and costs; "inside" information on service, maintenance, and reliability?

5. What is the availability of general-purpose software (e.g., spreadsheets, word processing, etc.) for the hardware and its costs?

6. What service and support are provided for the software? Review a standard contract.

7. Determine the supplier's history.
   a. How long has it been in business?
   b. How many clients does it have?
   c. What is its track record for system enhancements? What do enhancements cost you?
   d. What role do you as a client have in future development?
   e. Does it have a users group? How often do they meet and how many users attended their last meeting?

8. Investigate training.
   a. What is included and at what costs?
   b. How often is training held and where? How long does it last?
   c. How many of your people may attend?
   d. How is "remedial" training handled?

9. Determine the people with whom you will be dealing before and during installation and after the sale.

10. Consider how closely the package—software and support—suits your perceived needs.

V. Determine whether to make or buy.
   A. Determine the pros and cons of self-developed systems.
      1. Determine the development costs of a self-developed system versus amortized costs of "off-the-shelf" systems.
      2. Determine the "lost-opportunity costs." How much in savings will you lose while waiting for your own system to be developed?
      3. Determine the advantage of having a system designed precisely for your operations.
      4. Determine the disadvantage of being the *only* user of that system; there can be safety in numbers.
   B. Determine the pros and cons of "custom" systems.
      1. Investigate internally developed systems.
         a. How good is your software development group? Are you qualified to direct the project? Who will?
         b. What is their current development backlog? When can your system be delivered? Who will test it?

      c. Can they help you sort out your real needs from your perceived needs? How well do they know foodservice?

      d. Will they continue to provide advanced development and support? In a timely fashion?

      e. Where does foodservice stand in their list of day-to-day priorities?

      f. Will your system be centralized on the organization's mainframe or be within your control and operation?

      g. Who will write the documentation and provide training?

      h. What will it cost you to develop, to operate, and to maintain?

   2. Investigate externally developed systems.

      a. Locate and evaluate contract programming resources.

      b. Evaluate the same considerations as for internal development, only more carefully.

C. Investigate off-the-shelf systems.

   1. How closely do suppliers' systems match your needs?

   2. What features can you do without?

   3. What missing features are on the drawing boards? What is the track record of the supplier in meeting the development schedule? What features have been added recently?

   4. What "missing" features or applications can you get from other suppliers that will run on the same hardware?

   5. How willing are you to compromise? A good, experienced foodservice software supplier has had experience with a large number of operating, real-life foodservice systems. Test your perceived needs against what is being done by others.

VI. Develop an action plan.

A. Write the analysis.

   1. Analyze your operation.

   2. Determine the growth plan.

   3. Determine the probable effects on your people and organizational structure.

   4. Determine the probable effects on the larger organization of which your foodservice is a part.

   5. Evaluate the cost/benefit analyses.

B. Know the facts.

   1. Determine where you are.

   2. Determine where you want to be, both short-term and long-term.

   3. Determine how you intend to get there.

C. Present and sell the plan to your management.

D. Solicit specific proposals from the supplier(s) whom you have chosen as potentially acceptable.
E. Evaluate their proposals against your plan.
F. Invite finalists to make presentations to your management and to your staff.
G. Solicit the reactions of your key staff members.
H. Propose a selection to your management *if* you are satisfied that you have found a satisfactory solution.

16

Selection of Food Preparation and Service Equipment

PAUL HYSEN

During the past 30 years, Paul Hysen has earned national recognition as a foodservice specialist by creating quality effective and economically efficient foodservice programs and facilities. Although he is responsible for the overall corporate direction of The Hysen Group, he continues to remain active in individual project assignments to ensure that client needs are met. He has also lectured widely, has authored over 30 articles on foodservice issues, and has contributed to several books.

The actual performance of a corporate foodservice facility is dependent upon the proper and reliable performance of the facility's complement of mechanical and electrical foodservice equipment. The foodservice director is the individual with the greatest control over the process of selecting equipment for use in the foodservice facility.

The act of selecting and purchasing foodservice equipment is often a repeated occurrence in the typical foodservice operation. Generally, the department has a yearly budget allowance for the replacement of capital equipment items. The department also participates in periodic major renovation and enhancement programs during which a considerable amount of capital is identified for additions to and replacement of foodservice equipment.

The fact that the department's perceived success is intrinsically linked to proper equipment performance and that significant capital resources are allocated for equipment procurement requires that an equipment selection and procurement process be defined clearly to maximize the effectiveness of equipment expenditures made for foodservice equipment.

Note: Adapted from *Handbook for Health Care Food Service Management* by J.C. Rose (Ed.), pp. 177–183, Aspen Publishers, Inc., © 1984.

INDUSTRY STRUCTURAL AND ENVIRONMENTAL FACTORS

Before describing a process for equipment selection and procurement, a clear understanding of structural and environmental factors affecting the foodservice industry in general should be developed.

The typical corporate foodservice department is staffed with employees whose educational levels range from advanced degrees to technical or applied skills to little or even no formal education. Foodservice equipment is actually operated primarily by employees in the last category—those with little or no formal education. The foodservice department also acts as an entry point for many new employees who have no technical skills. Consequently, the selection process for foodservice equipment should include consideration of the type of employee who will be using each piece of equipment. Because it is quite possible that entry-level employees who possess low skill levels, low mechanical aptitudes, and a low interest level may be operating an equipment item, equipment should generally be selected on the basis of simplicity of operation and ease of employee orientation and training.

The quality of support received from the corporation's maintenance department is another factor that may significantly influence the equipment selection process. Although corporations are users of sophisticated and technically advanced equipment, this equipment is generally maintained under service contract with the manufacturer or a local service agency. In contrast, foodservice equipment is generally maintained by the maintenance division, which may or may not have the level of sophistication and quality needed for maintaining state-of-the-art equipment. Other segments of the foodservice industry similar in terms of dollar volume, such as hotels and large restaurant facilities, typically assign a full-time maintenance person or persons specifically to the foodservice component for the routine and emergency service of equipment. These types of facilities realize that income cannot be generated unless the production machinery is operational.

Other criteria for the equipment selection process should be ease of maintenance and records of high reliability. In more structured industries, such as aerospace and electronics, performance and reliability are measured in terms of "mean time between failures," and a manufacturer must provide certified data in support of this factor. We have yet to see this level of disclosure in the foodservice industry.

The foodservice equipment industry is a relatively small industry that consists of many individual specialty manufacturers. There are 500–600 companies in the United States manufacturing foodservice equipment. According to a 1982 survey of the National Association of Food Equipment

Manufacturers, more than 60 percent of these companies have sales of less than $3 million per year, which would indicate about 20 to 50 employees for the typical company. Less than 15 percent of the firms manufacturing foodservice equipment have sales greater than $10 million per year. The typical foodservice equipment company is therefore a small to medium-sized organization that has a historical and present orientation primarily to sheet metal fabrication or low-volume assembly of relatively unsophisticated components; its products have evolved through a market response process. The level of technical sophistication found in these companies is generally low, with any research activities being directed at specific applications rather than development and with a record that shows rather slow acceptance of recent technology. The low relative sales volumes for the typical foodservice manufacturing company have hindered their ability to integrate such items as microprocessors and other state-of-the-art electronics, chemical and mechanical innovations into their product line. In addition, low sales volume also suggests that most foodservice equipment manufacturers have inefficient distribution networks. Product support in terms of training, operation assistance, and service therefore varies widely according to geographic location and to the individual manufacturer's penetration in a specific area.

Small volume production, inefficient distribution networks, and construction with high-cost materials, such as stainless steel, tend to ensure high acquisition costs for a typical item of equipment. Combine these structural factors with limited capital budgets and increasingly limited space and the need to select highly productive, reliable equipment is even more apparent.

EQUIPMENT SELECTION PROCESS

A logical process can be described that will provide structure and guidance to the equipment selection process (Figure 16-1).

Functional Characteristics

The process starts with a macro-level definition of the item or items of equipment to be purchased. The first level of definition is rather straightforward; it identifies the generic item of equipment being considered, such as a dishwasher, a steam kettle, or a mixer. The next level of definition introduces the first real set of decisions to be made. This decision group requires that the primary and secondary purpose of the item of equipment be described, thus identifying the degree of flexibility that is desired and

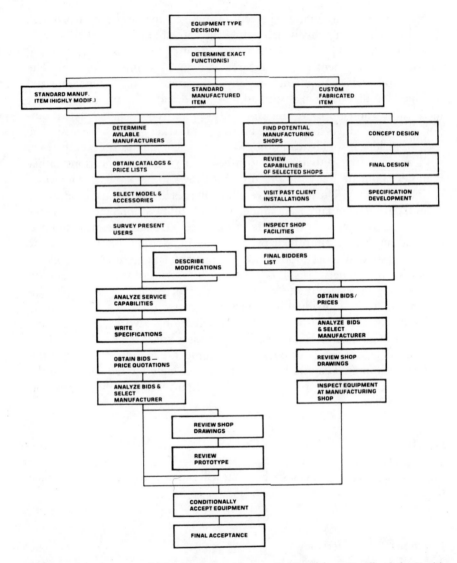

Figure 16-1 Equipment and Selection Process. *Source:* Reprinted from *Handbook for Health Care Food Service Management* by J.C. Rose (Ed.), p. 179, Aspen Publishers, Inc., © 1984.

the multiplicity of functions that should be performed. Is the unit to be strictly a mixer with a capacity of 60 quarts, or should the unit also have the capability to operate accessory equipment for slicing, dicing, and grinding functions? The more general purpose or the more flexible and multifunctioned a unit is, the less efficient it is for any one of the given functions. Thus, it behooves the selection team to weigh carefully the range of functions needed to be performed and the degree of specific dedication necessary for the equipment.

Another early consideration that is closely associated with the flexibility/ multiple use issue is the question of mobility or portability. Will the item of equipment be used in more than one location? Will it be used only during specific periods of the day? Does it have sanitation or cleaning requirements that would be enhanced by making the unit portable? There are both desirable and undesirable aspects to making a unit portable. Portability adds to the equipment cost, increases the maintenance requirements because of the installation of casters, and decreases the stability of the item because casters will never provide as rigid a mounting platform as a unit permanently secured to the building structure.

The requirements for flexibility and multiplicity of use also imply a commonality of various identifiable and definable criteria for a particular item of equipment. Does this item of equipment fit into an overall system, and thus are there size restrictions that need to be considered? If the item in question is a food transportation cart, will it be mated with other carts for transport or will it need facilities so that it can be secured in an over-the-road vehicle? Will this cart fit within a roll-in refrigerator? If the item of equipment is a tray-cart or a serving unit, tray sizes and pan sizes must be considered. Should the cart accommodate 18″ × 26″ bun sheets, 14″ × 18″ trays, 15″ × 20″ trays, 12″ × 20″ cafeteria pans, 20″ × 20″ baskets, or all of the above?

Standard versus Custom-Made Equipment

Another early and significant decision to be made is whether the item should be selected from a catalogue (i.e., that it be a standard, readily available item), or should it be custom-designed to meet a specific set of criteria. For certain items, this question does not present a problem. Ranges, fryers, steam cookers, and kettles are, in all but rare instances, purchased as standard catalogue items. In many cases, they may be custom tailored or highly modified or extensively accessorized, but they are still basically a manufacturer's standard model.

Work tables, service counters, cafeteria counters, carts, exhaust hoods and walk-in refrigerators do present a definite choice. A cafeteria serving counter or a hot food cart can either be selected from a manufacturer's catalogue or may be custom designed and fabricated.

Two popular misconceptions affect this decision. First, a picture in a catalogue may infer that an article of equipment is a manufacturer's "standard," presumably a readily available item. However, in reality it may only indicate that it has been manufactured at least once before and it may not actually be an in-stock item. Low production volume, as previously mentioned, suggests low, or in most cases, no inventory. Upon receipt of a confirmed order, the manufacturer will schedule the "standard" item of equipment for fabrication and assembly. Thus, a standard catalogue item of equipment may be nothing more than a custom-fabricated item built to a manufacturer's standard design, rather than to a design that perhaps suits your specific purpose better.

The other common misconception is that custom-fabricated equipment costs significantly more than standard catalogue equipment items. This may or may not be true and depends on the type of equipment considered. Certainly, to custom design and build a two-door reach-in refrigerator will result in a cost higher than purchasing a high-quality standard unit and with no increase in utility gained. Yet, if the item primarily consists of sheet metal or wood construction and has relatively simple mechanical and electrical components—for example, cafeteria serving counters or a cook's work table—then there may be a little or no difference in cost between a standard catalogue unit and a custom-designed and built unit. Custom-built equipment can even be lower in price than standard catalogue units because the item may be specifically tailored to meet your exact needs. If more than one item needs to be purchased—for example, if six identical portable work tables or a quantity of ten condiment stands are to be purchased—consideration may be given to obtaining price quotations for both a standard manufactured unit and a custom-manufactured unit. In this manner, a decision need not be made until the comparative analysis includes data concerning the exact price for either premise.

Equipment Procurement Sources

Regardless of whether the item of equipment will be selected from a catalogue or will be custom manufactured, the range of procurement sources must be identified. A number of methods and materials can be used in this process. Foodservice equipment dealers in the immediate geographical area may be contacted for information concerning available manufacturers for standard manufactured equipment items or custom manufacturing shops. Leading publications in the foodservice industry, food processing industry, and bakery industry typically publish yearly "buyers' guides" that categorize equipment by type and provide listings of manufacturer's names and addresses. Local, regional, and national trade shows are another excellent source of information not only on the range of available manufacturers for an item of equipment but also on state-of-the-art concerning the specific item type being considered.

Because the foodservice equipment industry is relatively small in relation to other consumer equipment industries, it has not seen the development of an unbiased consumer-oriented equipment evaluation and testing service. This deficiency does not obviate the use of the excellent consumer information service already in place that is provided by local, regional, national, and international associations of foodservice professionals, such as the Society for Foodservice Management (SFM).

Any evaluation process should include discussions with present and past users of the equipment being considered and, in the case of custom-fabricated equipment, in-depth discussions with present users of equipment constructed by prospective manufacturers. The evaluation process should also include on-site inspection at representative installations of both standard-manufactured and custom-fabricated equipment items. The on-site inspection process is particularly relevant in the case of complicated equipment items or systems or of mechanically or electrically intensive custom-fabricated equipment. Conveyor systems, exhaust ventilation systems, and food processing equipment would fall into this category. Much valuable information on performance, reliability and the manufacturer's continuing interest, support, and service can be obtained through on-site visits and telephone conversations with present users.

Equipment Specifications

The quality of any item of equipment is determined by more than the strength or weight of material used in its construction. Quality is as much a subjective evaluation as it is an objective evaluation process. Two manufacturers may both use 18-gauge stainless steel in the construction of a dish transportation cart. Both may use the same type, quality, and manufacturer of casters on their units. However, there may be wide differences between the way the two manufacturers attach the various pieces of material together; the quality of welding operations used; the quality of the surface finish of the material; the method, type, and amount of reinforcement used; and the general care and understanding taken in the design of the item. All of these factors are difficult, if not impossible, to describe objectively in a written, detailed description or specification and are better dealt with by visual, personal inspection. That is why it is necessary to create a list of acceptable manufacturers for a given item of equipment that is used to supplement qualitatively the narrative specification.

Whether selecting a standard manufactured equipment item or a custom-fabricated equipment item, the process of identifying acceptable manufacturers should be based upon an analysis of the manufacturer's normal response to qualitative issues, rather than to the often-used process specifying an item of equipment with as much detail as possible and then adding phrases such as "or equal—or approved equal." These phrases, which were developed in response to governmentally mandated requirements for competitive bidding, are still used in many government-financed projects. Competition may be promoted without the use of these phrases to the significant benefit of the equipment purchaser. The common interpretation by bidders or prospective manufacturers of the phrases, "or equal—or approved equal," is "or cheaper." The use of the phrases "or equal—or approved equal" destroys the diligent work accomplished by the equipment planning team because they allow interpretation of the requirements of the owner by individuals who are not party to the development of the detailed needs and specifications for the equipment. The original equipment planning team should be the only body authorized to determine what is "equal" to the needs that have been identified. A competitive and responsive bidding or quotation environment may be achieved by developing a list of at least three or four manufacturers who can meet qualitatively the planning team's requirements. Written specifications, regardless of how long or how detailed, can never replace the subjective qualitative analysis process. They should be used as a device to obtain comparable price quotations from a grouping of manufacturers similarly ranked according to quality.

Equipment Acceptance

The equipment selection process culminates in the receipt of price quotations from selected vendors for the specified items of foodservice equipment. The last piece of information is now available to enable the final identification of a vendor and a manufacturer, if more than one manufacturer is being considered for the final selection of the supply source. The equipment bids that have been received should be analyzed carefully to answer these important questions.

- Has the bidder quoted according to the exact and complete specification?
- Has the bidder quoted on all terms and conditions and not qualified its bid in any way?
- Are delivery schedules and payment procedures in accordance with the corporation's policies?
- Has the bidder included all applicable costs, such as freight, installation, start-up costs, factory supervision of installation crews, extended warranty, service policies, and applicable taxes?

After a vendor or manufacturer of equipment has been selected and the purchase order or contract is concluded with that company, a reverse communications process begins. The manufacturer or vendor now communicates to the planning team its interpretation of what will be supplied. This process includes the review by the planning team of what are commonly referred to as equipment brochures and shop drawings. These may consist of simple specification sheets, as in the case of standard manufactured equipment items, or more detailed shop drawings and other types of detailed engineering drawings of highly modified standard- manufactured equipment items or custom-manufactured units. The planning team should exercise diligence throughout this process to ensure that the contractor has understood completely the corporation's requirements and that equipment substitutions or construction modifications are not being made for the benefit of the contractor.

Many times more than one of a particular item of foodservice equipment, such as a transportation cart, serving counter, or a portable work table, are to be purchased. In this case the bidding specifications should require the successful contractor to provide a prototype or preproduction unit for review by the corporation. By accepting one unit early and then evaluating the preproduction prototype unit thoroughly, enhancements may be developed to address the corporation's needs more effectively. If a preproduction prototype is to be supplied, prospective contractors should be informed of this factor in the bidding phase of the process so that their cost structure may properly reflect the planning teams' desires.

Payment conditions to the vendor or contractor for an item or items of foodservice equipment should create a conditional acceptance situation that maintains the contractor's attention and interest throughout the installation and initial use period. A reasonable payment procedure would include a partial payment at the time of order placement and an additional payment when the equipment is conditionally accepted at the project site. A reasonable amount of money should be retained until the corporation/planning team is assured that the equipment or equipment items are performing to specified levels and have in fact been constructed in accordance with all provisions of the contract specifications. When it has been determined that the item of equipment meets all purchase specifications and conditions and is performing satisfactorily, final payment may be made to the contractor. At this time of final acceptance and payment, the warranty provisions and extended service policy provisions should begin. Many standard warranty policies provided by the manufacturers include the provision that the warranty period begins at the time of shipment from the factory. The purchase specifications should therefore state that the warranty period begins at the time of final acceptance.

SUMMARY

Growing technological development and marketing sophistication will present the foodservice professional with an ever-increasing array of products to select from to satisfy a given production or service need. Foodservice equipment products are not created equal nor are similar products necessarily equally appropriate for a given task. Even after the most appropriate and cost-effective article of equipment has been identified, it must be procured in a prudent and equitable manner and supported with responsive maintenance and service. The tasks associated with equipment procurement are not singularly or collectively difficult if they are identified as part of a systematic process.

REFERENCES

Avery, Arthur C. *A Modern Guide to Foodservice Equipment*. Boston: CBI Publishing Co., Inc., 1980.

Construction and Installation Standards for Food Service Equipment. Ann Arbor, MI: National Sanitation Foundation.

Equipment Guide for On-Site School Kitchens. Washington, DC: Superintendent of Documents, U.S. Department of Agriculture. Program Aid No. 1091, 1974.

Kazarian, Edward A. *Work Analysis and Design for Hotels, Restaurants and Institutions*. Westport, CT: The Avi Publishing Co., 1969.

Kazarian, Edward A. *Food Service Facilities Planning*, 3rd ed. New York: Van Nostrand Reinhold, 1989.

Kotschevar, Lendal H., and Terrell, Margaret E. *Foodservice Planning: Layout and Equipment*, 3rd ed. New York: John Wiley & Sons, Inc., 1985.

Puckett, Ruby P., and Miller, Bonnie B. *Food Service Manual for Health Care Institutions*. Chicago: American Hospital Association, 1988.

Rose, James C. *Handbook for Health Care Food Service Management*. Rockville, MD: Aspen Publishers, Inc., 1984.

PART V

Human Resources

17

Management Techniques: Our Greatest Resource— People

DEANNA HORMEL

Deanna Hormel is president of American Foodservices Enterprises, Inc. Prior to that, she had been director of foodservice for Hallmark Cards at its Kansas City headquarters since 1979. She has been involved in foodservice since 1960 when she began her career as a dietitian at Fort Hays State College. She joined Hallmark in 1968 as a dietitian and was promoted to foodservice director, corporate employee services administration in 1979. Deanna was a Silver Plate Award winner in 1988 and is a member of the Gold and Silver Plate Society.

There would be no reason to provide a chapter on management techniques and functions for the foodservice manager if we did not recognize our most necessary and valuable resource—our employees. This resource is now limited in our industry. However, through human resource development, you can change the word "limited" to "attracted to."

Because the B&I segment of foodservice is often an entry step into the corporate world, time spent in the foodservice area may be limited. This scenario is attractive to job applicants, giving B&I foodservices leverage over other facets of the industry. Corporate America provides benefits such as dental and medical benefits and retirement and profit-sharing programs, as well as opportunities, to attract people. Most corporations also have support programs, such as physical fitness and counseling programs. Another attraction in the foodservice of B&I is the 5-day work week.

ORGANIZATION

Organization is necessary to identify and group the work to be done so it can be accomplished effectively by employees. A good organizational structure can

- provide incentives for movement within the structure
- eliminate duplication of responsibilities

- separate management responsibilities from more technical aspects of the functions
- ensure meeting objectives through proper channels

As the organizational structure is established, inefficiency may develop if there are too many lines of supervision. The fewer the levels of supervision, the closer employees feel to the objectives of the organization.

Multiple reporting relationships should be kept to a minimum as a subordinate with two supervisors can find many excuses or alternatives for not completing the task. It can become very frustrating for the subordinate as well.

When developing an ideal organizational structure, do not consider the people currently in the organization as you do not want your structure to be reflective of personalities.

Organizational changes may need to be made as the direction of your organization changes. Remember to communicate to the staff the reasoning behind the changes. A new structure can be implemented more quickly when effected people have participated in its planning.

The following charts are examples of organizational structures that might be implemented in foodservice operations. Note the difference between the self-operator's chart and the contractor's chart (Figures 17-1 and 17-2).

The foodservice contractor's organizational structure is similar to the self-operator's chart. However, depending on the number of accounts, the Director of Foodservice would become a unit manager reporting to district managers or regional managers.

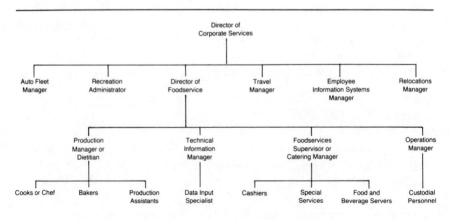

Figure 17-1 Organizational Chart of a Self-Operated Foodservice

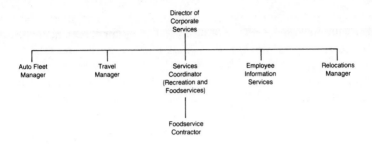

Figure 17-2 Organizational Chart of a Contracted Operation

The general responsibilities of personnel in these structures are described below:

- *Director of Corporate Services:* maintains efficient operations in the area of fleet, recreation and fitness, travel, foodservice, and communications; directs to those operations corporate philosophy in regard to the mentioned benefits
- *Director of Foodservices:* responsible for total foodservice operations, including long-range planning, budget, staffing, pricing, and càpital expenditures
- *Dietitian or Product Manager:* plans menus, assigns production responsibilities, purchases and forecasts needs, participates in product quality and research and development of recipes
- *Foodservices Supervisor or Catering Manager:* supervises the activities of cashiers and special services attendants; arranges for catered functions, determines the charges, and oversees the functions, such as retreats, receptions, meals for corporate jets, and executive dining
- *Technical Services Manager:* coordinates all software programs supporting the operations; maintains hardware needs of the department and monitors future programs to improve productivity and efficiency; provides formal training programs
- *Operations Manager:* responsible for sanitation of entire department to meet department, city, and state requirements; supervises warewashing, floor, and equipment care; interacts with corporate maintenance department for preventive and regular maintenance programs

All managers and supervisors are responsible for interviewing, hiring, and training personnel.

The foodservices director needs to encourage team effort on the part of foodservice managers as responsibilities and assignments can never be totally segregated from each other. Effective team efforts satisfy these criteria.

- Members must think of themselves as a team with an identifiable membership.
- The team needs to share a common purpose or objective; for example, product development.
- Team members must feel that their ideas and contributions are valued by other members.
- Team members must have an awareness of how they work together.
- The team, when necessary, must function as a single unit.

The director needs to provide structure and boundaries to the team effort. Team members must agree on work rules, limitations, and assignment of subtasks. Then by sharing ideas, feelings, and information and exploring possible courses of action, team members gain a feeling of "we." From this, the team will become creative in meeting the goal at hand.

Policies

Corporate policies are followed by employees in the foodservice. A contractor's employees will follow policies of the contractor's corporation. It is important for the contractor to be advised by the corporate administrator of the client's policies so they can be incorporated into his or her program for a particular unit.

The foodservice department should develop an agreed-upon mission. All foodservice managers should be a part of developing the mission and objectives for the operation. General policies of the foodservice operation will then be developed to address menu planning and preparation, costs, and vending.

An employee handbook for the foodservice area is important in communicating policies and procedures. It should be specific and easily read by the entry-level personnel. It should be a positive tool for emphasizing the importance of the position being filled.

Delegation

Delegating is essential in a well-executed management program. Effective delegation not only enables a manager to accomplish more but also helps develop the potential of subordinates. However, certain techniques must be followed if delegation is to be successful.

- Define your existing responsibility and authority.
- Identify the expected results of delegation.
- Determine ideal delegation.
- Know your subordinates' abilities and resistance level to change.
- Delegate as rapidly as the capabilities of your people will allow.
- Secure your subordinates' understanding and acceptance of delegation.
- Establish effective controls.
- Delegate technical work and routine and repetitive work.
- Delegate tasks to employees commensurate with their level of authority.
- Do not delegate final management decisions, decisions on overall technical problems, and work that team members cannot perform effectively.

In delegating, the manager must create accountability of results of the team effort. Develop measurable standards of delegated work, set checkpoints, require completed work on deadline, and rescind delegation when necessary.

Sometimes management has problems "letting go" or may feel guilty about delegating routine, repetitive work. The manager must maintain the attitude that delegation will be well received by subordinates if emphasis is placed on the opportunities for them to grow.

Morale will be at a high level as you place trust in employees' efforts. Everyone involved must realize that some mistakes will be made, as in any development process. Similarly, the accomplishments made during the delegation process must be recognized and commended through promotion, communication, or some other positive means.

LEADERSHIP

Business theorist Warren Bennis believes that the ability to lead is a skill that can be taught to—or at least learned by—everyone. Leaders he had interviewed shared four strategies in common.

1. attention through vision, exemplified by bringing people together
2. bringing meaning through communication

3. achievement of trust through positioning—being predictable, flexible, yet consistent
4. the deployment of self through positive-self-regard, which increases the confidence of the employees around them

Attention through Vision

Attention through vision might be described as *motivating*. The most effective method of motivating people is to provide an environment conducive to motivation, one that encourages and allows employees to develop motivation within themselves. Employees who are highly motivated receive a high degree of self-satisfaction from their accomplishments.

A climate for motivation is often developed by providing sincere praise, approval, and support to employees. The successful leader can inspire by infusing a spirit of willingness into people.

The esteem of the employee can be elevated by the manager who is sensitive to that vital need. Subordinates see themselves as their managers see them. We as managers must remember that others have drives to fulfill their needs just as we have drives to meet our needs.

Our needs vary as we go through the life cycle. Following the chart shown in Table 17-1, consider which element is most important to you at this stage of your career. Then consider what your employees might consider to be most important. Your subordinates would probably assign different importance to needs than you do as a manager. This exercise reminds us to recognize the individuality of our subordinates.

Table 17-1 Needs throughout the Life Cycle

	Age				
Needs	*20s*	*30s*	*40s*	*50s*	*60s*
Monetary rewards					
Company stability and one's own position					
Friendship and cooperation of managers, peers, and subordinates					
Appreciation and respect					
Potential for growth within the company					

Bringing Meaning through Communication

Motivation to accomplish goals tends to increase as people are informed about matters affecting goal achievement. Resentment is built up when employees have little information about their efforts.

Communication is successful when you

- speak of an applicable subject
- talk in easily understood terms
- anticipate emotional objections and are prepared to respond to them
- provide an association for retention
- encourage feedback
- encourage application of the information communicated

The more an idea is put to use, the better it is understood and remembered.

Managers must also develop a climate for subordinates to communicate upward. Such communication can be accomplished in small group meetings. However, there will always be a few employees who are uncomfortable asking questions, providing a suggestion, or stating their point of view in a small group. Therefore, try various strategies to elicit communication. One option is to encourage employees to submit questions on note cards and to deposit them in a closed box. Management could then respond to the questions verbally in group meetings. Another method is to have employees relay their questions to a coordinating staff member who does not exercise authority but who can pass on communication to management in an anonymous fashion.

A foodservice handbook outlining management structure in the foodservice should be presented to employees as they enter the foodservice department. This handbook should include policies on uniforms, checking in and out procedures, break and lunch times, smoking areas, vacation scheduling, and meal allowances. Include any information that is easily stated in print and helps the employee be comfortable in the department.

Remember to ask, tell, and listen as you communicate. Nonverbal communication should not go ignored. Messages can be conveyed through body language that should trigger the "ask" category of communication.

SELECTING EMPLOYEES

In most corporations, the personnel department is involved in the process of hiring employees. You must communicate to your personnel department the necessary qualifications for the candidates you wish to interview. When the candidates have passed the screening process, the decision to hire or not hire is yours. You will decide if the candidate has the specific abilities and background to "fit" into your foodservice organization. This decision may only be reached after repeat interviews.

In those interviews, ask the candidate to tell you about both successes and failures. Assess through questioning the candidate's orientation to service and ability to deal with people in a positive manner. Does the candidate have a concern for the quality and the attention to detail necessary to meet quality standards? Can he or she exercise flexibility and respond to pressures? Foodservice positions require an immense amount of diversity. Is the candidate enthusiastic and supportive of the foodservice industry? Assess other important qualities, such as self-confidence, creativity, and self-reliance. Talk to the candidate about both the advantages and the disadvantages of the job. Solicit questions. Once you have made a decision to hire, most personnel departments discuss salary, benefits, and promotion opportunities with the new employee.

In your interviews, be sure to observe the employment laws. Your personnel department should provide detailed information to you about the applicable federal and state laws.

When you are satisfied that you have chosen the best candidate and the hiring process is complete, a development or training process is necessary to enable the employee to use his or her capabilities to meet the demands of the job.

DEVELOPING AND TRAINING EMPLOYEES

At the outset of the training program, establish a positive relationship with the employee and alleviate any concerns of being tested or evaluated at this point. Put the employee at ease by talking about a recent vacation, family, or other pleasant topic that will establish a rapport conducive to an ongoing positive relationship. Then, assure the employee that the training will take place. This will produce a confidence level that will help put the employee at ease.

An important part of foodservice training is training in the use of motorized equipment. This equipment is often very dangerous without proper training in its use. Safety should be emphasized throughout the training process.

The use of videotapes is very effective in equipment usage training. Many corporations have an audiovisual department that can provide support to foodservice departments. Involve long-term employees in filming a training videotape as a motivator to all concerned. A detailed handout on how to operate each piece of equipment is an important reference tool and should accompany the videotape.

After you have demonstrated the process through videotapes or by example, have the employee tell you how to operate the machine, while you actually do it. Then have the employee do it while talking to you. Never begin a training program by letting employees operate equipment themselves.

Develop training records and check off the elements of training as they are completed. These are also helpful when filed for reference in relation to future promotions.

Follow-up to the completed training is critical. Often, employees may deviate from the correct procedure when they see others doing it differently. Or some details may not be retained. The follow-up session may come 30 days after training or earlier, depending on the task. Note on the training record the results of the follow-up.

The employee needs to receive reinforcement for completing the training successfully. Opportunities vary, depending on the operation. Recognition before peers, other managers, and superiors is almost always satisfying. Perhaps the employee can be given the opportunity to become a "trainer."

The most valuable aspect of the successful training program is the confidence level that results from its completion.

RETENTION

The benefits our employees want in exchange for their day on the job can be broken down into three components: knowledge, respect, and responsibility.

Knowledge

When top management makes decisions, they should not only share those decisions but also why they are taking certain actions. Often in management of foodservices, decisions need to be made quickly because service is of immediate need. The entry-level or hourly employee should be made aware of the philosophy behind those decisions.

Respect

Respect is regard for one another's humanity. Self-esteem is a part of respect and is improved by such factors as common courtesy among co-workers, recognition of each person as an individual, and good relationships among employees regardless of their role or status. Active listening can help induce respect. It grasps not only the facts but also the feelings that the employee is conveying. The listener should be attentive to nonverbal communication or a change in voice tone.

Responsibility

Employees need to understand what they are accountable for so they know what they can do to improve their performance rating. Allowing the employee some control over their responsibilities also improves self-esteem. Allow them to communicate their feelings about the product and the process in which it is handled. Including them in a blind taste test is a small way to involve them in the responsibility of quality assurance.

Often, the creativity of employees is underutilized. They have ideas about improving the quality of a product and its delivery. Feedback needs to be a two-way process. Participative management can be of great benefit when monitored closely.

In summary, follow these 12 steps to facilitate retention of employees.

1. Know each employee.
2. Listen to employees.
3. Keep employees informed.
4. Be fair and consistent.
5. Direct and lead through good example and clear instructions.
6. Give reasons for the directions given.
7. Be courteous and tactful.
8. Praise good work.
9. Control your emotions.
10. Be alert to changes in attitude or behavior of employees.
11. Correct problems or sources of irritation promptly.
12. Treat others as you would like to be treated.

PERFORMANCE STANDARDS

A key to the success of your unit is the development of performance standards that become a guideline to measure achievement of your objectives.

Standards should be established through a group effort so that they will be understood and accepted by your subordinates. The standards should be attainable, but should present a challenge. Finally, standards should be measurable. Has the desired action been accomplished? Accomplishments can best be judged if standards are quantifiable.

Where do the controls belong in performance of a corporate foodservice? Their place depends on whether you as a manager are responsible to self-operation or a contract company. However, the ultimate performance standard must satisfy the corporate philosophy for which the service is intended.

Developing Performance Standards

All standards described below are generally considered to be of equal importance to most corporations. However, there has been a recent concentration on service and convenience in our market. These two attributes do not stand alone, but must be supported by many other dimensions.

Service and Convenience

The operation must attract corporate employees as customers by meeting their needs in a friendly and pleasant atmosphere. Service personnel need to be sensitive to the customers and their varying reasons for being attracted to the facility. If the time element is important, as it is in many corporations, minimal motions and good dexterity play a role in performance. Many corporations allow employees lunch breaks lasting only 30–45 minutes. Service personnel need to perform with excellent communication skills as well. A smile and a brief pleasantry are often sufficient. Because indecisive customers may desire a suggestion for a menu choice, service personnel need to be prepared to advise them on ingredients in a particular menu item. If carry-out is a part of your program, the server needs to be prepared to package the food or offer the menu items on disposable ware.

Personnel handling monies not only have to be efficient in cash handling procedures and machine operation but also be friendly and occasionally responsive to customer concerns or complaints. For example, if a customer has any reservations regarding the size of a serving, they will likely be communicated at the cash register. All service personnel need to be able to call on a manager or supervisor to handle a problem situation. Service personnel need to keep their supervisor informed of customer feedback. Encouragement of prompt feedback helps develop teamwork that results in a successful operation. The service personnel need to understand that without the satisfied customer, their positions will become nonexistent.

Quality

In today's global society, your customers are well traveled. They have been exposed to various dining experiences outside the home. In the competitive public dining world, they have enjoyed many quality offerings. To dine in an operation on a daily basis, therefore, they expect quality. The ultimate control of quality is the responsibility of the purchasing agent and management. Quality in preparation is the responsibility of the employees in the production area. However, the cooks, bakers, salad, and pantry personnel cannot meet high standards without ingredients of high quality. A testing board might be necessary in establishing standards of acceptance. This group can be chosen at random if an appropriate cross-section of the corporation's employees is included. Offering a sampling of various preparations can be a good public relations exercise as well.

Quantity

Several methods of establishing quantity standards are available. A supervisor can measure time required to complete a task. Good employees may enjoy monitoring their own times. Quantity of work performed can be monitored by an office operating system that measures customers served at the cash register in a specific time frame. For a cash system, five customers served per minute might be an appropriate standard. Establishing a standard for labor requirements can be systematized by measuring meals served per manhour spent. Decide the required meals per manhour to meet your budget, and make this your standard. Other measurements of productivity are administrative costs per meal served and number of meals served per potential customers in a month.

Improvement in productivity comes from various elements, the most important of which are:

- adequate training
- reduction of employee turnover
- increased sales
- provision of labor-saving equipment
- implementation of efficient systems

When the operation allows, encourage "voluntary time off." After the employee has completed all assigned tasks, the supervisor can approve the employee leaving early. This will increase the number of meals served per manhour and reduce labor costs.

Department employees will work toward achieving the improvements in productivity if they are informed or can regularly monitor results. Post the results on graphs for easy reading. Highlight and announce records exceeded as improvement continues.

Develop a reward system for productivity improvements. This reward does not need to be monetary. However, many corporations have established "suggestion" programs that do make a one-time labor saving reward in dollars.

Safety

Safety standards should be relevant to the number or extensiveness of accidents incurred or caused. These standards should include proper signs in high-risk areas warning of wet floors, sharp objects, motors, etc. The training program should support the meeting of these standards. All electrical equipment must be unplugged before disassembling for cleaning. Knives should never be left in a deep sink of water. All spills should be cleaned up immediately.

Cooperation

Cooperation standards should be identified as teamwork, responding to supervision positively, and working well with co-workers.

Attendance

Attendance standards are somewhat complex. Most managers consider a lengthy illness or one associated with hospitalization as nonpreventable. On the other hand, a large number of days away, taken one at a time and spread out over a year's time, may warrant an unsatisfactory performance of attendance.

If attendance standards are not being met, it is often beneficial to have the employee establish an acceptable goal with the manager's assistance.

An incentive for improving departmental attendance can be recognition, as well as monetary. Most foodservice employees already enjoy the benefit of free meals so a complimentary luncheon will not be enticing. However, a gift certificate in a nearby restaurant could provide a dual benefit. The employee could critique the competition, as well as taking advantage of the gift certificate.

Measuring Performance

Once your standards are established, you must make all of your employees aware of the standards applicable to them and of how their performance will be measured.

Measure performance of the department as a whole. Doing so emphasizes the importance of teamwork. Post the performance results in easy-to-understand graphics. A more effective exercise is to meet in small groups for open discussions soliciting input from employees for performance improvement.

A new employee's performance should be measured at the end of the first 30 days. This measure will necessarily be brief because of the short time of employment. Exhibit 17-1 is a suggested measurement tool.

An annual performance review is appropriate in all operations. The review should be a two-way communication tool.

Passing an evaluation on to upper management provides checks and balances. Maintaining the evaluation for future reference enables a comparison of future performance.

Corrective action should correct first things first—those problems that are most pressing. Positive communication helps minimize your employee's emotional resistance to corrective action.

Move the controls down the organization to the point where the action takes place to reduce reaction time. Remember to provide rewards for correction, as well as for a strong performance. Recognition is often more rewarding than a monetary offering.

PLANNING

Planning the needs of your foodservice department well into the future is essential in today's volatile environment. Your corporation's facilities planning departments generally have a pulse on population forecasts of the facility you serve. When those numbers are made available to you, project the percentage of employee participation 10 years into the future. Identify labor, capital improvements, and facility space requirements to coincide with these customer projections.

You will then have the data needed to determine whether you should operate a commissary with various satellite operations. The remoteness of the customer and the long-term plans of department locations will affect this decision. If you have a facility sufficient to serve your projections, your long-term planning may be limited to forecasting new equipment requirements.

As technology continues to improve in foodservice, labor requirements may be reduced. Our future eating habits and service desires also need to be considered as we seek equipment and fixture replacement.

It is your responsibility as a manager to justify capital expenditures. Such expenses can be justified by projecting increased sales or cost reductions or

Exhibit 17-1 Measurement Tool for a New Employee

Name _____   Continuity Date _____
Date _____   Years under Present Supervision _____
                           Comments _____
                           _____

Service
  Outstanding
  Very Good
  Satisfactory
  Unsatisfactory
  Poor

Safety
  Outstanding
  Very Good
  Satisfactory
  Unsatisfactory
  Poor

Quantity
  Outstanding
  Very Good
  Satisfactory
  Unsatisfactory
  Poor

Cooperation
  Outstanding
  Very Good
  Satisfactory
  Unsatisfactory
  Poor

Quality
  Outstanding
  Very Good
  Satisfactory
  Unsatisfactory
  Poor

Initiative
  Outstanding
  Very Good
  Satisfactory
  Unsatisfactory
  Poor

Attendance
  Outstanding
  Very Good
  Satisfactory
  Unsatisfactory
  Poor

Time Missed
  Total Days _____
  Illness _____
  Hospitalization _____
  Personal Reasons _____
  Miscellaneous _____

Recommendation for methods to improve performance: _____

_____

_____

_____

_____

by offering a satisfying new service or project. Often, an equipment purchase is justified as a replacement to a unit that is depreciated and beyond repair.

Planning to maintain and refurbish an existing foodservice requires that you follow these four steps.

1. Write planning steps clearly.
2. List steps in proper sequence.
3. Identify people responsible for each step.
4. Provide information to those responsible.

Suppose your objective is to refurbish a foodservice without service interruption. Table 17-2 lists the steps in planning the refurbishing.

As you schedule implementation of refurbishing, take into account the day-to-day pressures of the operation. Build flexibility into the plan. Schedule starting and completion dates, allowing for unforeseen problems. Analyze the plans to see if any steps can be overlapped.

The refurbishing work can sometimes be scheduled during hours your foodservice is open by using plastic protection in production areas. How-

---

Table 17-2 A Refurbishing Plan

Program Steps	Accountability	Schedule	Budget
1. Chart areas needing refurbishing.	KR	August 1–5	
2. Arrange for cost estimates.	BB	August 7–10	
3. Write plan.	SL	August 14–17	
4. Get plan approval.	SL	August 21–25	
5. Distribute plan.	DH	August 28	
6. Replace chipped or cracked wall tile.	KR	Sept. 1–15	20 units
7. Replace broken floor tile.	KR	Sept. 17–20	20 units
8. Paint surfaces previously painted.	KR	Sept. 22–26	30 units
9. Upgrade equipment with cleaning or replacement.	KR	Oct. 1–20	60 units
10. Replace nonrepairable equipment or parts of equipment.	KR	Oct. 1–20	40 units

ever, some work may need to be scheduled during hours when the facility is closed.

Budgets represent the resources required to carry out the steps in the program. You must first determine the value of meeting the planned objective and then identify the resources required to meet the plan. Costs for those resources should then be listed on your chart (Table 17-2). You now need to decide if it is worth proceeding with the plan. If the refurbishing costs outweigh replacement costs, you may want to alter the original plan and costs, bringing the costs closer in line with the benefits.

ANNUAL BUDGETING IN THE CORPORATE FOODSERVICE

Your corporation philosophy determines whether the foodservice operates at a subsidy level, is break-even, or is a profit generator. Most corporate foodservices operate on a break-even basis.

The expenses in a typical budget are as follows:

- personnel
- salary
- tax and benefits
- outside maintenance
- communications
- transportation
- lodging
- meals
- supplies
- equipment
- laundry
- employee meals
- depreciation
- cost of goods

Sales that offset expenses are categorized differently, depending on the operation. One example of sales opportunities other than daily customer sales is carry-out catering.

A quarterly review with a forecast for the year remaining is helpful to upper management as an ongoing planning and communication tool.

It is important to share your plan and progress with other managers in the department because they influence the result. The goal of meeting budget requires team effort.

Follow these principles of effective budgeting.

- The value of specific objectives for which resources are to be allocated should be determined.
- The budget should be developed from the bottom up, as well as from the top down.
- Each manager should be accountable for proposing the budget covering his or her own operation.
- Each manager should be accountable for the expenses over which he or she has control.

18

Strategies for Recruitment and Retention

JOHN W. CHITVANNI

John Chitvanni is the president of National Restaurant Search, an executive search firm headquartered in Schaumburg, Illinois. He is a 22-year veteran of the foodservice industry, with 13 years of experience in restaurant operations. National Restaurant Search is the only executive search firm that specializes in the restaurant industry.

At one time, it was easy to obtain help in the restaurant industry. During the baby boom after World War II, there was an abundance of children; families were large and all of those children were going to school and looking for work. It seemed that there was an endless supply of waiters and waitresses.

The baby boom has long since passed. Suddenly, there are fewer high-school and college-aged individuals who want to work part-time. To add to the problem, there is more competition for this diminished number of workers. Thirty years ago, chains were not as prevalent as they are today, the B&I segment was not nearly as developed or sophisticated as it is now, and the hotel industry was a shadow of the giant it has become. Today, there is a wealth of restaurant chains, many new B&I-type accounts, and an explosion of growth in the hotel industry. With the decrease in the school-aged population usually available to the restaurant industry coupled with the increased competition in the marketplace, a large number of workers to choose from simply no longer exists.

As we look into the 1990s, we see that this labor pool is going to become even smaller. The United States is moving from a blue-collar industry and toward a service-oriented society. A great number of businesses are service related, and all of those companies are competing for the same type of employee who used to work in foodservice establishments and restaurants. There is increased competition, not only from within the foodservice industry as it continues to expand but also from new service industries. For example, there is now a burgeoning video industry, with videotape rental

221

stores on almost every street corner. This industry is using the same type of workers that the foodservice industry needs: young, school-aged part-time employees. So we have to be creative. We have to say, "Where can we tap new markets for people, or how can we redo our operations so that we can operate with less labor and be more efficient?"

As we look into the future, we can see that the challenges are going to be different than any we have faced before. We are going to have to rise to meet these greater challenges if we want the foodservice industry to grow effectively in the 1990s and beyond. If we do not adapt or change but continue with present practices, we are going to be in serious need not only of part-time help but also of managers. We must continue to try and develop more management people by professionalizing this industry and making it more attractive to others. And we must begin stealing management talent from other industries, rather than allowing other industries to steal from us, as has been the rule in the past.

MARKETING THE B&I FOODSERVICE INDUSTRY

One of the steps that we as an industry must take is to raise our image. For many years, this industry was not looked upon as prestigious, as it was in Europe. Many managers began in restaurants as dishwashers and worked their way up through the ranks. This fact, coupled with the lack of formal management training, is part of the reason why we had a lack of sophistication in this industry for such a long time.

To improve our image as an industry, we must begin to market our companies more effectively. We have to market our companies better in order to attract the best employees, especially the quality management that is necessary to make the company attractive to potential employees. When people are looking for a position, they are constantly comparing companies. The better a company looks, the better quality of individual it will attract.

One of the problems that the B&I segment has in successfully marketing itself is the ads that companies run to find new employees. Companies in this segment could do a better job of advertising for new talent. Merely running an ad that states, "You know about our company, come work for us because we have great benefits and great working conditions," is not going to attract the best employees. These ads must be creative to be effective.

The average person who decides to look for a position goes first to the newspaper. Research shows that the job seeker will look at the ads, select three or four that are appealing, and call them first. If an ad is creative and interesting, a corporation stands a much better chance of talking with this prospective employee first. The job seeker who is a quality candidate could be hired by your foodservice before any other corporation even has a chance to talk with him or her. This strategy not only markets the company successfully but allows the company to attract new employees a little faster than the competition, therefore giving the company the advantage of hiring quality labor first.

Today's prospective employees are very concerned with the quality of life that the corporation is offering, as represented by hours per week, nights and weekends off, benefits, incentive programs, etc. One of the advantages that the B&I segment offers over the hotel and restaurant segments of the industry is a better quality of life. B&I has better working hours; most operations are 9 to 5, Monday through Friday. Generally, there are no nights, weekends, or holidays. This improved quality of life is becoming more and more important, especially to people who are married and have families. These advantages have not been marketed as effectively as they could be. B&I should be getting a much larger share of the work force; it should have first pick of all the top talent, rather than getting too many "burnouts" from the restaurant and hotel industry who have worked the long hours, weekends, and holidays and then decided that quality of life is more important. The best way to remedy this situation is for foodservice companies to improve their images by doing a better job of communicating their positive attributes.

HIRING A MANAGEMENT RECRUITER

In order to hire top management talent, one of the most important steps that a foodservice company can take is to hire the best recruiter available. Hiring good employees is essential to the success of any business. In the past, all too often, the operator who was "a great guy" but who was a poor operator would end up in the personnel department. The company did not want to fire this individual, but did not know exactly what to do with him or her. As a general rule, companies now realize that, although this practice may have worked in the past, it does not anymore.

Hiring a good recruiter will give the company its fair share of the employment market. The good recruiter hires quality people, rather than playing the numbers game (a mentality that does not care what kind of worker fills a position just as long as the position is filled). In the numbers game, turnover, which is very costly, is high because the company is not hiring the right person from the outset. The numbers game is an expensive game to play.

Many companies today lack a sense of urgency in hiring good people. A good recruiter can bring this sense of urgency to the company. Too often, companies procrastinate when looking for employees. They might interview a candidate whom they like, but it will take anywhere from 3 to 5 weeks before the candidate has a second interview with one of the regional operators. By then, the candidate has had four or five other offers and is no longer available. Many good managers are lost simply because the hiring practice takes too long.

Another problem that arises in many companies is the loss of résumés in the personnel department shuffle. Many times, the personnel department does not recognize a good résumé or overlooks a good candidate because he or she is not a good résumé writer. A good recruiter, on the other hand, has a sense of urgency and is able to read a résumé and sort out "the trash from the treasures." The quicker someone gets into the interview process and the sooner an offer can be made, the greater the chances of being hired.

A recruiter is often paid a low salary, although the recruiter is really one of the most valuable people on the staff. The reason is simple: a company cannot grow and bring good results to the bottom line unless it has good people. Recruiters who know how to attract the best people return their salaries to the company many times over from the good performance of their recruits and the reduction in turnover. Experience shows that there is a direct correlation between companies with poor hiring practices and those with operation problems.

The kind of employee that a company hires is a direct reflection on that company. This is simple business sense. Poor employee performance can be attributed directly to the kind of employees who are working for the company. If a company can hire and keep good employees, then it will be successful.

A good recruiter can bring continuity and stability to a company. Many times, especially with larger companies, the left hand never knows what the right hand is doing. For example, a company will interview in the Northeast and find a quality candidate, but it has no opening for him. Another division of the company may have a need for that very candidate. Yet, because of lack of communication, the quality candidate is lost.

Operations people sometimes receive résumés and do not pass them on to the human resources department, or the human resources people hold on to the résumés and the operations people never see them. Operations people are always complaining that they do not have enough good employees, and recruiters are saying that they can never get the operations people to interview candidates on a timely basis. If such problems are not addressed, companies are going to be in serious trouble because in the shrinking labor pool of the 1990s employee "leftovers" will not be of good quality.

ATTRACTING HIGH SCHOOL AND COLLEGE STUDENTS

The B&I segment of the foodservice industry could do a better job of presenting a professional image, especially when it tries to attract college and high school students to special programs for foodservice. There are many more college programs available today that develop students and bring them into the foodservice industry, but we are not doing as much as we should with their graduates. We should be in the high schools actively recruiting these students for college programs. As an industry, we must improve our image to motivate more young people to commit to foodservice as a career. We also have to make it a better industry in which to work.

Many foodservice groups have contracts with colleges and universities. These are ideal places to recruit students. For instance, students who go through the four-year foodservice management programs should be encouraged to work in the school's foodservice facilities. In this way, they are trained on-site and are indoctrinated into the company's specific practices. In such a situation, it becomes evident who the good workers are. Therefore upon graduation, these people can be offered career opportunities with the company. They already know the system and the company's corporate philosophy, and the company knows it is getting a good worker. Such a program is an excellent source of new employees.

Most companies who have a foodservice program in a college or university take advantage of the student/employee program. Yet, these companies do not take the next step, which will be necessary to be successful in the 1990s. These foodservice companies must refine these college programs and broaden their scope. There is a need to develop a co-op program to handle adequately all of the incoming students. This would allow a foodservice contractor to farm out students to other foodservice accounts in the area. For instance, a contractor who operates the University of Illinois account would not only use students in the foodservice at the university but would also place some of the students in other accounts in the area. This accomplishes several goals: it exposes students to different types of accounts, gives them a higher level of experience, reduces the company's labor shortage, and aids in the development of future managers.

A similar program could be put together that would allow the students to take part in a 6-year work/study program. Northeastern University in Massachusetts does a fantastic job training engineers in a 6-year program. The students go to school two semesters, work one semester, go to school two semesters, and so on. This program allows students to earn money for their college education while receiving valuable on-line experience in the field. The companies save on payroll and have the opportunity to evaluate these workers thoroughly. At the end of the 6-year program, the student has a degree, as well as 2 years of work experience within the company.

The student is therefore able to step into a management role and be immediately productive. The company has paid this student very little along the way and yet is getting a fully productive manager. Under the old system, hiring and training someone was a "hit or miss" proposition. The company could spend a lot of money on training a new individual, with no guarantee of success. And even after the new employee goes through the training process, a few years of experience are needed before full productivity is attained.

Not only should foodservice companies be developing work/study types of programs within their college accounts but they should also be encouraging other colleges to institute similar programs. Next, they should go into high schools and begin recruiting on that level. Go into areas of the country where there is an abundance of teenagers who need scholarships or money to attend college. This would be the ideal program: "We'll let you work and go to school at the same time." We would also be developing a base of new professionals for the industry in the future.

Another possibility lies in high-school foodservice accounts. As we recruit some of these high school students, perhaps we could use them in our programs in their senior year by putting them to work in the kitchens of the high school. This would give them an even bigger head start on their career. Or a foodservice company can enroll students in a training program and place them at one of the colleges for which the company provides foodservice. The students obtain their education through that college. The result is that the company is recruiting in high school and receiving managers with an extra year or two of experience in the company's system. If the proper time and effort are put into this type of program, by the time the student graduates from college, the company has a well-trained manager or management candidate.

REDUCING TURNOVER

In order to keep good employees, especially the line workers, the foodservice industry is going to have to be competitive and create specific programs that will entice employees to remain with the company. We as an industry always need to hire new employees because of turnover. That energy should be directed at programs that will reduce turnover and retain employees. If a company can put together such a program, there would be no need to worry about the shrinking labor pool. For example, McDonald's has a program that allows employees to earn points for working. It is a system that awards one point for every hour worked and bonus points for every 3 months worked. Employees can redeem these points for cash, merchandise, or educational scholarships for family members. To make the scholarships more appealing, the employee's points are doubled if they are redeemed for scholarships. After 5 years, an employee can earn up to a year's tuition for a child or grandchild. This is just one example of a program that gives employees extra benefits, benefits that they appreciate. With programs such as these, employees are not as likely to leave to go to work down the street for an extra 25 cents an hour.

The cost of the McDonald's program is offset by the reduction in recruitment and turnover costs. Today, a company runs the risk of hiring three or four people before finding another employee as good as the one who left. The shrinking labor pool is forcing companies to run extra ads and spend extra time in interviewing. It is not easy to find a good worker who cares about the job. Companies should do everything they can to keep their trained, productive employees. The cost of keeping them is nowhere near the cost of finding someone as good to replace them.

Employee turnover is a major cost for all business today, and it will continue to be a major part of our budgets in the 1990s. Better training and development programs help employees become more productive. These programs also help them feel better about their jobs because they know what they are doing and they are comfortable with their positions. If employees are treated better by management and the company as a whole, they are going to stay.

At any of the major chains, the units with the lowest turnovers are the ones with the best managers. Why is that? Because these managers know how to treat their people well, they act in a professional manner, they challenge their employees, and they keep their workers happy. Bad managers run units that have no concern for the employee or treat employees poorly.

Generally, units with the highest turnover also rank near the bottom in terms of performance. Therefore, we have to train our managers better to become more conscious of the "people" needs. High turnover will continue until employees are treated like the valuable asset that they are.

Many companies do not think they have a problem because their turnover figures are lower than industry averages. Yet, consider, in addition to the percentage of turnover, the type of people who are being lost. Executive recruiters go after the top 5–10 percent of the work force, the top performers in the company. If a company's turnover rate is 20 percent and that of the rest of the industry rate is 100 percent, it assumes it is performing well. But is it really? If it is losing the top 5–10 percent of its performers to executive recruiters or to other companies that are recruiting, then the picture is not so bright. When the best are lost, the company's performance slips and the bottom line erodes.

Why do management employees leave their current employer? Surveys have shown that workers in general usually leave companies for reasons other than money. Although money usually ranks among the top five reasons, it is seldom the first or second reason cited for leaving. However, this is not true in the foodservice industry. In a survey published in the August 1988 issue of *Restaurants & Institutions*, money was the second most-cited reason for leaving a past position. For years, salary levels in the B&I segment have been lower than the restaurant industry in general because we can offer better hours. B&I operators have told people that they had to trade dollars for quality of life. Although quality of life is an important issue today, the survey indicates that compensation is still an important factor in job satisfaction. Yet, money is not the only form of compensation to be considered; increases in base salaries, improved benefits, and other perks will also help reduce turnover.

The most-often cited reason in the survey for switching positions is to achieve advancement and more responsibility. Many managers want to do more, but they find there is no room for growth. In a growing company in which a manager can look forward to being a district manager, he or she will be satisfied with the growth potential. Yet, in companies that have reached a plateau and where there is no room for advancement, managers become restless and start looking elsewhere. Therefore, we must develop programs or projects that will keep managers both challenged and feeling that they are still contributing. If they continue to find their work challenging, they will most likely wait until there is an opportunity to advance in the future.

When managers or hourly employees leave a company, it is important to know why they are leaving, where they are going, why they were unhappy, and what could have prevented the loss. It is important to identify top performers in a company and make sure that they are being treated fairly so that they do not leave. It is a defensive policy, a sort of "preventive maintenance" program, that needs to be installed to keep from losing good people. People want to be identified and they want recognition. They want to know that there are future plans for them with the company. Too many times, people become frustrated and leave, because they did not know that there was a future for them. They give their notice, only to find out that the company was about to promote them. So, at regular intervals, sit down and evaluate your people and make the evaluations meaningful. Give them goals to work toward. Give them special projects to work on that continue to develop them professionally.

Knowing how your employees see themselves and the company is very important to the success of your company. Gathering this kind of information for a company is sometimes referred to as a *climate study*. Climate studies are often done during a takeover to provide an incisive view of the employees and the climate or corporate environment.

During this study, the entire management team is evaluated. All key players, as well as a cross-section of the company at all levels, are interviewed. The results are then compiled into a comprehensive report that identifies the top performers in the company, the nonperformers, and the problem areas. This study allows top management to know if a particular department is not performing up to company standards. It is necessary for a company to know the strengths and weaknesses of its employees, as well as the general attitude of the workforce. Everyone is willing to fix a problem, but if the problem is not identified, how can it be fixed?

TRAINING MANAGERS

Most contractors involved with B&I foodservice are on the right track in client relations, but even more needs to be done in training managers how to deal with the corporate client. It is a major part of retaining accounts. The client is the most important customer the manager has and must be kept happy or the account could be lost. Many times, accounts go out to bid not because of price, but because of lack of performance.

Training managers and keeping them challenged are two of the major challenges facing foodservice companies today. If promises are made to the managers, follow-through is crucial. Many times we tell managers that they should run the operation as if it were their own, yet we do not give them the autonomy to do so. We tell them we do not care what their ideas are because we are running a system, and we want them to work only within the system. In such cases, the manager has no voice in matters. Any good manager has a lot of ideas, but these ideas are stifled. Thus, this manager becomes an unhappy employee.

One approach is to give managers a discretionary budget. It does not have to be large, but it gives them some money to spend in ways that they think will improve the operation, such as special promotions, new equipment, merchandising aids, or improved signage. Because they have to account for how the money is spent, managers are forced to think of new ways to improve the business. This exercise makes them better business people and gives them a sense of being part of the management team, a sense of value.

If we can teach our managers to become better business people, to understand the P&L's, what cash flow means, and what it means to buy a new piece of equipment, we will be developing a part of the management team that could become very valuable in the future. In the past, we taught our managers how to run the system, but if we just continue to train managers to run the system and nothing else, we really will not have an employee who will help us in the future. If we involve managers and teach them to be better business people, they will be more satisfied and more challenged and will feel as if they are contributing to the growth and development of the company.

The development of managers is certainly beneficial to the company in the long run. These managers will be better able to sit down and discuss new programs and new ideas with the clients. They will be better able to develop their own people so that their assistant managers can one day take their place. If we can teach our managers to be better business people, then they can better adapt and react as the company grows. The company is then able to grow with less supervision and is able to pass on the training and the knowledge from level to level, as opposed to passing on the systems of how to run the operation.

ATTRACTING NEW TYPES OF WORKERS

Hourly employee compensation is another area in which the foodservice industry needs improvement. In today's society often both members of the household must work full-time to support their families and their life-styles. Many times, the money we pay these people is not enough to justify the expenses they incur on behalf of their jobs. For instance, it is just not practical for many of these hourly workers to put their children in day care programs and go to work for $5 or $6 an hour. Therefore, these people are going to work elsewhere for more money so they can be able to afford the day care for their children. We are losing out on a potential workforce that the industry utilized for years: mothers. In the past these mothers worked during the lunch hours and would be home when their children came home from school. This is no longer the case because now many are forced to work full-time.

There are other different areas to find new employees. These new sources include the handicapped and the older worker. By hiring handicapped workers, companies are tapping a very under-utilized labor source. Companies may also receive tax breaks and money for training programs when they hire handicapped workers. The older workers and the semiretired are also proving to be a useful labor source in the foodservice industry. The industry shied away from these older workers in the 1950s and 1960s, but this labor group has become very effective. Older workers might not be able to move as fast as a 19-year-old, but they make up for that lack of speed in other important ways. Older workers tend to be much more conscientious and more dependable, often have more common sense than their young counterparts, and can make up for their diminished quickness with increased hospitality.

CONCLUSION

The ultimate key is to be able to market your company effectively to attract new employees. Equally as important as attracting new employees is training them properly and, once they are trained, retaining them. The labor pool is becoming smaller and smaller, and companies will continue to scramble to compete for quality employees. There will always be turnover; it is inevitable. But, if we work to keep the good employees whom we have and work to create new programs in colleges and schools, we should be able to supply the need for new employees. By doing this, we can then grow and develop from within, and we should not have any problems as we face the 1990s and the year 2000.

Acknowledgment

The author would like to recognize Earl L. McDermid, president of Earl L. McDermid & Associates, for his input in this chapter.

Glossary

A

Account Executive: The individual, employed by the contractor, who is responsible for the client's services and who deals directly with the client's liaison.

Area Treatment: Interior design and decor of the cafeteria, dining area, and/or vending area.

B

B&I: The Business & Industry segment of the foodservice industry.

Bain Marie: Large metal table with a recessed top into which water is fed and heated. Used to maintain foods at serving temperature. A water bath.

Bid: Financial and/or operating proposal submitted to an individual or company requesting the opportunity to provide a given service and/or product.

Bussing: To manually clear soiled dishes, utensils, trays, etc. from tables.

C

Central Kitchen: A single kitchen that prepares food to be consumed in more than one service location.

Check Average: Total dollar sales received divided by the total number of persons served.

Client: The company, institution, or individual who employs a foodservice contractor.

Cold Pan: Depression in serving counter for display of cold food. Can be either electrically refrigerated or manually filled with ice.

Company-Operated Foodservice: A foodservice operation that is maintained and operated in-house.

Contact: The individual with whom another person is in regular, direct communication concerning his or her operation, service, or product.

Contract: The legal agreement between a company, institution, or individual (known as the client) and a professional foodservice contracting company (known as the contractor) to provide foodservice based on the specifications of the submitted proposal.

Contracted Foodservice: A foodservice operation that is provided by an independent contractor on a predetermined fee basis.

Contract Vending: A vending operation that is installed and operated by an independent contractor. The contractor retains title to the vending equipment.

Convenience Foods: A product that is purchased precooked, portioned, and ready for reconstituting and serving. Because of the increase in food costs, convenience foods are usually uneconomical in industrial cafeterias.

Conventional Oven: An oven with the heat source, either gas or electric, located beneath the deck; air is indirectly circulated.

Convection Oven: A gas or electric oven that uses a fan for distribution and control of air circulation. More energy efficient than a conventional oven; prepares food in less time with less shrinkage.

Cover: Table setting for one person. The number of meals served per meal period is usually referred to as "covers."

Cover Charge: Fixed fee for admittance, independent of the charge for food and beverage. A cover charge may be required when a corporate foodservice operation is also open to the general public.

Custom Sandwich: A sandwich made to order at a customer's request. The term usually refers to a cold sandwich as opposed to a grilled or carved-to-order sandwich.

D

Demographics: A statistical evaluation process whereby the total available population is segmented according to certain factors, such as geographic location, age, sex, and position in the workforce. In B&I, demographics usually refer to sex, exempt/nonexempt, age group, and work shift.

Dish Dispenser: A spring-activated device that raises stacks of plates or loaded warewashing racks to service level position. May be built into another piece of equipment or a free-standing portable machine. Also available in heated units.

Disposable: Paper, plastic, or other product that is designed and intended for a single usage, after which it is discarded. The term "single service" is more commonly used today.

Dual Temp Refrigerator: A combination refrigerator-freezer.

Durable Equipment: Permanent pieces of equipment used in preparation, service, or storage.

E

ECR: Electronic cash registers that have the capability of maintaining detailed information on all product sales.

EDP: Electronic data processing.

Employee Dining: Foodservice provided in an industrial or institutional setting. Also called in-plant feeding, this term makes no distinction between company-operated and contracted operations.

Entree: A dish served as the main course of the meal, usually meat, fish, or poultry.

Ethnic Foods: Food normally associated with certain nationalities or religious groups.

Expendable Equipment: Items that must be periodically replaced because of loss or breakage, such as chinaware, flatware, or kitchen utensils.

F

Fee Account: An agreement whereby a client operation assumes the responsibility for all costs incurred (including losses); in addition, the contractor is paid a fixed or predetermined fee for its management services.

Fixed Expenses: Basic costs that remain constant and do not fluctuate with increases or decreases in sales and/or volume. Examples are depreciation, rent or square footage charges, and management fees.

Food Cost: The ratio of cost of food purchases to sales income, expressed as a percentage.

Food Slicer: Equipment designed for slicing meat, cheese, and vegetables. Can be adjusted for varying slice thicknesses for accurate portion control.

Food Transport Cart: Portable refrigerated, heated, or noninsulated truck used to transport perishable and nonperishable food items from one location to another. May also be used for storage purposes.

Furnishings: Items, such as tables, chairs, carpeting, and draperies, that must be replaced more frequently than durable equipment but less frequently than expendable equipment.

H

Holding Equipment: Refrigerated or heated equipment used to store food from the time it is prepared until it is served.

I

Incumbent Operator: The individual or company (contractor) that is currently providing food or vending service to the client.
In-plant Dining: *See* Employee Dining.

L

Liaison: The individual employed by a client who has the responsibility of coordinating the activities of the contractor with the needs of the client.

M

Management Fee: Monies paid by an individual or company to a contractor for providing a given service, usually defined by a written contract or agreement.
Management Fee Contract: *See* Fee Account.
Management Fee If Earned Contract: An agreement whereby a contractor is reimbursed for all costs and expenses; however, additional fees must be earned by accomplishing pre-agreed-upon objectives and guidelines.
Manning Chart: A chart that graphically illustrates the projected labor requirements for an operation, showing the number of cafeteria employees, their function, and time schedule.
Manual Foodservice: A type of service where food is dispensed by serving people working in a cafeteria line, as opposed to vended foodservice.
Market Segmentation: The identification of particular groups within the available customer base by applying demographic factors, such as sex, age, exempt/nonexempt, and work shift. *See* Demographics.
Marketing: The process of identifying the needs and desires of the available customer base and developing or designing a product that will satisfy

those demands, making the product available at times and places convenient to the consumer, and communicating to the consumer the availability of the product.

Menu Cycling: To repeat the same set of menus after a predetermined interval of time. The length of cycle will vary depending on the type of facility.

Menu Matrix: Establishes the "sales mix" of product sold and is used to determine food cost.

Menu Pattern or Plan: A listing of the number of entrees, vegetables, salads, desserts, and beverages that will be offered for sale at each meal period.

Merchandising: Any marketing or promotional technique that is designed to stimulate sales. May encompass food displays, platter presentations, use of promotional materials distributed by processors and manufacturers, or use of merchandising materials prepared in-house.

Microwave Oven: A cavity into which microwave energy, generated by magnetron tubes, is transmitted at the speed of light. Food is cooked in a microwave oven by the conversion of microwave energy into heat within the food.

Modular Equipment: Equipment of all the same design, height, and color that can be used free-standing or in any combination.

O

Overproduction: Items that have been prepared but not sold or consumed at the conclusion of the meal for which they were produced.

P

Participation Ratio: Total available population at a given location divided by the number of customers actually using the foodservice facility. This ratio may be established by meal period, break period, on a daily basis, or other variables.

Participation Stimulators: Special events, promotions, and merchandising designed to increase sales and/or patronage.

Pass-Thru Refrigerator or Freezer: Cabinet with refrigeration system located on top and with dual-access doors front and rear to facilitate loading and service. Fans inside the cabinet circulate the air.

Per Capita Spending: Total dollar sales received over a specified period of time divided by the total available population (not the actual number of foodservice participants.)

Permanent Ware: Flatware, tableware, and glassware designed for repeated usage, usually for the life of the product.

Point of Purchase (POP): Merchandising materials that are used to stimulate sales and are displayed for maximum customer impact. Materials are often developed around a special promotion or holiday. Materials may be either provided by processors and manufacturers or developed in-house. Examples of point-of-purchase advertising are table tents, banners, and window signs.

Point of Sale (POS): Physical location of cash register or other payment system for cafeteria or dining rooms.

Point of Service: Physical location of food and beverage service.

Portion-Pak: Prepackaged, individual servings of condiments in disposable packaging.

Preportioned: Food items that are purchased in a fully trimmed, portioned state, ready for cooking.

Product Cost: The combined costs of all food ingredients and items purchased from an outside source that are used to produce an item for sale.

Productivity Rate: A measure developed to determine the level of work produced by an individual or group. May be expressed as sales dollars realized per labor hour, customers served per labor hour, meals served per labor hour, etc.

Profit-Limitation Contract: An agreement that restricts a contractor's profits to a set percentage of sales and/or to a predetermined dollar amount. Any excess profits are retained by the client.

Profit and Loss Contract: An agreement whereby the contractor pays all costs and expenses incurred in a foodservice operation and retains all receipts from sales. The net profit or loss related to this business is borne by the contractor, not the client. The client does not subsidize the operation, and the contractor pays the client no commission.

Profit and Loss Statement: A formal accounting of income matched against expenses incurred in the operation of a particular facility to determine the current profit level; usually produced monthly.

Projected Profit and Loss: A tabulation of anticipated revenues and expenses for a specific operating location in order to determine potential profits.

Promotion: Communicating to the consumer about the availability of a particular product or planned event in order to stimulate interest and increase sales.

Proposal: A bid submitted by a contractor that includes a complete description of the type of foodservice to be provided and the fees that will be charged.

Publicity: An indirect effort to increase sales by making the consumer more aware of the operation. This is accomplished by creating news—something unusual, exceptional, or special about the operation—that will merit coverage by newspapers, magazines, or other media.

Q

Quartz Oven: High-speed oven, designed specifically for the heat conditioning of bulk-packed frozen foods. A quartz plate at the top of the oven diffuses infrared wave lengths throughout the oven for uniformity of heat.

R

Reach-In Refrigerator or Freezer: Cabinet with the refrigeration system located on top. Fans inside the cabinet circulate the air. Interior shelves are usually adjustable. Doors are located on the front of the cabinet.

Resident Service: A vending installation where a contractor permanently assigns a maintenance worker to the client's premises.

Return On Investment: The amount of money earned after taxes in relation to the total dollar investment required to operate a specific facility. Usually expressed in percentage form.

Running Rate: The current average rate for a cost category, computed over a period of time.

S

Satellite Operation: Point of service located away from the main preparation and/or service location. Food for a satellite operation is customarily prepared in a central kitchen and then transported by cart to the serving area.

Schedule of Releases: A listing of the segments that comprise a given meal period or work break, giving the release time and number of employees per each given segment.

Scramble System: A cafeteria layout that separates various segments of the point of service for more rapid flow, decreased customer queuing, and increased merchandising potential.

Shortfall: A negative variance of actual performance from budget or forecast.

Single Service: Paper, plastic, or other product that is designed and intended for a single usage, after which it is discarded. Also referred to as disposables.

Slippage: *See* Shortfall.

Steam Cooker: Cavity into which live steam is injected under extreme pressure. Steam is in direct contact with the food to be cooked.

Steam-Jacketed Kettle: Floor- or wall-mounted kettle usually constructed of stainless steel and/or aluminum, with a space between the body of the kettle and the outer wall that is filled with steam. Kettles have safety valves, pressure gauges, and inlet valves. Stationary kettles usually have a draw-off faucet. Used primarily for preparation of large quantities of soup, gravies, stocks, and sauces.

Stock Pot: Steam-jacketed kettle in which bones, meat, vegetables, and seasonings are simmered for many hours; end product is the bases used for soups, gravies, etc.

Straight-Line System: For many years, the traditional cafeteria layout in which all food stations were connected in a single straight line. A slower method of service than the scramble system because of customer queuing and frequent back-ups.

Subsidy: Monies allocated or spent to underwrite the direct costs of foodservices not recovered from sales income.

Supplementary Vending: Vending equipment scattered throughout an installation to provide back-up for a more complete centralized manual or automatic cafeteria.

T

Tempered: Food brought from a frozen to a thawed state by holding under refrigeration for a specific period of time.

Theme Days: Special event days that feature appropriate ethnic foods, decorations, and/or entertainment and are designed to stimulate additional customer sales, participation, and continuing interest.

Tracking: Monitoring or measuring actual performance against established goals.

Tray Conveyor: Conveyor belt carrying soiled trays, dishes, flatware, etc. from dining area to dishroom.

V

Variance Costs: Costs that increase or decrease in a direct relationship to increases or decreases in sales.

Vended Foodservice: A type of service in which all food and beverages served are dispensed through automatic merchandising equipment.

Vending Commissions: Dollar amount or percentage of sales paid to a client by the vending contractor.

W

Walk-In Refrigerator: Refrigerated rooms used for bulk storage of items.

Y

Yield: The amount of fully prepared, ready-to-consume food or beverage product that should result if directions for a specific recipe or procedure are properly followed.

Index

NOTE: Page numbers in italics refer to material in illustrations.

About the Editors

Joan B. Bakos is former editor, associate publisher, and vice president of *Restaurant Business* magazine. Joan devoted her impressive 30-year publishing career to covering the foodservice industry. She joined *Fast Food* magazine in 1967 and was named editor in 1969. She was also managing editor of *Chain Store Age* restaurant division, and before that was associate editor of *Restaurant Management* magazine and *Restaurant Equipment Dealers* magazine. Joan has been named to the Academy of Women Achievers by the YWCA of the City of New York and holds the Jesse H. Neal Certificate of Merit for Editorial Achievement.

Guy E. Karrick is communications director for the Society for Foodservice Management and served as the project director for *Dining in Corporate America*. In this capacity he is responsible for all the Society's publications, including the SFM Report, SFM Annual, and special reports. Guy joined the association in 1984 upon graduating from the University of Kentucky with a B.A. degree in Communications.

DATE DUE